T0293224

Columbia University Press
Publishers Since 1893
New York   Chichester, West Sussex
cup.columbia.edu

Library of Congress Cataloging-in-Publication Data
Names: Lidow, Derek, 1953- author.
Title: The entrepreneurs : the relentless quest for value / by Derek Lidow.
Description: New York : Columbia University Press, [2022] |
    Includes bibliographical references and index.
Identifiers: LCCN 2022007092 (print) | LCCN 2022007093 (ebook) |
    ISBN 9780231199148 (hardback) | ISBN 9780231552967 (ebook)
Subjects: LCSH: Entrepreneurship. | Industrial management—Environmental
    aspects. | Management—Technological innovations. | Risk management. |
    Value added.
Classification: LCC HB615 .L4933 2022 (print) | LCC HB615 (ebook) |
    DDC 658.4/21—dc23/eng/20220321
LC record available at https://lccn.loc.gov/2022007092
LC ebook record available at https://lccn.loc.gov/2022007093

Cover design: Lisa Hamm

THE ENTREPRENEURS

The Relentless Quest for Value

Derek Lidow

Columbia University Press / New York

THE
ENTREPRENEURS

For Arel and Teel, two wonderful role models

Contents

Preface

Stumped No Longer

I was asked by a student on my first day teaching at Princeton, "What's the key to being a good entrepreneur?" I knew I didn't know the answer. In preparing for my teaching position, I had done enough reading and asking around to know that no one else knew the answer either. To answer this question required knowing the answer to two even more fundamental questions about entrepreneurship: what good does it do and how does it do the good it does? I have spent the past twelve years looking for the answers. I would like to share with you what I've found.

Answering these questions provides many valuable insights on how we can help entrepreneurs make the world more sustainable and equitable. As we will soon see, we will not succeed without entrepreneurs leading the way. Entrepreneurship is an even bigger deal than we think. We have become so accustomed to the enticements of entrepreneurs that we do not even notice how much of our lives they control. Entrepreneurs may bring us mind-blowing playthings, but we must also hope that they invest the time and effort to make the world sustainable and equitable because it cannot happen without them. My findings make me optimistic that we can.

I feel fortunate to be writing this book. First, I have a unique set of experiences that give me an unusually broad perspective on the subject. I have a PhD in applied physics, which taught me how to ask questions and find answers by exploring, analyzing, and precisely and practically describing mysterious phenomena in greater detail than anyone else. After graduate school I had a career at an established semiconductor company, where I held many different positions and ultimately became CEO. I then did what few successful big-company CEOs do: I left to start my own company from scratch. After successfully selling the company I founded and led, I was invited to teach entrepreneurship at Princeton. While here I have written two books related to what it takes to be a good entrepreneur. My first book, *Startup Leadership*, outlines the fundamentals of creating and leading enterprises and teams that create value for everyone involved. My second book, *Building on Bedrock*, describes the who, what, when, where, and how of successful entrepreneurship today. Researching and writing those books laid the foundation for me to tackle the more ambitious project of discovering where and how entrepreneurship has evolved into its present form, where it is headed, and whether we can change the trajectory of entrepreneurship for the better.

Second, I feel very fortunate to be able to write this story now. Nobody has yet written it. Countless scholars have researched, analyzed, and contemplated the role of business and economic structures in shaping society, but we've mostly overlooked the role of entrepreneurs. That is analogous to studying trees without any concerted effort to study the role and evolution of seeds. Part of the reason that scholars have overlooked entrepreneurs is our inability to agree on a definition. No widely accepted or debated economic theory explicitly models the impact of entrepreneurs.

The understanding of the story of entrepreneurship has rarely brought academic prestige. Hence the absence of effort.

I am also fortunate to be writing this book at Princeton. Because my role is to teach students about entrepreneurship, I have been fully and completely supported in my efforts to better understand the subject. The university's world-class scholarly support staff and facilities have been essential in finding evidence of entrepreneurship in so many places and within so many types of material. Many of my academic colleagues at Princeton and elsewhere have provided essential leads (all thanked profusely in the acknowledgments).

Finally, I am writing this book after many recent pivotal discoveries identified entrepreneurial behavior further in the past and in more places than realized. This book would be much shallower if it had been written fifteen years ago. Past attempts to summarize entrepreneurial behaviors by the likes of Marx, Schumpeter, and others were constrained and incomplete, as the world had not yet discovered many facts and stories that I have found essential in writing this book.

A Fascinating and Entertaining Story

The story of how and why entrepreneurship became so ubiquitous and impactful is both fascinating and entertaining. For example, I found archeological records that show hunter-gatherers making a small assembly line to produce jewelry. Who knew that jewelry making was the world's oldest profession? We have ancient documents that introduce entrepreneurs from four thousand years ago. By name. We hear them celebrate their successes and lament how stressed out they feel. We feel their relief in finding investors. Four thousand years ago some even formed limited-liability partnerships that closely resemble those used by venture capitalists today. We meet fascinating entrepreneurs from long ago in almost all places in the world behaving in ways that are both familiar and surprising.

I want to share these stories. They've been extracted from diving deep into archeological, anthropological, and historical records. These stories are not just for academics; they will fascinate almost everyone. These stories led me to the answers I was looking for, and I think they will help everyone develop valuable new insights about entrepreneurs.

The only antidote to our many existential problems is knowledge. We must understand what entrepreneurship is capable of accomplishing and the crucial role it has always played in driving human progress, for better and worse, in order to inspire more people to responsibly perform this essential function for the rest of us. This book will illuminate, for the first time, what entrepreneurship really does—and has always done—so that we can all reap its benefits.

(I note here that to make this book as enjoyable as possible, I do not use footnotes, which I find distracting. Instead, I have included extensive notes in an appendix. There you will find the most relevant references I used in writing the book. The notes will help you dig deeper, if you are so inclined, into the story of entrepreneurship.)

THE
ENTREPRENEURS

Introduction

An Indispensable Problem

Society must have farmers before it can eat; foresters, fisherman, miners, etc., before it can make use of natural resources; craftsmen before it can have manufactured goods; and merchants before they can be distributed.

—Sima Qian, *Shiji*, c. 94 BC

Ten inches tall and seventeen feet in length, the *Qingming Shanghe Tu* depicts a day in the life of a large city of the Song dynasty (960–1279 AD). This painted scroll is a revered masterpiece in China and an acknowledged milestone in the global history of art. It also provides us a captivating glimpse into the impact of entrepreneurship on everyday life a millennium ago.

The scroll (figure 0.1) unrolls from right to left, taking the viewer on a journey from a morning in the countryside to an afternoon in the bustling city center. The city itself is located next to a river thriving with commerce. Its streets are clogged with vendors and customers of every class and status. There is even a high-stakes action set piece: a boat, its towline broken, careens toward the bridge in the center of town, causing panic all around.

Every detail is rendered crisply, down to the signs in shops listing their products and services. A fortune-teller's shop advertises three services: "determining auspicious days," "fortune-telling," and "prognostication." Other signs list the names of the shops' owners: "Wang Family Paper Goods," "Lord Wang's Inn—Suitable for Long Stays," "Li Family Shipping Company."

Entrepreneurs are everywhere along the scroll: artisans, innkeepers, street vendors, traveling merchants, traders, wholesalers, along with shops of every type, including pawn shops. We can tell the classes apart by their clothes: laborers wear short leggings, students and humble civil servants wear scarves around their necks, merchants wear half-length robes over full-length pants, and higher-ranking officials and scholars wear full-length robes. Some restaurants, particularly the informal ones, appeal to a range of

0.1 Detail from the Qingming scroll.   *Source*: Alamy.

classes, and the fancier ones, located in extravagant, multistoried structures, are clearly intended only for wealthier clientele. That said, all classes can be seen enjoying their free time, spending what money they can spare on food, drink, and entertainment. They are also enjoying having choices. Thanks to the efforts of large numbers of entrepreneurs, many offering similar products or services, these citizens can go beyond satisfying the necessities of life. They are living large.

When customers of all classes can spend freely on goods and services offered by large cohorts—swarms—of entrepreneurs, you have an entrepreneurial golden age. The Qingming scroll depicts one of these times. It began with entrepreneurial innovations that made more terrain suitable for growing rice. China in the Song dynasty and the preceding Tang dynasty benefited from these innovations, which lowered the cost of food and added to the wealth of many small landowners. Having more food to sell spurred entrepreneurs to innovate new ways to sell it, leading to a cycle of entrepreneurial innovation that rapidly expanded the scale of their combined achievements. Driven to get customers to buy even more food and drink, Song dynasty entrepreneurs developed the business of hospitality. Their innovation thrives to this day.

Ten Millennia of Impact

There have been many other entrepreneurial golden ages throughout history. The entrepreneurial wealth creation we see today is far from unprecedented, as many would claim it is. Examining the similarity of entrepreneurial behaviors and outcomes over the past 9,000 years or so—as far back as explicit entrepreneurial behavior can reasonably be traced—yields profound new insights into exactly how entrepreneurs increase the standard of living of entire civilizations as well as affect society in powerful and surprising ways. As entrepreneurs shake the world, governments, religions, and other groups respond, attempting to influence the direction of these entrepreneurial efforts, with varying degrees of success. Entrepreneurship creates a dynamic within societies, amplifying the tension between change and regulatory constraint.

This book is about the impact of both entrepreneurs on society and society on its entrepreneurs. Entrepreneurship has created most of what we view as essential for living in today's world. We venerate our entrepreneurs, and yet we still underappreciate their impact—both positive and negative—on society. The following partial list of ten millennia of entrepreneurial innovations, listed in approximate chronological order (table 0.1), shocks my students:

0.1 Some Entrepreneurial Innovations

Jewelry

Mining

Specialized standardized tools

Standardized pieces of clothing

Metal tools, including weapons

Import/Export

Markets

Spices

Mortgages

Caravans

Taverns/Inns

Prepared foods

Renting assets (including land, houses, and slaves)

Venture capital

Dyes

Banking, including interest bearing deposits

Shipping and logistics

Apartment buildings

Advertising

Printing

Publishing

Plantations

Spirits (high alcohol content drinks)

Factories

Retail shopping experiences and department stores

Packaged foods

Programable machines

Steam Engines

Newspapers

Steamships

Railroads

Steel

Metal (wide span) bridges

Synthetic colors

Pharmaceuticals

Plastics

Bicycles

Electric motors

Electric lights

Cable cars, trams, and subways

Combustion engines

Cinema/movies

Wireless communications

Household appliances

Air conditioning

Elevators

Automobiles

X-Ray machines and most other medical equipment

Airplanes

In-line production/assembly line

Airlines

Semiconductors

Software

Personal computers

Online shopping

Smartphones

Apps and services delivered by mobile phone

Social Media

Video calls and conferencing

This list does not include the many critical services that entrepreneurs have successfully taken over from governments, scaling to make them accessible to much wider swaths of the population. For example, construction has been dominated by entrepreneurs since before 1760 BC, when Hammurabi posted laws concerning penalties for shoddy construction. I don't include it because the first structures were not built by entrepreneurs. Likewise, lawyers, doctors, and other professionals are not on this list even though most have been entrepreneurs since their professions emerged as specialties available to the public and not just the ruling elite who initially employed them. I also omitted once-essential items that are now obsolete, such as phonographs, telephones, and carriages.

Consider what life would be like if these entrepreneurial innovations had never existed or never been made widely available. The world we know simply would not exist. Entrepreneurship's impact on how we live has always been enormous, so ubiquitous and profound that we usually take it for granted. In fact, entrepreneurs are the primary shapers of our culture.

Consequences

Entrepreneurship's impact on society is always profound, but that does not mean it is always exclusively to the good. In fact, it tends to run amok in predictable ways. Understanding and acknowledging the negative consequences of entrepreneurship can help society mitigate those consequences before they get out of hand. For example, only within the last few years have we truly begun to grapple with the negative effects of digital technology on our privacy, social lives, politics, and other key areas of life. For years after the introduction of these tools, as smart phones, social media, and other innovations proliferated with mind-boggling entrepreneurial speed, people and their leaders remained willfully blind to the potential dangers.

As we'll see, by considering past entrepreneurial outcomes, we could have predicted our present concerns and worked to reduce some of these negative effects, leading to less runaway detrimental impact. Society's capacity to anticipate and mitigate the unintended consequences of entrepreneurial innovations becomes clear as we look to the past.

Concern about the unintended effects of entrepreneurship is ancient. Most of us know Daedalus as the father of Icarus, the boy who flew too close to the sun. The full story is more intricate—and more salacious—than most realize. In classical times, the myth of Daedalus was widely known to be a parable of the perils of entrepreneurship.

Daedalus was the Greek ideal of a pure entrepreneur: a self-directed individual who utilized his "mechanical arts" to profit by selling his skills to the highest bidder. In the myth, Pasiphaë, queen of Crete, falls in love with a beautiful snow-white bull given to her husband, King Minos, by the god Poseidon. Wishing to mate with the bull, she asks the famous innovator Daedalus to build her a mechanical cow to hide within (figure 0.2). Using Daedalus's creation, Pasiphaë becomes impregnated by the bull, giving birth to the monstrous Minotaur. The half-man, half-bull monster then feasts on the best young men and unwed women of the kingdom.

In desperation, King Minos contracts with Daedalus to design a structure to contain the Minotaur. Daedalus devises a cunning labyrinth for the purpose, and King Minos considers the technology so important that he imprisons the entrepreneur within his castle to keep its secret. To escape, Daedalus devises wings—feathers held together by wax—for he and son Icarus to fly to the mainland. Unfortunately, Icarus ignores his father's warnings and flies too close to the sun. His wings melt, and he plunges to his death.

0.2 Pasiphaë, Daedalus, and the wooden cow. Roman fresco from the northern wall of the triclinium in Casa dei Vettii (VI 15,1) in Pompeii.

Source: Wikimedia Commons, https://commons.wikimedia.org/wiki /File:Pompeii_-_Casa_dei_Vettii_-_Pasiphae.jpg.

Daedalus's skills were extraordinary, but the point of the myth was that his dazzling creations had horrific unintended consequences. Learned citizens of Greece and Rome were more alert to the potential unintended consequences of entrepreneurial innovation than we are today. As we will see, the governments of Athens and Rome worked to keep their entrepreneurs focused on the best interests of their citizens. As a result, the classical world enjoyed the benefits of an entrepreneurial golden age of extraordinary length and richness.

Dictators by Default

Entrepreneurship affects what we can and cannot do more than any other facet of society, certainly more than governments and organized religions. Entrepreneurs dictate what we wear, where we live, how we live, how we decide what is right and wrong, and even who we love, whether through matchmaking or a dating app. Countless incidents throughout time and place show that entrepreneurs as a class tend to pick and choose which rules to follow, and societies implicitly allow the latitude to do so even as those societies try to restrict their behaviors for past breaches of trust. Most legal strictures limiting behavior were prompted by entrepreneurs who pushed the boundaries of acceptability. Innumerable, often arcane restrictions on, among other things, where and when we can get our food and drink, how we can entertain ourselves, where we can go—and how quickly we can get there—have all been enacted into law because at one point or another, an entrepreneur took advantage or endangered too many people for rulers to ignore. Crucially, these impacts accumulate over time. Once an innovation takes hold with the public, once Pandora's box is opened, it is impossible to take it away completely.

We have ignored this essential dichotomy, this indispensable problem. Entrepreneurship, throughout time and place, has delivered us almost all that we feel makes life livable, if not enjoyable. It also is the force that germinates many of society's biggest challenges and most of our planet's existential threats. Rulers and religious leaders have occasionally tried to steer entrepreneurs toward doing what they want them to do, but the attempts have been sporadic and ill-conceived. We need to understand this dynamic, this push and pull between societies and their entrepreneurs. This will yield an essential understanding about what we, not just rulers and politicians, can do to better align our entrepreneurs with our overall well-being.

We must start with facts, the most important being that entrepreneurship, more than any other factor, determines how we live our day-to-day lives. Not even contemporary practitioners fully understand it as a function or its full impact. Even well-meaning entrepreneurs can end up harming society when they misjudge the nature of the force they're unleashing. The consequences of this lack of understanding are enormous and will become irreparable if we do not quickly educate society about how entrepreneurship actually works, its extraordinary capacity to affect the world in positive and negative ways, and the many effective ways in which that capacity can be controlled and directed by society. As you will see over the next twelve chapters, few historical threads could be considered more crucial or more relevant to today's problems to follow. In addition to helping mitigate the unintended consequences of unchecked entrepreneurial activity, clearing up myths about entrepreneurship will help us unlock even greater benefits from it.

One of the most pervasive and damaging of these myths is that entrepreneurship is somehow unique to the modern age, to the world of computers and electric cars. In fact, the practice of entrepreneurship dates to before the first human settlements. Likewise, entrepreneurship is intrinsic to virtually all forms of economic or societal structure. It predates them all. Nor is modern entrepreneurship in any way centered in the United States, let alone Silicon Valley. The young white male techie in his open-plan coworking space represents only the tiniest fraction of today's story—half the working population tries entrepreneurship at least once. Women and minorities play a huge, underrepresented role.

In fact, nearly everything we take for granted about entrepreneurship is wrong, if not outright misleading. Clearing up these misunderstandings and opening a window into entrepreneurship's true nature is another central purpose of this book.

What Is a Good Entrepreneur?

The final objective of this book is to use our understanding of the past to seek an answer to a question of profound importance: what makes a good entrepreneur? Is it simply someone who knows how to start companies that grow quickly and make lots of money for lots of people, as most would answer the question today? Are high-profile role models like Elon Musk, Jeff Bezos, and Oprah Winfrey prime examples? Intelligent people once thought of Elizabeth Holmes as an ideal entrepreneur, the next Steve Jobs, until a reporter at the *Wall Street Journal* exposed the fact that her company's highly touted blood-testing machines didn't actually work as she had confidently claimed. Perhaps there is more to the definition.

Though the field of business ethics technically exists, it is moribund. The history of business has been essential to the formulation of widely accepted ethical standards of business, but its focus has been the professional management of business enterprises. Legal systems and social structures rely on a shared definition of what is or is not ethical behavior to better formulate laws and preemptively exclude bad actors from responsible positions. People in most parts of the world expect ethical businesses to deliver products and services and implement employment practices in compliance with existing laws, rules, and regulations. We expect ethical businesses to produce verifiable accounting records. Businesses are considered corrupt and illegitimate if their business emanates from a bribe or physical threat.

No such shared and accepted ethical model exists for entrepreneurs and their creations. Some argue that it is essential for entrepreneurs to "move fast and break things," even to flaunt currently existing laws, which, after all, can't be expected to anticipate and allow for major innovations. Others say that entrepreneurial businesses should be held to the same standards as any other organization. Without a collective understanding of the historical ramifications of these different attitudes, how can any society be expected to take the right approach? Entrepreneurs unleash the forces of change in a way and on a scale that professional managers of established businesses never will. Therefore, a system of entrepreneurial ethics must be developed to suit. We will look at the historical justifications of such a system in the coming pages.

A Primal Self-Powered Societal Force

Understanding why entrepreneurship is so impactful requires us to discover how it emerged as an activity and how societies react to individuals trying to improve their well-being by doing something valued by their neighbors. The lack of study of the emergence of entrepreneurial behavior has impeded our ability to properly define it, let alone appreciate and effectively nurture it.

I have tackled this dichotomy of no understanding without a definition, yet no definition without understanding. Going back and forth from sets of potentially relevant archeological artifacts to potential definitions ultimately yielded answers to the question, "Was this artifact evidence of entrepreneurial behavior?" The result is a new, compact, practical, and insightful definition of entrepreneur. (I will spare you the iterations, but you can read about them in the appendix.)

Entrepreneurs can be defined as individuals who

1. are *self-directed* in their actions;
2. are *innovative in ways that create perceived value* within their local culture; and
3. *entice others to offer them something of value* in return for delivering their innovation.

The power and usefulness of this definition will emerge as our story unfolds. For a start, it applies in all places and for all times past and present. It allows us to start our journey analyzing the earliest evidence of entrepreneurship. We'll start with exploring some interesting archeological sites.

Furthermore, our time-invariant definition of "entrepreneur" provides us a filter we can then use to identify the specific mechanism that stimulates entrepreneurs to appear in significant numbers in almost all social groups. I call it "entrepreneurial swarming." This mechanism explains a great deal about entrepreneurship; for example, why entrepreneurs group in enclaves, why they form similar businesses, why there are so many of them, why entrepreneurs achieve a higher status in some societies and not others, and why rulers often cannot stop entrepreneurs from appearing, no matter their brutality.

It also explains why and how entrepreneurs—as a group—are so innovative. I call this manifestation of entrepreneurial swarming the "entrepreneurial innovation cycle" (EIC). Understanding the EIC tells us how to stimulate entrepreneurial innovations, the world's most potent force of change. Entrepreneurs who understand the EIC will find new opportunities to explore and exploit.

These insights are delivered in the first two chapters. The rest of the book addresses the implications of swarming and the entrepreneurial innovation cycle: how entrepreneurs have led us to create the abundance of products and services that we enjoy, along with our value systems and laws, as well as our existential problems of sustainability and inequality. We will understand how entrepreneurs have pushed us to where we are today, for better and worse.

Illustrating the impact of entrepreneurship requires us to get to know entrepreneurs over a 10,000-year span and in all parts of the globe. This story is too big and rich to tell in a linear fashion. I have organized the stories in chapters 3 through 8 to illustrate and enrich our understanding of the impact of entrepreneurial swarming and the EIC. Chapters 9 through 11 describe the consequences of that impact. Within these chapters I usually start with a rich and representative story before using linear timelines for the rest of the stories. To help digest the scale and scope of the stories in each chapter, I have created a graphic that depicts the journey we'll take in each chapter. In the last chapter I focus on how our findings can lead us to better align entrepreneurial action with improving overall well-being and sustainability.

Throughout the book the stories of past entrepreneurs will underscore that we are not powerless in controlling what the most ambitious entrepreneurs want us to want, whether that is good for us or not. Most historical attempts to control entrepreneurs, by rulers of all types or other social leaders, have been misguided and ineffective. By the final chapter practical mitigations will become evident to proactively deal with the adverse consequences of entrepreneurial innovation. Understanding these mitigations also helps us to finally answer the question that started this all: "What is a good entrepreneur?"

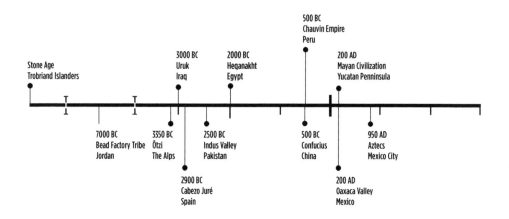

CHAPTER 1

Emergence

Jostling and joyous,
The whole world comes after profit;
Racing and rioting,
After profit the whole world goes!

—Ancient Chinese jingle described by Sima Qian in the *Shiji*, ca. 94 BC

Much of what we know about the origins of entrepreneurship has been discovered accidentally. Over the past few decades, exciting archeological finds and exacting scientific analyses have shown that entrepreneurship dates to a time even before humans lived in permanent settlements, proving that the concept is more primal than we had previously thought.

For some of this newfound knowledge we have to thank Helmut and Erika Simon of Nuremberg, Germany. They are the couple who found the mummified remains of Ötzi, the so-called Iceman, on a hike in the Alps in September 1991. At 1:30 in the afternoon, the Simons were still ten thousand feet up in the mountains, so they decided to take a shortcut through Tisenjoch

Pass to avoid a treacherous, shadow-obscured descent to the base. As they hurried along, something off the trail caught their attention—a brown lump sticking up out of the ice that they recognized as a human torso.

Deaths are frequent in the Alps, particularly at high altitudes on dangerous terrain, so the Simons assumed they'd found a hiker who had recently met an untimely end. They took a photo and reported their find to the local authorities, who visited the site the next day. The next four days were spent digging the body out of the remains of a receding glacier. By the end of the excavation, the local Austrian authorities were pretty sure the corpse didn't belong to a modern hiker at all but to a human being thousands of years old. The next day, a helicopter flew the remains to the Institute of Forensic Medicine in Innsbruck.

Since that day, Ötzi has been extensively studied by experts from around the world. His body now resides in his own museum in Bolzano, Italy (see figure 1.1). According to researchers and scientists, he was murdered around 3250 BC, shot in the back with an arrow fired from about two hundred feet away. He was killed near the top of the ridgeline, but, judging from tree pollen he'd ingested with his food, on the previous day he'd been on the valley floor seven thousand feet below. There, probably in a village, he'd gotten into a knife fight in which his right hand was gashed down to the bone near his thumb. He obviously had been in pain when he hiked those seven thousand feet up into the mountains. For Ötzi, a wound like that was par for the course. He knew violence. Blood found on his knife, arrows, and clothes indicates that at some point in his past, he had knifed someone, shot at least two other people, and likely carried a fourth wounded or dead person to some location on his back.

No one knows what Ötzi did to make enemies or accumulate his wealth, but from the quality and workmanship of the objects found

1.1 Ötzi and his tools.

Source: Wikimedia Commons, https://commons.wikimedia.org/wiki/File:Ricostruzione_otzi.jpg.

with him, it is clear he was not a subsistence farmer or goat herder. His bones indicate that he'd walked many miles in his forty-some years of life. Some speculate that he may have been a trader or a hunter, perhaps a medicine man. Judging from the quality and diversity of what he carried, he was an astute customer. And where there were customers, there must have been entrepreneurs who made specialized goods that those customers believed were worth trading their hard-earned wealth to acquire.

Researchers marvel at the technology and craftsmanship associated with the kit found on Ötzi's body: his collection of tools, special-purpose clothes, and medicines. His boots were constructed using several sophisticated technologies required to tan and inter-connect three types of animal hides, each used specifically for either the soles, interior, or covering. A fine mesh of bark in the boots' construction held hay in place to act as thermal insulation. His boots could even convert into snowshoes when necessary. Their design was so sophisticated, a Czech scientist tasked with replicating them decided they must have been made by a special-ized cobbler.

Knapping—the skill of making useful tools such as flint blades, cutting tools, or arrowheads out of pieces of rock—was a highly valuable skill in Ötzi's time, one that had been refined for over a million years. In the sparsely populated and isolated Alpine villages of five thousand years ago, each style of knapping was likely associated with a specific individual. Looking at the condi-tion of Ötzi's recovered flint knife and two arrowheads, scientists determined that he was barely competent at knapping himself; he sharpened his blades as a specialist never would. His flint knife and each arrowhead were originally fabricated by knappers living in different villages that were widely separated from one another. We know he didn't get them all in one place: the flint material was mined in three different regions of the Alps, and the knap-ping styles are similar to the types of blades recovered near where the flint was mined.

The refined copper axe Ötzi carried would have been a highly coveted object. Copper toolmaking was perhaps the most special-ized skill set of the time. It required multiple steps, special tools, and sophisticated pyrotechnic, refining, and metalworking knowl-edge. Chemical analyses reveal that the axe came from southern Tuscany, more than five hundred miles from where he lived. Since Ötzi's murderer didn't take his axe or any of his other valuable objects, it's unlikely he was murdered by thieves or in retaliation for being one himself.

Ötzi's tools, clothing, and medicines made up a sophisticated and complimentary set of items needed for hunting and defending himself while traveling long distances in cold weather. We know he strategically assembled this kit for his livelihood and survival, but how did he get all the individual items? He didn't steal them, nor did he receive them all as gifts. Primarily he traded for them. We cannot tell what Ötzi handed over in return, but we do know that he was a customer of various skilled artisans and, probably in the case of the axe, traders. These artisans and traders were self-directed individuals or small family groups who delivered specialized and coveted tools—in other words, entrepreneurs.

A Natural Resistance

Entrepreneurs existed long before Ötzi. Important evidence of the ancient practice of entrepreneurship comes from observing the Stone Age–like cultures that still exist, untouched by modernity. Perhaps the best-studied of these cultures are the Trobriand Islanders, who live in the western Pacific off the coast of New Guinea. Slightly over one hundred years ago, the Trobriand culture was vividly described by the pioneering anthropologist Bronisław Malinowski. In his book *The Argonauts of the Western Pacific*, Malinowski detailed a society that used only Stone Age tools and practices and had little contact with the world outside their archipelago. He observed the complex, ritualized ways these villagers exchanged goods and services among themselves and with neighboring villages and distant tribes. Malinowski cataloged seven distinct forms of trade practiced in the archipelago, six of which were highly prescribed in terms of rituals that set specific constraints on which objects or services could be traded.

Unsurprisingly, Malinowski's observations are consistent with the trading practices of many globally dispersed cultures observed by subsequent anthropologists. A group that is isolated, and whose members are dependent on one another, cannot remain cooperative unless it has rituals, myths, and taboos that prescribe how and when materials, goods, and services can be shared or exchanged. Game theory tells us that it is dangerous for any individual in a group or clan small enough that everyone knows one another to take advantage of someone else in the group or clan. They may get what they wanted, but they also may be evicted, shunned, or physically harmed for doing so.

At the time Malinowski researched the Trobriand society, their most important and revered form of trade was the *kula*, a form of ceremonial exchange. Guided by ancient rituals, myths, and taboos, Trobriand Islanders used stone tools and plant materials to build oceangoing canoes (see figure 1.2). They then paddled for

1.2 Trobriand Islanders set off in a canoe.

Source: Plate XXIII of *Argonauts of the Western Pacific*, https://www.gutenberg.org
/files/55822/55822-h/55822-h.htm#pl23.

days across open ocean to visit residents of neighboring islands to exchange boar tusk ivory armbands for seashell necklaces. Danger was omnipresent. Participants feared mythical evil flying witches known to cause shipwrecks during the journey. The risk of death was nonetheless worth taking because of the honor that came with possessing one of the armbands or seashell necklaces. Those involved were expected to possess their treasure only briefly; ritual prescribed that everyone exchange their treasures with another trading partner living on a different distant island on the very next trading expedition. Just being able to describe one of the well-known ornate items firsthand, however, would make the possessor a legend.

Though a great honor and revered ceremony, entrepreneurial behavior was explicitly banned from the *kula*, under penalty of death. In his book, Malinowski includes the Trobriand myth of the flying canoe, which illustrates both the extent to which Stone Age entrepreneurs, using their special skills, can change the fabric of their societies, as well as the violent reactions they can provoke in doing so. In the myth, a Trobriand chief convinces the men of his village to go on a *kula* alongside a friendly group from the neighboring village of Kitava. Unexpectedly, Mokatuboda absurdly orders his men to build their canoe in their mountain village instead of on the beach.

Before departing for a *kula*, the headman of each canoe recites his own secret leadership spells in the privacy of his home, using ritual objects that he then brings along. (Magic was, and still is, an important "technological product" among the Trobriands; a Trobriand could make a decent living performing magic spells that produced rain or caused someone to fall in love with their "customer.") The myth does not reveal what spells were recited, but when the protagonist taps his adze against the skids that hold his heavy vessel—filled with people, stocks, and valuable armbands—his canoe takes to the sky.

When the neighboring villagers arrive at the first trading destination, they are shocked to find a canoe already anchored there. They ask the crew how they got to the destination before them but receive no answer. The same scene plays out at each of the other islands visited during the *kula*. When the neighboring villagers finally return home, they see the protagonist and his crew are already marching their newly acquired treasures off the beach. At this point it hits them: the other canoe flew. Villagers, including the chief's brother, feel cheated and kill the protagonist. The Trobriands have lived contentedly without flying canoes ever since.

The chief with the magical powers was murdered for knowing and practicing a unique skill exclusively for his benefit, something that was clearly unacceptable within Trobriand society. Trobriand culture prohibited the hoarding of powerful magic—that is, technology—for personal benefit, even for a chief. All societies, even the most ancient, have limits as to how much they will allow entrepreneurs to take and how much they expect them to give.

Gimwali

The seventh form of trade practiced by the Trobriands was *gimwali*, which Malinowski describes as "trade, pure and simple": "The main characteristic of this form of exchange is found in the element of mutual advantage: each side acquires what is needed, and gives away a less useful article. Also we find here the equivalence between the articles adjusted during the transaction by haggling or bargaining" (378).

Trobriands considered gimwali undignified and potentially dangerous. When it occurred, it was conducted with total disregard for ritual and taboo. Gimwali was not transacted within a clan, nor was it practiced in public when established clans interacted with one another. Malinowski observed this frowned-upon form of trade taking place almost exclusively between people whose tribes had no formal ties.

Throughout time, most entrepreneurial behavior has been limited because of its ability to incite jealousies and desires that are dangerous to the well-being of groups in which members relied on one another for support. While evidence points to our ancestors exchanging goods with one another over long distances for over a hundred thousand years, most of these exchanges were made in an effort to maintain peace, often in the form of reciprocal gifting. Contrary to a common association of entrepreneurship with all forms of trade, most prehistoric trade was not entrepreneurial in nature.

Understanding the nature of entrepreneurship requires an understanding of when and how individuals have acted to maintain a balance between benefiting themselves and benefiting others. Our struggle to balance give-and-take started long ago.

The Bead Factory Tribe

The archeological record shows that humans have always loved ornaments, painting their faces and bodies with ochre, ash, or other dyes or, once they had developed the appropriate technology, making and adorning themselves with jewelry. We have evidence of Paleolithic body ornaments dating as long ago as forty-five thousand years in Europe, East Africa, and Western Asia. These were usually made from materials like stone, ivory, shells, horns, and animal bones that were easy to paint and connect with one another. During the transition from the Paleolithic to the Neolithic, about ten thousand years ago, humans developed the necessary knapping skills to carve stone into shapes, figures, or statuary. Beads are found regularly throughout the archeological record from that point on.

Starting more than nine thousand years ago, a small number of hunter-gatherers, probably an extended family group, spent their winters in a wadi, or valley, in modern-day eastern Jordan. Within a day's walk of Wadi Jilad lies a colored marble outcrop that led this group to spend a considerable amount of time and effort perfecting marble bead and pendant making. They created processes that enabled them to produce different styles, sizes, and colors in large quantities and in a range of shapes: discs, barrels, and cylindrical beads as well as triangular, oval, and rectangular pendants (see figure 1.3). Their ornaments would have been

1.3 Sample of stone pendants from eastern Jordan, 6950–6400 BC.

Source: From Katherine Wright and Andrew Garrard, "Social Identities and the Expansion of Stone Bead-Making in Neolithic Western Asia: New Evidence from Jordan," *Antiquity 77*, no. 296 (2003): 267–84.

sought after at a time when most such ornaments were crudely fashioned from seashells.

The extended family group that produced these ornaments created or procured flint drills, miniature mortars, and sandstone abraders that ensured uniformity in their production. Working together on a large flat stone table, they created a type of assembly line, with each bead-making step performed on a different quadrant of the smooth, hard surface. One person chiseled blanks; another roughly ground the blanks into the desired shape and size; another drilled the hole; another polished the bead. Four people working together could produce at least four beads or pendants a day. Their streamlined and efficient production techniques enabled the group to produce almost a thousand beads during their winter stay. These quantities far exceeded what they needed for personal use or what they would have given out as lavish gifts. The relative uniqueness of a uniform, smooth, and colorful bead or pendant would have made them highly valuable.

The group would have engaged in many dozens, if not hundreds, of exchanges wherever they spent their summers, probably near the Azraq oasis east of Wadi Jilad, near where other tribes were learning to domesticate sheep and goats. These bead producers imported the first sheep and goats to Wadi Jilad, which they likely received in some trade, giving them a more stable source of food outside of hunting and gathering. Although no one knows for certain how these bead-manufacturing hunter-gatherers exchanged their beads with others, the large quantity of beads points to their using some equivalent of Trobriand gimwali, "trade, pure and simple."

This high-volume bead-producing family provides insight into the evolution of entrepreneurship. First, the group acted in ways that are clearly distinguished from other families, tribes, or clans of the time in that region. Second, the members invested considerable time, effort, and resources in becoming highly specialized in this unique set of skills. Finally, they deliberately produced far in excess of what they needed to remain independent and well provisioned in the face of unpredictable droughts and generally inhospitable conditions. This self-directed investment in special skill development and excess production in order to facilitate beneficial cooperative exchange can be considered proto-entrepreneurship, if not pure entrepreneurship.

The Neolithic bead-producing people of Wadi Jilad are probably not the first distinctly entrepreneurial hunter-gatherers, but they are a serendipitous example: they left evidence that didn't get washed or worn away. Sharp-eyed, meticulous archeologists will likely find more examples of proto-entrepreneurs among the hundreds of archeological projects currently under way, or in the reexamination of projects past. Entrepreneurial behavior is not unique to the people of the Wadi Jilad, the Trobriand archipelago, or the Tyrolean region of our old friend Ötzi. It has appeared in numerous early societies, pre-hierarchies, and pre-economies. There is no evidence for what triggered entrepreneurial behavior, however. For the hunter-gatherers in Wadi Jilad, the beautiful and accessible marble outcrop might have been the inspiration for their "bead factory." Or maybe the group suffered in a drought and sought to create tradable assets to enhance their ability to survive. Perhaps the group found a particularly fertile winter wadi that left them with more free time to build better tools and opulently adorn themselves. They could have been motivated by many factors, but that motivation resided within these hunter-gatherers before any society assigned them the task. Entrepreneurship is primal because it appears in the earliest and most basic of human structures and relationships.

Five-Thousand-Year-Old Factories

An even starker prehistoric example of entrepreneurship than the bead factory tribe can be found on a farm in Spain that raises wild, acorn-fed pigs to produce the finest jamón ibérico (Iberian ham). Here, located on top of a hill in the hilly southwestern portion of the country within sight of the border with Portugal, you'll find the prehistoric, copper-tool-making factory at Cabezo Juré (see figure 1.4). Besides acorn-bearing oak trees, these mountains contain the richest veins of copper ore in the world. The excavation site is the pride of the rural community, and though every schoolchild in the region visits it, as a tourist you'll need permission from the family that owns the farm and from the local town council.

1.4 Structures excavated at Cabezo Juré.

Source: Huelva Buenas Noticias, https://huelvabuenasnoticias.com/2015/03/03/el-cabezo-jure-testigo
-de-la-actividad-minera-en-la-provincia-en-el-2-500-antes-de-cristo/.

The extended family group that built Cabezo Juré must have known about the copper in the region when they decided to live there. Before settling on this location they had likely searched for several years for the greenish rock outcrops that indicate high concentrations of copper. They were not locals; around 2900 BC, this part of Spain was home to pastoralists who tended sheep and goats. Copper technology was unknown to them—no copper tools or artifacts have been found among the remains of the contemporary indigenous culture. Five thousand years ago, this westernmost part of the Mediterranean basin had no significant contact with the advancing civilizations on the eastern side of the sea. The closest copper-refining site was over a thousand miles away in southeastern France.

The site was ideal for these foreign travelers. Cabezo Juré overlooks the fertile plains below, with abundant green-colored surface rocks that would have advertised the rich reserves to a group experienced in copper mining and production. A small river nearby would provide fresh water. Once mined and refined, the copper could be used to produce a wide variety of tools, knives, punches, saws, and axes, all in great demand throughout Europe at the time. With no other source of copper tools for thousands of miles, Cabezo Juré was a classic entrepreneurial opportunity just waiting to be exploited.

The settlers built a fortified stone house and warehouse at the top of the hill. The house contained a deep stone-lined cistern for storing large amounts of water in case of drought or siege. They built four high-temperature furnaces with forced ventilation on the southern-facing slope of the mountain, where uplifting breezes would provide extra oxygen and make the fires even hotter. Smelting copper from crushed cuprite requires temperatures above 1,200 degrees Celsius. Achieving this temperature demonstrated highly advanced technology back then. The furnaces were larger and featured more sophisticated ventilation systems than any found in the western Mediterranean. Unique stone tongs found at the site were used to grab and manipulate scalding hot molds. Their pyrotechnic expertise was cutting-edge. On the northern-facing slopes, the group built lower-temperature kilns for working and molding the refined copper into tools. Small huts that housed about a dozen families of workers stood nearby.

The factory's efficient layout and ideal location made it so lucrative that it operated for almost seven hundred years. Refuse found around the stone house indicates that the factory owners lived on a high-caloric diet of wild game, whereas the workers subsisted on only a third of the calories by eating meat provided by local pastoralists. Artifacts discovered in the house show that the family accumulated great wealth, acquiring finely made objects from around the Mediterranean. Their factory brought them into contact with long-distance traders who possessed refined crafts.

Cabezo Juré was deliberate, innovative, and exploitative. Its creators were self-directed and utilized specialized skills that were considered highly desirable throughout the Mediterranean. The founders produced their tools in fortified isolation and in high quantities; they were not subject to any rulers or chiefs. The extended family group was also independent of any known social order and were not subject to taboos, rituals, or constraints in how they exchanged their wares. The behaviors of this copper-making clan clearly parallel those of present-day entrepreneurs. But what did the behavior of early entrepreneurs look like on an individual level?

Stressed-Out Ancient Entrepreneurs

Heqanakht is one of the earliest entrepreneurs we know by name. From his correspondence and financial reports we can almost hear what he was thinking, though he lived thousands of years ago in

ancient Egypt. The first impression we might get of this early entrepreneur is that he was incredibly stressed out. The detailed and
meticulous directions he gave his overseer and family on how to
accumulate more wealth were an effort to keep his family fed and
his staff paid, all while trying to add to his surplus wealth, which
was rapidly being depleted.

Heqanakht's papyrus letters and records were discovered in 1921
by the Egyptologist Herbert E. Winlock. Winlock had been sent to
Egypt by the New York Metropolitan Museum to uncover ancient
tombs and return with artifacts. Heqanakht's papyri were found
among other debris in a small, previously unexcavated tomb. Tied
with twine and with their seals in place, the eight documents were
in excellent condition, having been left untouched in a dry tomb
for thousands of years (see figure 1.5).

It took forty years for the contents of the papyri to be published
and another forty of analysis before the documents made complete

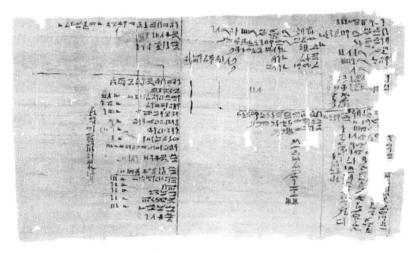

1.5 Heqanakht Letter V, ca. 1961–1917 BC.

Source: New York Metropolitan Museum of Art, https://www.metmuseum.org
/art/collection/search/545449.

sense to historians. These are perhaps the oldest letters known. Deciphering their vernacular was challenging, as they are written in a script that had never been seen before. Some of the writing is likely Heqanakht's own, but he also dictated some of it to a female scribe with a different writing style. It appears the papyri were sealed into the tomb by accident, probably left there after the scribe had finished her transcription but before a courier arrived to pick them up.

Heqanakht lived in Thebes, Egypt, four thousand years ago. He ran several businesses while also working for a vizier, a powerful official appointed by the pharaoh. Heqanakht's responsibility was to set up and run a business for Vizier Ipy that would provide enough income in perpetuity to pay the priests who would watch over his tomb and protect him in the afterlife. While viziers were powerful, they did not pay their staff well, and Heqanakht had to make his own money on the side to support his extended family, who lived two hundred miles to the north of Thebes near Memphis.

At the time the letters were written, around 2000 BC, Heqanakht appears to have been away from his family for several years. He is in a bad mood as he starts his correspondence, berating his overseer, Merisu, for sending him old barley. (He may have needed extra rations to eat and pay for services beyond what he received from the vizier.) Heqanakht also complains that his new wife is being treated poorly by the servants and demands that this behavior stop immediately. One employee in particular would have to be dismissed. He then delivers the news that he would have to reduce pay and rations for everyone in the household back home. In ancient Egypt, barley was used for barter, so rations and pay were described in terms of standardized measurements of the grain. Heqanakht explicitly lists the new pay and rations for twelve members of his household, including his mother and wife. Households were like small enterprises and included family members, other dependents, and servants. Heqanakht had at least twenty-three mouths to feed.

According to the papyri, Heqanakht had to take these measures to free up assets he wanted to immediately invest in additional land on which he planned to grow more grain. To find the best property, he tasks one of his employees with traveling to another district and contacting elite landowners there to arrange the purchase of "wet land," not poor-yielding "dry land." Another employee is sent to visit Heqanakht's debtors to get them to pay him what they owe. The documents specify the type and quantity of grain in which he expected payment, mentioning that an equivalent payment in oil would also be acceptable.

In one letter, Heqanakht orders that a large quantity of flax that had been harvested from his land be taken to a woman named Sitnebsekhtu, who runs a workshop in another town that processes flax into linen cloth. Linen was another standard unit of barter at the time, and Heqanakht was clearly ensuring he'd have some purchasing power available, even if he and his household had to eat all the grain they produced.

The papyri packet also includes accounting records for the previous three years of output and expenses. Although Heqanakht never uses terms to denote profit or surplus—Egyptians would not explicitly calculate profits for another thousand years—his accounts are written so that a surplus or deficit is easy to discern. Today, we recognize them as profit-and-loss statements. These accounts prove that Heqanakht was an entrepreneur, self-directed and skilled in generating revenues from multiple sources while living in a highly regulated society dependent on ancient Egyptian forms of negotiation and trade.

From these accounts we can also see that output had been 30 percent lower for the previous two years due to poor flooding of the Nile, while in an earlier year his businesses had enjoyed a healthy surplus. Because of poor harvests, Heqanakht had been forced to use up most of his surplus to maintain his household's pay and rations. Now he had to cut those rations to enable him to rent fertile new land in the hope of ensuring that his household would have enough food to survive for at least another year if the Nile's poor flooding continued. Unfortunately, there are no records of what actually happened to Heqanakht after he lost these letters in the tomb.

Ancient Egypt is usually thought of as an empire completely controlled by the pharaoh. That official narrative was inscribed on monuments and royal tombs of the past, which was how Egyptologists first learned about this culture. Heqanakht's papyri, along with other translated writings and tomb drawings discovered after those first inscriptions were found, have built on that narrative. They describe a life in which people had to hustle to feed themselves and their families or to acquire the objects they desired. Even under the strongest and most successful pharaohs, the state-controlled institutions were not effective in collecting and redistributing everything the population needed, let alone wanted.

Illustrations from tombs of midlevel administrators and officials depict men and women sitting under canopies offering food, textiles, pots, sandals, and other necessities in exchange for pouches filled with metal flakes, baskets of barley, and other goods. What we understand from Heqanakht and these illustrations is that even in centrally controlled societies, entrepreneurs have appeared as far back as history goes to fill a population's unmet wants and needs.

Ancient Partners of Power

Unlike in ancient Egypt, entrepreneurs were a respected and important part of Mesopotamian life, playing a critical role in the success of the first major civilization as agents of local and long-distance trade and exchange. A merchant class arose from these entrepreneurs supported by virtually every king of every city-state in the region.

The city-state of Uruk dominated Mesopotamia politically from 3700 to 3100 BC. Uruk's location, near fertile bogs and navigable waterways, kept its citizens fed, but the landscape lacked other critical materials required for building the first major city. There was no local access to hardwood, stone, metals, or beautiful minerals such as lapis lazuli, used by elites and temple priests for ornamentation to display their status and power.

Over this six-hundred-year period, Uruk's rulers tried to centrally manage its long-distance trade by creating dozens of fortified trading outposts to secure trade routes to obtain logs from present-day Lebanon and copper from northeastern Turkey. Archeological evidence shows that many of these forts were unwelcome and subsequently attacked by local populations. They required considerable resources to protect and maintain, resources the city-state could not afford given Uruk's fast growth and need to defend itself from rivals that envied its power and prosperity and sought to emulate its tactics.

By 3100 BC, all Uruk's trading outposts had been either destroyed or abandoned, so the ruling elite of the city-state tried a new strategy to maintain a flow of goods into the city. The rulers and city administrators began to invite citizens they knew and trusted to take individual responsibility for specific trade missions. To induce traders to undertake their risky missions, administrators consigned to them the materials they could trade. The city owned a surplus of textiles and baskets that Uruk's citizens had made and paid in tribute, a form of taxation. The city further incentivized traders with the opportunity to keep whatever profits they earned from their actions. It was up to the traders themselves to get as much copper or timber as they could in return for the baskets and textiles they were given on consignment. If they did not bring back the minimum amount, however, they were liable for the difference. The city charged the traders interest on the value of their consignment to ensure that they returned as quickly as possible.

The strategy worked so well that within a few generations, other Mesopotamian city-states copied this consignment trading system. Some merchants amassed significant assets and wealth independent of the ruling elite. Regional trading was so vigorous and important to the well-being of the culture that explicit rules were enacted in many city-states requiring entrepreneurs to document their contracts. They also had to keep written records to reasonably adjudicate the disputes that would inevitably arise. We're fortunate to have found and translated many of these tablets.

Within a few generations of empowering independent traders, they began to write about their "profit," or *mās*, which also meant "interest," as in an extra payment in addition to the original loan. From that point forward, the archeological record is awash with tens of thousands of records of Mesopotamian entrepreneurs, describing what they produced or sold, how they acted, and what they needed to do to capture this profit.

The system of using entrepreneurs to direct and control long-distance trade between city-states (what today we would think of as the city-states' supply chains) remained in place throughout the region until Alexander the Great took control around two thousand years later. The records describe ancient Mesopotamia as a dynamic entrepreneurial culture that, in many ways, worked the same as Silicon Valley does today, as have many other entrepreneurial societies throughout time.

In this example, we see how the world's oldest major civilization embraced and encouraged entrepreneurial behavior: Mesopotamian culture revolved around city-states ruled by ambitious kings who controlled territories poor in resources that were critical to the prosperity of their kingdoms and the support of their elites. These kings adopted a successful and resource-efficient strategy of forming, and then supporting, an entrepreneurial class independent of the ruling elite that innovated and mastered skills associated with all types of trade.

Global Behaviors

The Indus Valley civilization also had a thriving entrepreneurial culture. As the most geographically expansive and diverse culture on the planet in its heyday (2500 to 1900 BC), it spanned the western Himalayan drainage basin, running two thousand miles north to south and five hundred miles west to east. Its two great cities, Harappa and Mohenjo-Daro, had the most advanced urban amenities of the time, including indoor plumbing and toilets. The ubiquity and uniformity of their stone weights and measures show that they maintained set rules and regulations. They even produced standardized clay and stone seals that were used for marking property ownership. But how they governed themselves peacefully for such a long time remains a mystery. There are no records of large public buildings or showy palaces, nor is there evidence of any central warehouses where food would have been collected for redistribution. The daily lives of those cities' inhabitants also remain obscure. These mysteries are even more tantalizing because this civilization had a writing system that we have yet to decipher.

What we do know is that as early as 4000 BC, members of the Indus Valley civilization were traveling significant distances and climbing or descending considerable heights to exchange their surplus goods, manufactured or harvested, with others. The village of

Mehrgarh, located about a hundred miles north of Mohenjo-Daro, included a central market. There, archeologists have found extensive evidence of foodstuffs and commodities grown or produced in distant parts of the region. Items from the highlands are very different from those of the lowlands or the seashore, and apparently some among the population were highly motivated and felt safe enough to travel extensively to acquire things they found unique, exotic, or desirable.

The general population, not just elites, particularly valued high-quality pottery and jewelry in the form of beads and bangles. The cultural demand induced craftspeople to innovate and specialize to make their products more desirable, spurring the move of production from their homes to separate workshops as early as 3300 BC. Indus craftspeople developed a long list of remarkable technologies that enabled them to transform and manipulate materials to produce new colors and complex patterns in refined shapes and a wide variety of sizes. The most culturally prized objects, stoneware bangles for the arms and legs, were produced in neighborhoods surrounded by walls, and only in the two large cities. Due to this arrangement, it has been speculated that bangle producers wanted to protect their secret of producing unique ceramic lusters by firing them in tightly controlled atmospheres. It is unknown whether the bangle makers were entrepreneurial, because their craft may have been controlled by some other group, perhaps a trade association, meaning that they may not have been self-directed in their actions.

On the other hand, entrepreneurs were almost certainly among the Indus Valley pottery and bead producers. While they tended to congregate in neighborhoods, theirs were not closed off, and they could also be found in other cities and towns. They produced products that varied and used diverse techniques to make them. There was no centralized control or standardized methodology.

They were, by all accounts, self-directed, at least those who were not precisely and unthinkingly following the actions prescribed by their entrepreneurial ancestors.

Cuneiform tablets mention that at least a few Indus Valley traders made it all the way to Mesopotamia, which means they had contact with that region's entrepreneurial traders. Persian Gulf traders of the time also would have been exposed to the entrepreneurial behavior of their Mesopotamian brethren and may have passed some of those practices and behaviors to the Indus traders they dealt with. (Indeed, Indus Valley jewelry and seals have been found along the coast of the Persian Gulf and in Mesopotamia.) Though no one knows for sure, it's safe to suspect that Indus Valley long-distance traders were as entrepreneurial as the craftspeople who supplied them.

Governmental need spurred entrepreneurship in Mesopotamia; governmental neglect spurred it in ancient Egypt. In the Indus Valley civilization, it was their cultural appreciation for diversity among their craftspeople, particularly those who made jewelry and pottery, that inspired entrepreneurs to innovate.

At the Bottom of the Celestial Order

Unlike Heqanakht, Ötzi, or some of the other ancient entrepreneurs discussed so far, we know the name Zidong not by accident but because he was a disciple of Confucius and the first entrepreneur to be mentioned in Chinese literature. Confucius conferred on Duanmu Ci the name Zidong and refers to him this way throughout *The Analects*, the compendium of Confucian sayings compiled after the philosopher died in 479 BC. Zidong was a wealthy merchant when he came to study with Confucius and his other disciples. To Confucius, Zidong was emblematic of what Chinese culture considered a good entrepreneur: loyal, intelligent, and strategic; a person to whom profit-making was of lower priority than creating harmony for his family, and who revered his leaders, elders, and ancestors. Zidong understood his place in ancient Chinese society and his responsibilities to others.

Entrepreneurship was also implicit in a core Chinese belief that everyone has an appropriate place in a harmonious society. Of greatest importance to order, and therefore at the top of the natural hierarchy, were strong and learned leaders; followed by farmers, who produced what was needed for life; then artisans, who created products that made living easier and more enjoyable; and, finally, merchants, who sought to profit off the work of others.

But entrepreneurs existed in China long before Confucius's time. The Chinese character for profit is "li," a combination of the characters for "rice field" and "the sharp point of a plow." The character has an ancient provenance, showing up before 1000 BC. Clearly, people noticed that Chinese farmers who invested in sharp plows had greater yields and were wealthier. The character also meant "auspicious," as in good fortune. "Profit" and "good fortune" were synonyms in ancient China.

Determining the earliest roots of Chinese entrepreneurship can only be speculative, given the currently available historical record. By the beginning of the Shang dynasty in 1460 BC, there were two large bronze-making workshops outside the walls of Zhengzhou Shang City, which may indicate that some bronze ritual vases and utilitarian objects, like belt buckles, were produced by independent artisans and not controlled by the ruling elite. Prior to this date, all workshops—bronze or otherwise—were located in close proximity to the palaces of local rulers. Merchants may have acted independently to facilitate the trade of some local exotic foodstuffs, crafts, or perhaps even fine textiles. Merchants were a well-established part of Chinese social hierarchy from around 1000 BC at the latest, five hundred years before Confucius, but evidence of either merchants or independent artisans before the Zhou dynasty is scant.

Continental Connective Tissue

Entrepreneurs developed independently and in many forms throughout America. The Chavín, dating from 850 to 200 BC, allowed self-directed industry and trading. The wealthy and sophisticated Chavín culture encompassed all of the Peruvian coast and the watershed of the central Andes. The archeological record from 500 BC on shows evidence of a wide assortment of pottery types and styles produced in many locations, all using different techniques and materials, making their way to the capital. The distribution of utilitarian ceramics points to Chavín rulers' encouragement of and reliance on entrepreneurial behavior centered in the surrounding towns and villages to provide residents with goods and diverse foodstuffs.

Mesoamerica also contains evidence of a system that relied on independent artisans and traders. From extensive studies of the Valley of Oaxaca, we know that villages specialized in producing certain types of goods, baskets, tools, and foods by 200 AD. This production was located in and around individual homesteads with easy access to market plazas, which were connected to one another by roads. During this same period, Mayan rulers, like the pharaohs, controlled the production and trade of high-status objects such as jade and metals but left the production and trade of other items to individuals.

Farther north in central Mexico, an entrepreneurial golden age of both utilitarian and luxury goods flourished around 950 AD.

A specific group of people, the *pochteca*, carried out all long-distance trade throughout the Triple Alliance, commonly referred to as the Aztecs. The pochteca were self-directed in how they negotiated and traded, but they had to pay taxes and satisfy the needs of the ruling elite in return for their monopoly position in long-distance trade. This is normal, of course. Entrepreneurial activities are always subject to the constraints imposed on them by rulers and governments, and that was no different in the case of the pochteca. For example, a subgroup, the *tlatoani*, were expert in procuring slaves required for sacrifice and menial labor in large construction projects, while another subgroup, the *tencunenenque*, focused on procuring objects for the ruler to demonstrate power and prestige, as well as providing useful information about distant towns and tribes to rulers and military leaders.

During this time, both utilitarian and luxury goods were created by independent artisans, often working in specialized neighborhoods with workshops attached to their homes. Trade and political networks facilitated the transfer of goods over roads and waterways, enabling the expansion of production to supply local, regional, and export consumption. Production and trade thrived during the Triple Alliance, and contemporary conquistador accounts marveled at the activity and breadth of products available in the markets when they arrived in 1521; "more varied than a European city" they wrote.

An Everywhere Behavior

Evidence exists throughout ancient history of entrepreneurial behavior that developed independently of any urbanization or social hierarchy. Hunter-gatherers practiced entrepreneurship to take control of their own future. The beads produced in Wadi Jilad required extensive effort, and far more were manufactured than the group could have wanted for themselves, or even for the purpose of lavish gifting. This excess production helped the group ensure their livelihood. The Cabezo Juré clan also expended immense effort in traveling thousands of miles looking for an ideal location to produce copper tools—they, too, wanted control.

The archaeological record proves that entrepreneurship eventually develops in all urban cultures throughout the world, while many systems develop in turn to control, restrict, or encourage entrepreneurial behavior. The extent to which people can choose to make or collect desirable assets for themselves in exchange for performing specialized skills varies with the level of trust that develops between rulers and their citizenry.

The kings in Mesopotamia and the Aztec empire trusted a distinct class of entrepreneurs to oversee the trade that was essential to their power and legitimacy. Whoever governed the city-states in the Indus Valley appears to have encouraged widespread entrepreneurial behavior in both the production of goods and trade. Mayan, Egyptian, and Chinese rulers controlled the distribution of prestigious goods and foodstuffs around their capitals but deferred to entrepreneurs to supply the commodities needed and wanted by more distant citizenry, or simply ignored them. Entrepreneurship eventually appears within every form of economy and every type of society, however it is controlled.

As entrepreneurship develops, it changes the societies in which it operates. It expands the breadth of the goods available as entrepreneurs work to improve their standard of living, which also improves the standard of living of the people they deal with. An essential by-product of entrepreneurship is that it forces change on its customers, not by physical force but by force of desire and consumption. Societies do not require entrepreneurs to exist, nor do entrepreneurs coerce rulers of city-states or kingdoms to let them operate—their legitimacy comes from satisfying desires that rulers cannot.

Entrepreneurship is a primal force that drives some people living in groups to expend huge amounts of energy and take risks to deliver products and services to others. As a force that shapes how societies operate and what they consume, it is clearly something we need to understand much better.

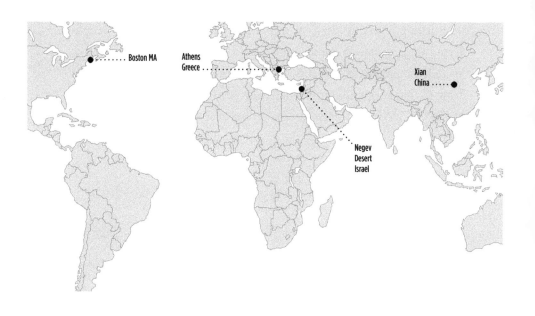

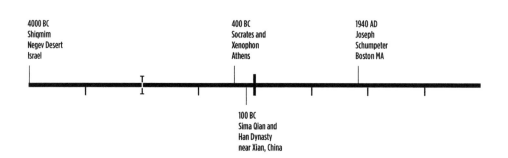

4000 BC
Shiqmim
Negev Desert
Israel

400 BC
Socrates and
Xenophon
Athens

1940 AD
Joseph
Schumpeter
Boston MA

100 BC
Sima Qian and
Han Dynasty
near Xian, China

Boston MA

Athens
Greece

Xian
China

Negev
Desert
Israel

CHAPTER 2

The Core of Entrepreneurship

But whether [entrepreneurship] be for good or ill, it is upon us, beyond our power to alter, and therefore to be accepted and made the best of.

—Andrew Carnegie, *The Gospel of Wealth*, 1889

A s we saw in chapter 1, most societies larger than a few thousand individuals, no matter how ancient or technology-free, have tolerated or even encouraged entrepreneurs and benefited from their efforts. There are fundamental reasons societies encourage entrepreneurs, chasing the benefits of entrepreneurial innovations while accepting the unintended consequences of their innovations. Many wise people through the ages have wondered what has driven this widespread acceptance.

A Historic Question

Sima Qian (ca. 145–86 BC) was the son of a court historian in the early Han dynasty (see figure 2.1). As an ardent follower of the

2.1 Portrait of Sima Qian.

Source: Wikipedia, http://diq.wikipedia.org/wiki/Image:Sima_Qian_%28painted_portrait%29.jpg.

philosophy of Confucius and therefore a loyal son, he dedicated his life (and, as we'll see, his testicles) to fulfilling his father's dream of researching and writing a complete history of China. The *Shiji* (*Records of the Grand Historian*) is considered one of the great works of history; it was required reading for the Chinese intellectual elite and aspiring bureaucrats for two millennia.

As he viewed it, Sima Qian was assembling and documenting an unbiased history of China to ensure it would be known for eternity. He was outspoken about the wisdom that could be derived from understanding history. In fact, he felt so strongly about the importance of an unbiased view of history that he felt compelled to disagree with Emperor Wu's assessment of the role his generals played in losing a battle to nomads near China's northern border. As a result, he was accused of treason and sentenced to death. As a court official, however, he could accept castration and humiliation instead, with an expectation of suicide. He chose castration and humiliation but indefinitely postponed his suicide so he could finish his history.

Sima Qian's extensive review of documents found in archives throughout China led him to believe that entrepreneurs played a critical role in creating the empire's great wealth. In a chapter translated as "The Biographies of the Money-Makers," he writes, "Society must have farmers before it can eat; foresters, fisherman, miners, etc., before it can make use of natural resources; craftsmen before it can have manufactured goods; and merchants before they can be distributed." He makes it clear that profit was the driving motivation for the wealth accumulated in China, quoting a famous ancient Chinese jingle:

> Jostling and joyous,
> The whole world comes after profit;
> Racing and rioting,
> After profit the whole world goes!

Sima Qian goes on to describe specific individuals who accumulated massive wealth that equaled or exceeded that of rulers; he clearly felt that these people were important enough that subsequent generations should appreciate and respect their accomplishments. For instance, he details how a Mr. Chou was taken captive in one of the many wars that ravaged China as the Zhou dynasty collapsed. Chou was stripped of his wealth and forcefully resettled in a distant part of the kingdom. He then used his knowledge of iron smelting to "accumulate wealth until soon he dominated the trade among the people of Tien and Shu." Sima Qian mentions three other iron smelters—it was a hot technology in China around 300 BC—who amassed fortunes equal to or exceeding that of feudal lords. The entrepreneurial Ping family's influence was such "that so many people in Tsou and Lu abandoned scholarship and turned to the pursuit of profit." He then describes successful slavers, whom he acknowledges as controversial; merchants, some of whom accumulated vast agricultural landholdings and large herds of animals; rags-to-riches ranchers; and moneylenders. The *Shiji's* implied definition of "money-maker" is similar to what some would consider a contemporary definition of entrepreneur: a person who creates wealth by chasing after profit. These people intrigued Sima Qian just as entrepreneurs intrigue us today.

An Idealist's Essential Skill

Profit-seekers also fascinated Socrates (ca. 470–399 BC). We usually think of Socrates as the person whom Plato described in *The Republic*, someone who abhorred profit-seeking, but that is an incomplete understanding. Socrates greatly respected some entrepreneurs. In fact, his views are similar to those of Confucius, a contemporary. Profit-seeking was a benefit if the citizen devoted those profits to the glory and well-being of their city-state and fellow citizens.

Socrates's views on profit-seeking were documented by Xenophon (ca. 430–354 BC) in his book *Oeconomicus* (see figure 2.2). The book details a dialogue between Socrates (an acquaintance) and an esteemed estate-owning Athenian citizen. It begins with Socrates questioning what an estate manager is, making it clear that estate management is about managing not only the land you own but also your physical and social assets so that they yield profits. The dialogue makes clear that estate management

2.2 Bust of Xenophon.

Source: Kgl. Museum, Berlin, https://en.wikipedia.org/wiki/Xenophon.

is something every citizen should aspire to do well; they should strive to be observant and thoughtful while seeking advice to improve the profitability of all their assets. Esteemed estate managers are men who understand how assets yield profits, work in partnership with their wives, hire and train people to be attentive to profits (Socrates is humorously instructed to be a more profitable farmer), and inspire their slaves by praising and rewarding them for good work and for mastering profitable skills. The book's advice is still relevant today if you substitute "worker" for "slave" and take away the gender specificity.

Xenophon and Plato were contemporaries, both members of Socrates's retinue of young Athenian men. Whereas Plato dedicated his life to disseminating his master's teachings, Xenophon left Athens at the age of twenty-nine to lead ten thousand Greek mercenaries to help Cyrus the Younger overthrow the Persian king. When the rebellion failed, Xenophon was forced to lead his troops through hundreds of miles of hostile territory to safely return to Greece, winning great acclaim. He then went to work for the king of Sparta, Athens's mortal rival, demonstrating an unusually open-minded political pragmatism very different from Plato's idealism. Socrates left a big impression on Xenophon; indeed, he was so impressed that he went on to write four Socratic dialogues and reminiscences. He was particularly attentive to the master's practical advice and descriptions of the real world. Xenophon may have been particularly interested in documenting Socrates's opinions on estate management and profit-seeking in *Oeconomicus* because he built and managed his own estate.

Since the age of Socrates, people have sought to understand the profit-seekers who created wealth for their communities. Entrepreneurs have fascinated us for millennia, even before the word "entrepreneur" was first used by Richard Cantillon in his 1730 seminal treatise on economics, *Essay on the Nature of Commerce in General*. Since Cantillon coined the term, economists have dominated attempts to define and describe what an entrepreneur is, creating in the intervening three centuries at least fourteen schools of thought on how entrepreneurs influence the creation of wealth. Entrepreneurs, of course, have mostly ignored the debate. They've been too busy seeking profit.

What Is It?

Today "entrepreneur" and "entrepreneurship" are so widely used that they can mean just about anything. Virtually any two people discussing the topic of entrepreneurship, including academics, will have different ideas about who qualifies as an entrepreneur.

Hundreds of articles have been written on the subject—mostly in the 1980s and 1990s, when entrepreneurship as a subject was beginning to be taught in universities—but academics have now given up trying to agree. Most people just assume that everyone shares their opinion, so definitions are rarely given, and confusion ensues. The word "entrepreneurship" long ago escaped into the wilds of the vernacular, mutating in meaning as it was dragged along by the currents of culture.

There are three major schools of thought about who counts as an entrepreneur. Contemporary dictionaries tend to focus on somebody who starts and runs their own company. These definitions require that a person has accomplished something: they've started a business that has survived long enough for them to lead it for a period of time, often unstated. There are many variations on this baseline definition: whether the business has to be incorporated, have an employee, have revenues or profits, pay taxes, or meet other conditions. This category of definition is particularly attractive to people who want to count entrepreneurship among their own binary list of accomplishments.

Another category of definition revolves around how an entrepreneur thinks or acts. For example, an entrepreneur might be defined as someone who is trying to start a company or actively looks for ideas that could make money. A popular definition among professors of entrepreneurship is someone who is effective at building systems or processes with very few resources. Into this category we can also put definitions of entrepreneurs as risk-takers, although to be useful, it also requires an accompanying definition of risk. An extreme version of this category comes from the Austrian school of economics, which theorizes that every adult is an entrepreneur because everyone decides what to buy and how to spend their time based on their own unconscious assessment of the risks versus rewards of what they consider worthy of doing.

A third school of thought revolves around the entrepreneur as hero, someone who has special abilities that enable them to innovate and facilitate "creative destruction," resulting in unprecedented progress or disruption. People who use this category of definition are often enamored with that phrase, which they incorrectly attribute to Joseph Schumpeter and which is actually taken grossly out of context. Schumpeter first described the role of entrepreneurs as the agent of economic innovation in his 1911 book, *Theorie der wirtschaftlichen Entwicklung*, which was translated into English in 1934 and became the first edition of *The Theory of Economic Development* (see figure 2.3). This work is considered a landmark in identifying a primary role for entrepreneurs as agents of growth and progress (although Schumpeter's theory has many similarities with Richard Cantillon's original description of an entrepreneur). Twenty-seven years after writing *Theorie*, Schumpeter explains the

2.3 Joseph Schumpeter, ca. 1930–40.

Source: Wikimedia Commons, https://commons.wikimedia.org/wiki
/File:Joseph_Schumpeter_ekonomialaria.jpg.

concept of creative destruction in his 1939 treatise *Business Cycles*. Without explicitly using the term, he describes a process whereby less productive enterprises are replaced with more productive ones over long-term economic cycles. In that book, he reiterates his 1911 theory that entrepreneurs play a critical role in reinvigorating economic productivity and growth at the start of new long-term business cycles.

Schumpeter explicitly uses the catchphrase in his next book, *Capitalism, Socialism, and Democracy*, when identifying the nature of "industrial mutation" in capitalism—not entrepreneurship. There he states the following: "The opening up of new markets, foreign or domestic, and the organizational development from the craft shop and factory to such concerns as U.S. Steel illustrate the process of industrial mutation that incessantly revolutionizes the economic structure *from within*, incessantly destroying the old one, incessantly creating a new one. This process of Creative Destruction is the essential fact about *capitalism*. It is what capitalism consists in and what every capitalist concern has got to live in" (emphasis added).

No mention of "entrepreneur" or "entrepreneurship" appears in this or neighboring sections. In this book, Schumpeter abandons his earlier theory connecting entrepreneurs to innovation, superseding it with a theory of corporate-based innovation. As we will see, in the years between writing his first book focusing on entrepreneurs and his third book associating innovation with industrial mutation, entrepreneurship was sidelined by big business. The catchphrase is not even Schumpeter's—it was coined by the German sociologist Werner Sombart in his 1913 book, *Krieg und Kapitalismus* (*War and Capitalism*). The concept ultimately was first described by Marx, whom Schumpeter credits, to explain a fundamental flaw in the structure of capitalism. It is ironic that many entrepreneurial enthusiasts use "creative destruction" to laud heroic entrepreneurs when the term was originally meant to describe a flaw in the capitalist system.

A Definition for the Ages

Unfortunately, none of the foregoing constructs help us consistently identify entrepreneurs from the historical or archeological records. We need a definition that applies to both Heqanakht and Oprah Winfrey, as well to the actions of both bead-making hunter-gatherers and Cornelius Vanderbilt. As our bead-makers were entrepreneurs before any social structures, economic systems, or markets existed, the definition must be independent of all social or economic constructs. *Entrepreneurs helped to create social structures and economic systems, not vice versa.* Most critically, we need a definition that enables the identification of entrepreneurial activity in archeological records—otherwise we'll just generate more babble.

Based on the examples used throughout the book and many others that we do not have the time, space, or attention span to visit here, entrepreneurs can be defined as individuals who

1. are *self-directed* in their actions;
2. are *innovative in ways that create perceived value* within their local culture; and
3. *entice others to offer them something of value* in return for delivering their innovation.

These three characteristics define a unique, identifiable set of people across time and place to the present day. Most important, we can spot these individuals in archeological and historic records. These individuals mattered.

I offer additional support and describe the derivation of this definition in "Notes on the Definition of 'Entrepreneur'" at the end of the book.

Self-Direction

Humans are social animals. Groups are integral to how we are raised, how we interact with one another, and how we survive. Entrepreneurs, on the other hand, act individually in their creation of value. They choose which societal norms and rules to accept; they decide if they will risk being beheaded or put in jail because they ignored specific rules or laws. In terms of the archeological record, we look for individual or small-group activities that have taken place independently of political or social hierarchies. As described in the previous chapter, in Zhou dynasty China, we looked for evidence of workshops outside palace walls as an indication that they were free of the emperor's control. Because archeologists and anthropologists are very interested in documenting social and political hierarchy in their research and observations, we are often on solid ground in using their findings to extrapolate self-directed behavior.

This criterion has implications. People whose actions are directed by others—whether a strongman, politician, boss, parent, or legacy social ritual—are not entrepreneurs. Many people mimic successful entrepreneurial behaviors by creating value as others have done, but these mimics do so without deliberation. For example, a person who derives wealth from the produce of lands or a business they inherited and maintains the value creation routines already in place is not an entrepreneur. Farmers who inherit their farm and follow the practices of their ancestors are not entrepreneurs, but if a farmer inherits a farm and then creates a more effective method for milking cows that breaks from tradition, trades away the excess production, and thereby measurably captures more value for the family—*that* farmer has become an entrepreneur. This same filtering applies to people who take over or inherit existing businesses.

The self-direction requirement is also effective for filtering business managers from entrepreneurs, or in determining when a startup becomes a business. Business managers might have discretion in how they make moment-to-moment decisions, but they cannot act independently of the expectations of their bosses or the policies and procedures that define their roles. Entrepreneurial enterprises create their own policies and procedures and are led by entrepreneurs who set their own expectations, unconstrained by any higher authority. Societal expectations, laws, or rulers' edicts may attempt to constrain entrepreneurs, but *they choose which to follow*, accepting the personal risks of any consequences.

Entrepreneurs are different from businesspeople who, more often than not, maintain and build on something an entrepreneur started. Steve Jobs and Steve Wozniak were entrepreneurs when they founded Apple Computer. But Jobs's goal was to create a successful business, so, acting on advice from professionals he admired, he hired Mike Markkula and Michael Scott to run the company. While Jobs envisioned and evangelized new computers and Wozniak dreamed up technical innovations, the two Mikes implemented their ideas by running Apple as a professionally managed business, not a startup. Apple prospered over hundreds of other competitors because Steve Jobs chose to run Apple this way.

Likewise, primal businesspeople carried on the valuable practices established by the entrepreneurial founders of places like Cabezo Juré and the bead factory in Wadi Jilat. Most of the descendants of the founder of Cabezo Juré were likely not entrepreneurs, but some of their successors may have been if they broke from tradition to significantly improve the productivity or distribution of copper toolmaking.

Of course, being self-directed isn't the only criterion; otherwise most teenagers would be entrepreneurs.

Innovative in Creating Value

Entrepreneurs must do something their local culture considers valuable—valuable enough to want to trade with them. They create value by introducing an innovation that makes their product or service desirable and unattainable other than by trading with them. The innovation does not need to be unique to the world, just to some local group.

Innovation is different from invention. Invention is the demonstration of a new and creative way of accomplishing a task. Patents are given to inventors after an examiner has determined to his or her satisfaction that nobody has ever thought of the product or the method of accomplishing something. Louis Pasteur's method for making milk safe was an invention. Innovation occurs when some group (it doesn't have to be big) adopts the product or activity as better than anything they've known before. Pasteur did not spend time, nor was he interested in, developing the manufacturing processes to make milk that was safer, still affordable, and available whenever and wherever it was wanted. Milk entrepreneurs were the innovators who figured out how to controllably boil large cauldrons of milk and then bottle and distribute the product while it was still fresh. Groups of people pay for innovations, not the underlying invention, if there even is one.

Entrepreneurial innovation is usually incremental and often has nothing to do with a recent invention. Innovations may be aesthetic, as in a color combination that some group finds extremely pleasing and some item of clothing they need to wear. Offering standard products at lower prices than ever before is an innovation that is easy to convince shoppers to embrace; in this case the innovation is often efficiencies that the entrepreneur has developed for cutting out overhead costs or in methods of negotiating, or both. Offering in another place an item that an entrepreneur sees working in an existing locale can be innovative if it can be done reliably and affordably (that's where the innovation comes in). People being offered what they could not easily access before are grateful to the entrepreneur. A new bakery is an innovator when it offers crispier croissants to a neighborhood where croissants are soggy. The croissant cravers in the neighborhood embrace the new bakery as the best around and gladly spend their money to keep the entrepreneurial baker in business.

The notion that innovation can be incremental yet still valuable means that many, if not most, of the features of entrepreneurial products and services are derivative or copycat. For anyone to want the copycat requires that it be different in some discernable way from the original. Today, the difference might be as small as a logo that has meaning to some group. This feature of entrepreneurship means that entrepreneurs who are in close proximity or whose products can be easily compared must engage in a constant game of leapfrog: "I copy your incremental innovation and now add to it another incremental distinction." Once the croissant bakery opens and has gained many customers, others will copy what they do. So entrepreneurs have to keep innovating to keep customers from buying croissants from the copycat bakery that was opened by another entrepreneur in a location with more foot traffic. This cycle of incremental leapfrog innovation cumulatively drives much of the progress in the world. I will describe this phenomenon in greater detail after I finish describing the third and final component of the definition.

As a final comment, not all self-directed innovators are entrepreneurs. There are some brilliant artists and craftspeople—and almost all hobbyists—who gladly give away the marvelous products they make to those around them, receiving only gratitude or a spontaneous gift in return.

Enticing Others

For entrepreneurs to keep delivering desirable products and live off their self-directed actions, they must reliably receive something more valuable in return. Value for the entrepreneur, and the society in which he or she lives, is created only when more valuable objects are exchanged for a product or service created with less valuable materials and resources. The innovativeness of the product or service is what makes the customer feel good about an exchange to the point that they willingly hand over objects of greater value.

These exchanges do not happen accidentally. They only happen when people—that is, potential customers—know the product is conveniently available and appreciate its innovativeness. For this to happen, entrepreneurs must *entice* people to meet in a safe place, take the time to understand the product or service, and agree to engage in barter. This is what the Trobriands called *gimwali* and what the academic community would call "double opt-in exchange."

Many exchanges have taken place over time in which one or both parties were compelled to participate by either force or threat of social ostracization. As we saw with the Trobriands, almost all their exchanges were prescribed by ritual and constrained by taboos dictating that an infringing person faced social ostracization or even a communally sanctioned death sentence. Fragile societies cannot risk the festering animosities created when a person feels taken advantage of by someone considered a peer. These animosities can lead to violent schisms that jeopardize the community's survival. Trobriands rarely experienced violence associated with the performance of ritualized exchange. Trade-induced violence was self-limiting because if enough Trobriands felt taken advantage of by one person, even a chief, then the myth of the Flying Canoe basically gave permission to kill the offender.

Mutual gifting is another common form of exchange that is not entrepreneurial, because giving a gift in many cultures creates a social expectation that a gift will be given in return; the receiver faces dire social consequences if they don't hand over an equivalent gift or supplication. Redistribution of goods, tribute payments, and transactions where prices are dictated by third parties, such as guilds or governments, are not double opt-in exchanges.

Many forms of double opt-in exchange have developed through time. Mesopotamian merchants used written contracts whereby value received today resulted in another party receiving items of greater value at a later date. Insurance, loans, options, bills of exchange, licenses, subscriptions, and time payments are all forms of double opt-in exchange, most of which were invented by entrepreneurs. Today we call these types of transactions "arms-length." Markets facilitate double opt-in exchange by providing a physical or virtual location for buyers and sellers to meet and trade, but even today many double opt-in exchanges do not happen in markets; rather, they occur as one-off gimwali-like negotiations with an entrepreneur or between entrepreneurs.

I Can Do That Too

Once an entrepreneur personally benefits from performing a skill, those nearby notice. Some of them inevitably try to perform the same skill and deliver a similar product. Each will do it a little differently, as each has his or her own personal set of resources, traits, and skills. Successful copycat attempts will then be noticed by other potential entrepreneurs; in this way an increasing number of copycat entrepreneurs radiate out geographically, chaotically, from the first successful entrepreneur.

Schumpeter called this effect an "entrepreneurial swarm." Although he used "swarm" descriptively, the term has subsequently acquired a more scientific definition, and some academics have developed mathematical models to describe it. In general, swarms act as if they have a shared intelligence, as each member of the swarm pursues the same common goal. In the case of entrepreneurs, swarms pursue new value highlighted for all by a past or present innovation.

Figure 2.4 illustrates how an entrepreneurial swarm develops and evolves with time. In period 1, an initial person, whom I call an "instigator," offers some product (or service) not previously available, enticing some people within the community to offer something of value to possess it. The existence of the new product and the instigator's increased wealth are noted within the community. In period 2, a few members of the community decide they can do something similar and offer copycat products. This initiates the swarm, but every member of the swarm has unique capabilities, so the way each makes and delivers their product will be incrementally different, as will be the value they receive for it.

As the number and distribution of these exchanges expand, they are noticed by more people in the community and eventually in neighboring communities, which, in period 3, inspires more copycats and further increases the size of the swarm. The swarm's increasing size makes it harder for every member to find enough customers and be offered equivalent value in exchange for their product, forcing some members in period 4 to drop out.

Understanding Entrepreneurial Swarming

1

A person (**instigator**) uses a skill to create something that makes some people (**customers**) happy enough they give something valuable in return.

INSTIGATOR — PRODUCT

INSTIGATOR — PRODUCT — CUSTOMER

People witness the successful exchange.

2

Some of the people witnessing the successful exchange decide they want what the instigator has, and try to **perform the same skill** and deliver a similar product (**copycats**).

INSTIGATOR — PRODUCT

COPYCAT — PRODUCT

COPYCAT — PRODUCT

COPYCAT — PRODUCT

COPYCAT — PRODUCT

COPYCAT — PRODUCT

3

Successful copycat attempts are noticed by yet other potential entrepreneurs and the number of **copycat entrepreneurs increases, forming a swarm.**

4

Some copycat entrepreneurs are **unable to keep up** or are **unsuccessful** in adopting the most beneficial innovations, and leave the swarm.

2.4 How entrepreneurial swarms work.

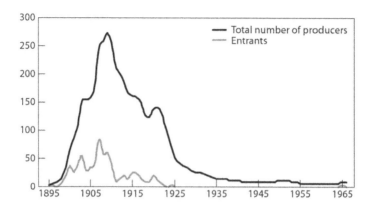

2.5 The size of the automobile swarm in the United States, specifically, the number of firms founded by entrepreneurs who produced automobiles, 1895–66.

Source: Steven Klepper, Experimental Capitalism: The Nanoeconomics of American High-Tech Industries (Princeton, NJ: Princeton University Press, 2015), fig. 2.1.

Figure 2.5 shows the size of the swarm that formed after the first automobile was offered in the United States.

Swarms form for almost every innovation that generates large amounts of value. Swarms persist through generations of incremental waves of innovation until new innovations completely capture the former's value-creating potential. That still represents an enormous number of entrepreneurial swarms. Some, like the swarm that formed around copper tools, are still going after six thousand years. The size of every swarm eventually peaks, but how fast and at what number of members depends on the product, the capabilities within the community surrounding the instigator, and how fast news of the innovation travels (today this is often near the speed of light and no longer a major variable). The sheer number of swarms that exist, and the numbers of global members of each swarm, mean there are huge numbers of entrepreneurs in the world. The estimate today is around one billion.

The Entrepreneurial Innovation Cycle

Entrepreneurial swarming drives innovation. Within every swarm, some members will be motivated to capture more value than the rest. They work more hours to deliver more product than anyone else, and they hire people or use slaves. Others in the swarm try to capture more value by improving product desirability. Still others try to produce the product faster, with fewer or different materials, or by leveraging techniques or technologies they may have learned from another activity.

Entrepreneurs wishing to not drop out of their swarm or increase their pace of asset accumulation try copying what others have done to capture more value. Some will be inspired to use a mix of strategies to innovate their own improvements, some of which will also be copied. The diversity in motivations, skills, traits, resources, and experience sets within the swarm creates an array of incremental improvements—innovations—in the supply of the product, its design, and the methods by which it is made. This desire to copy and improve on the successful techniques used by others to prosper creates a uniquely entrepreneurially accelerating scale and scope of innovation that I call the "entrepreneurial innovation cycle" (EIC).

The sequence of events that drive the EIC is illustrated in figure 2.6. Period 1 represents the status of a swarm that has recently formed and where the diversity of motivations among the members has resulted in different outcomes in supplying similar products. These disparities trigger some members in period 2 to develop their own methods for making more product and getting their increased supply to more customers. For example, as long ago as six thousand years, we find some copper entrepreneurs developing specialized hearths while others developed molds to speed production of the copper tools they could not

How Entrepreneurial Swarming Causes the Entrepreneurial Innovation Cycle (EIC)

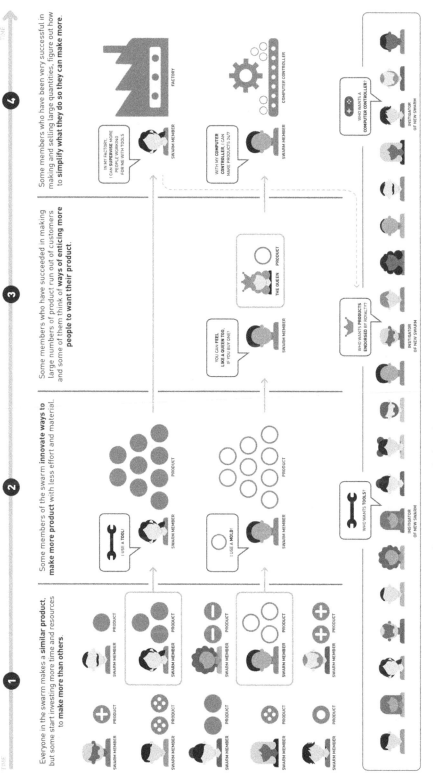

2.6 Understanding the entrepreneurial innovation cycle (EIC).

make enough of. These innovations are then copied and some improved on by many members of the swarm, stimulating wave after wave of innovations to *scale up supply*, with some waves more impactful than others. The cumulative incremental modifications of the product and the methods by which it is produced often also increase its desirability.

Many members of the swarm do not have the skills or time to copy some of the innovations used to scale up supply. The need some have for help often sparks a new set of entrepreneurs to form around the initial swarm. Members of the new swarm offer the tools, machines, and services to help those in the swarm who might otherwise be left behind in their scaling up of supply. Individuals in the initial swarm who are unable to keep up or are unsuccessful in adopting the most beneficial innovations, with or without the help of these specialist entrepreneurs, become exhausted, disheartened, or bankrupted and leave the swarm.

In period 3, some on the leading edge of the swarm encounter a new problem: they've delivered their product to everyone they can find who wants it. Further efforts to scale supply prove frustrating because the product sits unsold. Some individuals in the swarm must now innovate ways to get existing customers to want even more and to get others with no immediate need for the product to want it after all. Six thousand years ago, some copper products entrepreneurs figured out that if they made very ornate products for their most powerful customers, others would want similar products to display their power or importance. "Objects of astonishment" have been a proven way to scale demand ever since. As is always the case with entrepreneurs, the successful methods to scale demand for copper objects were copied by others within the swarm. Again, eventually a new swarm of entrepreneurs develops to provide demand enhancement services and products to members of the initial swarm. This entices more and more customers to want more and more of the product.

Keeping up with all the methods and techniques, as well as supervising all the people and machines needed to scale supply and demand fast enough to stay successful, is exhausting. For every entrepreneur, there is a limit to the scale of supply and demand they can effectively implement and supervise. In period 4 some entrepreneurs direct their innovative skills toward simplifying the tasks they're required to do to stay in control of their enterprise. Back in the Copper Age, some entrepreneurs used other entrepreneurs to refine their copper ingots, thereby simplifying the number of hearths, tools, and refining steps they needed to tend to and master. As with the scaling of supply and demand, a new swarm of entrepreneurs develops to offer their products and services to the more successful members of the initial swarm who need to simplify their tasks to scale up even more.

The initial swarm of entrepreneurs stimulates many waves of innovation to create more and more value for its ambitious members. The efforts of members of the initial swarm also inspire many new swarms to form to support their innovations with products and services that supplement and simplify the tasks required to stay competitive.

The nature of entrepreneurial swarming, with the EIC's requirement that swarm members continuously augment their skills, results in a highly impactful naturally occurring cycle of innovations. This is not the "invisible hand" described by Adam Smith; it is the invisible shove that drives ever-accelerating innovation. The entrepreneurial innovation cycle acts within entrepreneurial swarms while also creating new swarms. The EIC is the force that underpins much of the growth in the standard of living and well-being the world has enjoyed. Enormous scaling has enormous impact.

Unintended Consequences

The EIC adds ever-increasing aggregate value to the world, but it also scales aggregate risk. Entrepreneurs create risk for everyone whether or not we want it. Entrepreneurs scale risk because scaling supply, demand, and simplicity also scales unintended consequences. Swarms of entrepreneurs and their customers create an intensity in the pursuit of value creation that diverts time, energy, resources, and attention away from considering medium- and longer-term consequences. Innovations always have consequences because innovation requires change—changes in natural resources and daily routines that may be more or less healthy or dangerous for everyone. Consider the changes to society sparked by Henry Ford's development of the affordable assembly-line-produced automobile. It changed family structures, landscapes, and commercial processes while also fostering dangerous driving situations and pollution.

The EIC changes what we produce and how we produce things, which change the face of the earth and the chemicals that surround it. It also changes who accumulates wealth and who benefits or suffers from the innovations and the value they create. These accumulating entrepreneurially induced changes stoke social tensions between those who benefit from the changes and those who do not.

The consequent risks are often further amplified when entrepreneurs individually choose which laws and social norms they follow and adopt. If one entrepreneur increases their value capture by flaunting a law or social norm, others in the swarm will, too. As each entrepreneur accepts an individual risk of legal action or social shaming, society lives with the consequences when the previously aberrant behavior is propagated by means of the EIC. British and French slave traders were often socially shunned, but they still forced slavery on populations and enticed people to own slaves. Their actions created major issues that sparked social unrest and war. Poachers supply entrepreneurs with parts of rare species to sell at high prices that endanger entire ecosystems. It used to be considered an invasion of privacy to pry into people's private lives; now every minute detail is available to advertisers on Facebook and Google whether consumers like it or not.

The EIC accelerates with population density and the speed of communication as more people see or hear about how others benefit from their entrepreneurial actions. It also accelerates with the development of new technologies that mitigate previous constraints of energy sources, materials, processing, or precision. As society's entrepreneurs accelerate around this cycle of scaling, the consequences pile up at a quickening pace, and the rest of society gets increasingly reactive.

Entrepreneurs take risks that no established business entity or government can. Some entrepreneurs grapple with these risks, but the rest of us do, too, whether we like it or not. Entrepreneurial scaling challenges the status quo. In response, society tries to control entrepreneurs through words, theologies, social dictates, or laws. Four millennia ago, Hammurabi defined laws to constrain entrepreneurs, such as limiting interest rates that could be charged on mortgages. Today, we argue over laws to limit software companies that invade our privacy. This dynamic between entrepreneurial innovation and social, religious, and political attempts to control it runs through all civilizations and all times. Along the way, it has sparked economic, political, and legal change as well as social unrest, inequality, and war, which we will examine later in the book.

Clusters

Another consequence of the EIC is the resultant geographic clustering of entrepreneurial swarms and consequent concentrations of wealth. The entrepreneurial benefits of operating in proximity to other entrepreneurs attempting to exploit new techniques or technologies are tangible and significant. Unless an entrepreneur invests significant effort in keeping their methods secret, those secrets will become known, first to those in closest proximity, irrespective of patent protection.

Clustering facilitates the copying of best practices. It also facilitates specialization in skills that speed improvement in product design and processing. An individual entrepreneur will gravitate toward using what they personally do best as the basis for how they try to improve their specific version of the product or service.

We can see examples of an entrepreneurial cluster even in the archeological record. Metal refining and metalworking were technologies that transformed civilization and defined the end of the Neolithic era. Around seven thousand years ago, individuals and small groups experienced in techniques used for firing clay to make pottery experimented with creating higher-temperature fires required for producing copper out of green materials like malachite. This more refined copper and its alloys were used to make small tools such as awls (needles to pierce leather). With improved processes, entrepreneurs produced larger luxury goods like standards and sculptures to satisfy demand for public displays of power from a growing number of elite families. The development of metallurgy and its diffusion throughout the Mediterranean basin initiated swarms of entrepreneurial activity, some creating entire new settlements.

Shiqmim is located in the northern Negev desert in present-day Israel, between the borders of Jordan and the Gaza Strip (see

2.7 Location of Shiqmim in the northern Negev Desert.

Source: M. Faerman, and P. Smith, "Has Society Changed Its and Children? Evidence from Archaeo-logical Sites in the Southern Levant." In *Nasciturus, infans, puerulus vobis mater terra: La muerte en la infancia*, Francesc Gusi i Jener, Susanna Muriel, and Carme Olària (Castelló, Spain: Diputación de Castelló, Servei d'Investigacions Arqueològiques i Prehistòriques, 2008), 211–30fig. 2.

figure 2.7). The village was settled rapidly around sixty-five hundred years ago along what was then a river fed by a seasonal watershed. A series of settlements from the same period appeared nearby. Within a few generations of its settlement, many families built individual independent workshops to produce copper tools and objects. Their copper production technology appears nowhere else in the archeological record of the Levant during that time, so the technology was not widely known or disseminated. It appears to have been a closely held secret back in 4000 BC.

The copper-containing malachite used in the production processes of Shiqmim was dug out of the side of a mountain sixty miles away, indicating that the inhabitants invested considerable effort and resources in copper tool production. The ore was smelted and then processed into increasingly purified copper as the material moved through two or more workshops in Shiqmim or neighboring settlements before being hammered or molded into a finished tool like an awl or a mace head. The volume of production exceeded what the families would have needed for their own purposes. There is no evidence of elitist differentiation in the village that would have created any demand for mace heads to demonstrate status. The molded and finished tools were exported throughout the Levant in a form of exchange that we cannot identify. The number and independence of the workshops indicate that this area of the Negev was a locus of ancient entrepreneurial activity, a proverbial Chalcolithic (i.e., Copper Age) Silicon Valley.

The scale of entrepreneurship surrounding copper tool manufacture evolved through the Copper and Bronze Ages. Sixteen centuries after copper tool production began in Shiqmim, the technology had diffused throughout the Mediterranean basin, probably by people who learned the technology in one hamlet and then moved to another. In some of the hamlets that acquired the skill, other inhabitants started their own production. Some hamlets turned into production centers. We do not know what motivated these copper technology migrants to move or flee. Some of the migrant metallurgists may have moved on to marry or find food as the climate changed, but others may have been entrepreneurs seeking opportunity through some mix of reward and social status, like the founders of Cabezo Juré.

We will examine the consequences of swarming and the EIC for the rest of the book. In the next chapter I focus on how the groups

that cultures try to prevent from being self-directed actually succeed as entrepreneurs. By understanding the significant constraints
outsiders overcome by joining entrepreneurial swarms, we further
understand entrepreneurship as a vastly underappreciated, potent
force of social change.

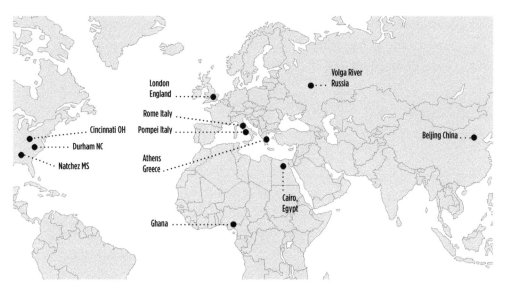

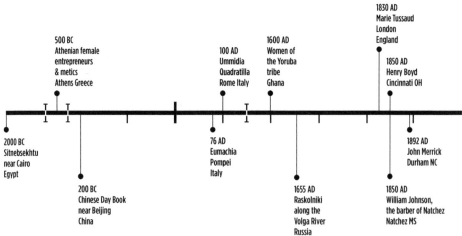

London England
Volga River Russia
Rome Italy
Pompei Italy
Cincinnati OH
Durham NC
Natchez MS
Beijing China
Athens Greece
Cairo, Egypt
Ghana

1830 AD
Marie Tussaud
London
England

500 BC
Athenian female
entrepreneurs
& metics
Athens Greece

100 AD
Ummidia
Quadratilla
Rome Italy

1600 AD
Women of
the Yoruba
tribe
Ghana

1850 AD
Henry Boyd
Cincinnati OH

2000 BC
Sitnebsekhtu
near Cairo
Egypt

76 AD
Eumachia
Pompei
Italy

1892 AD
John Merrick
Durham NC

200 BC
Chinese Day Book
near Beijing
China

1655 AD
Raskolniki
along the
Volga River
Russia

1850 AD
William Johnson,
the barber of Natchez
Natchez MS

CHAPTER 3

Outsiders

You can not depend upon any one else to do it for you.

—Irene Hartt, *How to Make Money, Although a Woman*, 1895

W ritten histories and archeological records highlight the struggles and successes of the elites, leaving many other stories untold. The study of the past is inherently biased toward the politically, economically, and socially powerful. For one thing, their monuments and luxury items are far more likely to resist the erosion of time than the meager possessions of nonelites. For another, elites have long compensated people to record their successes, something commoners could never afford to do. For most of history, what is written, and the methods of preserving the legacies of the powerful, have been controlled by privileged males. The powerful have no interest in acknowledging others' efforts, particularly the accomplishments of those who flaunt or overcome societal constraints, thereby exposing imperfections in that society—and the elites whom those flaws unfairly helped.

In this chapter, we look at the entrepreneurs who ruling elites have tried, explicitly or implicitly, to hide from history: women, slaves, ethnic and religious minorities, the underclass, and immigrants—in other words, outsiders. Over the past few decades, we have begun to be able to discern outlines of the roles historical outsiders have played in shaping the societies in which they lived. Of course, we have not discovered nearly as many details about those outsiders as we have about entrepreneurs who were privileged males. Evidence that outsiders were successful entrepreneurs in their own right and for their own self-directed purposes has only recently emerged based on closer review of the archeological record and of very early written records. Minorities, by definition, represent a smaller percentage of the population than women do, making them more difficult to spot archeologically and in the earliest historical records. When writing became more common, after 500 BC, we find more evidence of outsider entrepreneurship. The entrepreneurial strategies that outsiders developed to overcome the additional constraints they faced are both illuminating and valuable.

"The scope of woman's work to-day is larger than it ever was before," Irene Hartt wrote with justifiable optimism in her 1895 book, *How to Make Money, Although a Woman.* "It is a great thing now to be a woman." Women made great gains in independence in nineteenth-century America, with large numbers entering the workforce and many becoming entrepreneurs. This blossoming of female entrepreneurship did not happen in most other countries at the time, and, sadly, much of that momentum was lost as better-financed men formed bigger, copycat versions of the businesses that women pioneered.

Although this chapter describes some of the ups and downs faced by women, minority, and other outsider entrepreneurs, its focus is on the historical constraints outsiders have faced and the strategies they have used to overcome them. Outsiders are essential participants in entrepreneurial swarms. They are forced to participate in ways different from those of their privileged male counterparts, using unique methods of scaling and innovating to ensure that their investments of time, energy, and resources circumvent the constraints they face. Thus, outsider entrepreneurs are often the most resourceful, innovative, and ambitious members of the entrepreneurial swarms they join, even as the ruling elite ignore them or explicitly repress their wealth and influence.

The constraints that societies place on women, slaves, minorities, the underclass, and immigrants never completely curtailed their entrepreneurial ambitions. Laws and religious proscriptions have prevented women in many societies from leaving their homes or controlling their own assets. Often, women seen in public without a husband or male guardian were considered sexually promiscuous, a threat to the stability of society. Many minority groups were prevented from owning certain types of enterprises or even doing business with members of the majority group. These constraints and others made it extremely difficult to be self-directed, to master skills other than those practiced in the home, or to entice strangers to engage in any public form of exchange. Yet, some outsider entrepreneurs have thrived in every society, whether through cunning, persistence, or both.

The efforts of outsiders to overcome the additional obstacles society places in their way have changed the course of history, albeit more subtly than the actions of privileged entrepreneurs. To be self-directed, master and practice their special skill, and entice strangers to engage in mutually beneficial exchange, outsiders must simultaneously stand out and fit in. The strategies outsiders have used to succeed are fundamental and universal.

Always Shining Through

Recall Heqanakht, our stressed-out Egyptian friend whom we met in chapter 1, dictating letters to direct the efforts of his employees in various real estate, moneylending, and trading enterprises. One of his letters he scribed himself. This letter was destined for a fellow Egyptian entrepreneur, a woman named Sitnebsekhtu, who ran a four-employee workshop turning flax into linen cloth. When communicating with his employees, Heqanakht conveyed his demands with emotion and urgency. His letter to Sitnebsekhtu clearly indicates he is writing to a business equal. High-quality linen cloth was a freely exchangeable commodity in ancient Egypt, so Sitnebsekhtu provided a very important service by turning flax reeds into this money-like commodity, and she was paid handsomely for it. This four-thousand-year-old document describes a business transaction between a male and a female entrepreneur in which the man shows trust in and respect for the woman.

Egyptian tomb paintings show women merchants wherever male merchants are shown—perhaps not in equal proportions, but they are there (see figures 3.1 and 3.2). Other than the clothes they wear, men and women merchants in tomb paintings are depicted as equals. Women are not smaller in size, as are some of the foreign traders arriving by boat, nor are they shown dealing in less valuable goods.

During this same period in Mesopotamia, the first quarter of the second millennium BC, women merchants also appear in documents, fleetingly but with apparently equal status. Independent women traders lived in Kanesh, a vibrant Anatolian trading colony of Assur. Though few, they were present, and their houses were average in size. Unfortunately, the cuneiform tablets found in their homes have yet to be translated and published. Historians have not given these artifacts the attention they deserve.

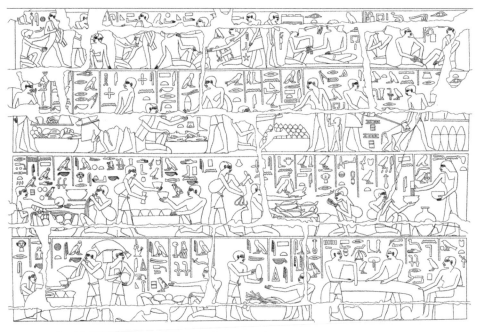

3.1 Market scene from the tomb of Niankhkhnum and Khnumhottep.

Source: Nicky van de Beek, "Saqqara Scenes: Women in the Marketplace," https://nickyvandebeek
.com/wp/wp-content/uploads/Beek_N_van_de_Saqqara_scenes_Women_in_the_marketplace.pdf.

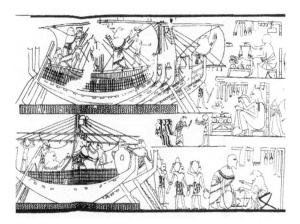

3.2 Detail from the tomb of Kenamun in Thebes.

Source: Hélène Bouillon, "On the Anatolian Origins of Some Late Bronze Egyptian Vessel Forms,"
Anatolia Antiqua XXIII (2015): fig. 2. https://journals.openedition.org/anatoliaantiqua/342.

Around the same time, in a different part of Mesopotamia, Hammurabi's law explicitly denoted in feminine tense the regulations pertaining to tavern owners. While many of the laws explicitly concerned women and assessed lesser damages for their personal injuries, none of Hammurabi's other laws concerning entrepreneurs explicitly assigned women entrepreneurs a greater or lesser penalty, value, or position. The only exception was the law concerning taverns, which conveys the sense that women dominated the Mesopotamian industry that fed and housed travelers.

We find a similar situation in ancient China. Chinese texts written before 200 BC are extremely rare. Among the few that archeologists have recovered from graves are several "day books." These combined almanac and astrological forecasts and were assembled by professional prognosticators for individuals of means. Written on thin wooden strips strung together with rope, these texts were found near the heads of the deceased, appearing to have been important in helping the buried individual make decisions during their life, afterlife, or both. A section of these books is usually concerned with "Giving Birth to Children" and offers forecasts for what will happen to a child born on each day of the sixty-day calendar cycle then in use. One such prognostication reads (see figure 3.3) as follows:

> If one gives birth on an *yihai* day: the child will be fine and become rich.
>
> If one gives birth on a *dingchou* day: the child will be good at using words but may have a milky film over his corneas [i.e., be a blind bard].
>
> If one gives birth on a *gengyin* day: if a girl, she will become a merchant, if a boy, he will enjoy fine clothes and jewels and be wealthy.
>
> (Quoted from Barbieri-Low's *Artisans in Early Imperial China*)

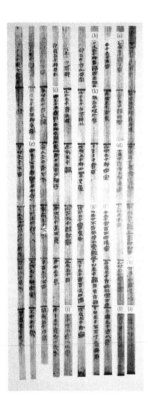

3.3 Text of "Giving Birth to Children" from Daybook Text A, ca. 216 BC.

Source: Cultural Relics Publishing House.

The forecast for each day mixed and matched some combination of gender, profession, physical characteristics, and level of wealth and status. Becoming a female merchant or successful female artisan was portrayed as a positive outcome for women in ancient China. They were there even if we can't easily identify them from what has been left behind.

Behind Closed Doors

Women's standing in ancient Greek society was highly constrained by cultural norms and legal regulations. Together, plays, records of trials, political speeches, and books written for a literate citizenry give us a good sense of women in Athens public life but only an insinuation of the private lives of female Athenian entrepreneurs. They were expected to be seen in public only with an appropriate male guardian. Legally, they could not own property other than gifts they received, and they could not transact any exchange more valuable than a bushel of barley. With pity, Athenian texts mention women who did business in public. Selling things like vegetables or ribbons in the market was considered servile, but a market known as the *gynaikeia agora* served only women. We know of several women who were successful tradespeople, even some who supplied materials for public buildings and temples, but they were the exceptions.

That said, women were highly respected for being entrepreneurial within their prescribed wifely duties. Socrates, as described by Xenophon in his *Oeconomicus*, explicitly states, "I think that the wife who is a good partner in the household contributes as much as her husband to its good; because the income *for the most part* is the result of the husband's exertions, but the *expenses are controlled mostly by the wife's management*. If they both do their part well, the estate is increased, if they act incompetently, it is diminished" (emphasis added).

Writings such as this imply that Greek women were encouraged to pursue home-based profit-making activities. Wives of the middle class and many elite households managed, trained, and organized slaves to produce clothing, accessories, and delectables for both the household and the market. Because women couldn't directly sell their products, slaves did it for them. The profits from these sales added to the wealth of the household. Though the income was not legally controlled by the wife, many directed how some or all of it was used.

The Greek model—women prevented from publicly selling their wares but privately practicing valuable skills as long as their products were offered indirectly to strangers—has been a common starting point for female entrepreneurs in both Western and non-Western cultures.

Women began deviating from this model in larger numbers in ancient Rome. The unprecedented growth of Roman cities made the middle class and commoners anxious about where they could get the goods they needed and less concerned about who they got them from. We can document many hundreds of examples of successful female entrepreneurs in Rome and throughout its empire. For example, Eumachia, a woman that lived in Pompei, was the town's most successful fuller, an establishment that cleaned and dyed clothes. She was wealthy and successful enough to help pay for a temple on the forum that honored all fullers, male or female. A statue depicting her as if she were divine was placed prominently in the temple (see figure 3.4).

3.4 Eumachia, the most successful fuller of Pompei, depicted in a statue found in a temple erected by the fuller guild.

Source: Wikipedia, https://en.wikipedia.org/wiki/Eumachia.

Let Me Oblige You

The constraints restricting the entrepreneurial actions of outsider entrepreneurs vary depending on time, place, and the group in question. For example, a set of Athenian laws specifically constrained the entrepreneurial activities of immigrants, known as *metics*. Metics were allowed to live in Athens provided they registered with the government and found a citizen sponsor. They were prevented from owning property and required to pay an additional tax. Their actions and what types of businesses they could start were further constrained by having to find an Athenian sponsor. Athens was welcoming to immigrant entrepreneurs offering products and services that its citizens weren't interested or skilled enough to provide. Metic entrepreneurs served an important role in Athens as long-distance traders, particularly of grains, by trading with relatives or people they knew back home. Others possessed valuable skills, such as blacksmithing. This is a common theme with outsider entrepreneurs: just do what the majority would rather not.

Slaves were a different story. Almost all Greek slaves were captured foreigners who were sold into slavery by entrepreneurs. They had virtually no rights and could be physically punished for disobedience, whereas citizens and metics could not. Most slaves were forced to do the dangerous, backbreaking, and dirty jobs that Athenians of any class, not even metics, were willing to do. Even so, we know of successful slave entrepreneurs because some were written about. Others left temple offerings with short personal descriptions that show specific evidence of their endeavors. Some Athenian citizens, following the advice of Xenophon and Socrates, incentivized their slaves to run businesses on their behalf, with profits going toward buying the slaves' freedom. Convincing their masters of their business abilities, many slaves ran businesses, and some successfully bought their own freedom despite the extraordinary constraints they faced. For example, a slave banker named Passion played a critical role in developing banking practices in Athens and even was granted Athenian citizenship after he was freed. Many of his innovative banking practices remain to this day. Ironically, some slaves in ancient Athens, despite not being able to own property, faced fewer entrepreneurial constraints than female citizens.

Outsider entrepreneurs have historically offered to do what wealthy men did not know how to do or did not want to do for themselves. Making money from acting servile in the eyes of the elite has helped many outsiders, including the very poor, live more comfortable lives; the lucky and ambitious ones have even become wealthy themselves. Many societies, from ancient times to the present, have counted on very large numbers of entrepreneurs to provide services, particularly personal services, that are essential to keeping citizens healthy and happy enough not to revolt.

(Let me correct a pervasive falsehood: prostitution is not "the world's oldest profession" and it is not a business historically run by women or outsiders. According to the earliest records from ancient Mesopotamia, what we would think of today as prostitution was actually a temple-controlled activity. Only when prostitution was no longer controlled by the state did entrepreneurs move in. At that point, the use of slaves made brothels a profitable entrepreneurial business for men—and a few women. The lone woman selling her sexual services is not an example of a historically successful entrepreneurial strategy for women to make money.)

Taking Over

The Athenian women who were pitied for selling vegetables and ribbons in the marketplace were the start of a far more important story. Women vegetable hawkers have been found worldwide in markets serving the lower classes since the first mention of central markets in literature, around 500 BC. In a similar fashion, self-directed, independent, skilled washerwomen have been common in societies around the world for thousands of years. Women providing services, such as making and selling clothing accessories (like ribbons), aimed at other women have typically faced few constraints beyond pity and the potential wrath of a husband. As is true in almost all swarms, many of these businesses are subsistence, but some are not.

The Yoruba of Western equatorial Africa—present-day Nigeria and Benin—are a tribe with an ancient lineage. Archeologists find evidence of important Yoruba urban centers dating from at least two thousand years ago. Without a written tradition, we must rely on oral histories passed down through generations to trace entrepreneurial practices hundreds of years back.

The Yoruba have traditionally been a male-dominated society, with men controlling both the political and economic hierarchies. The production and sale of virtually all things of value have been controlled by chiefs and rulers, leaving only the crafting and trade of low-value items to entrepreneurs. Commoner women have been expected to stay home, cook, take care of children, and help their husbands with their entrepreneurial endeavors. But there is an important exception among the Yoruba. Because traditional Yoruba meals require significant amounts of fuel to prepare, and fuel is relatively expensive in the region, it has been less expensive for even the poor to buy prepared foods than to buy the fuel required to cook it themselves. For as long as the oral historians can recount, Yoruba women have controlled the business of preparing and offering food for sale. This endeavor is truly entrepreneurial, in that women keep their earnings. Men, though they have always dominated all other aspects of Yoruba entrepreneurial endeavors, have left this business to women.

For millennia, personal services have been socially unacceptable ways to make a living and therefore have been ceded to outsider entrepreneurs. Personal service entrepreneurs have often gone on to create thriving businesses. William Johnson, the so-called barber of Natchez, has a museum dedicated to him in Mississippi (see figure 3.5). Natchez was the center of Southern slave-trading until the Civil War. Johnson, born a slave, was bought by a relative when he was eleven. This may have been Johnson's brother-in-law, who owned a successful barbershop in Natchez. Johnson apprenticed with this brother-in-law and, in 1830, bought the shop from him for $300. It was around this time that Johnson started keeping a diary, which is how we know so much about him today.

A determined and savvy entrepreneur, Johnson expanded the business, and within only a few years, he was considered a

3.5 William Johnson, Jr.

Source: BlackPast, https://www.blackpast.org/african-american-history/johnson-william-jr-1809-1851/.

prominent citizen in Natchez by both whites and the free Black community. Known for his skill with scissors and sartorial style, Johnson grew his barbershop to a value of $3,000 within five years of buying it. His prominence and wealth enabled him to marry the attractive twenty-year-old daughter of a prominent local free Black family. Over the next sixteen years, Johnson and his wife had eleven children. He continued the tradition of training other young Blacks to be barbers while acquiring slaves of his own, owning sixteen at the time he died, murdered in 1851 by a Black neighbor over a boundary dispute. Fortunately for historians, Johnson accumulated enough wealth that his family could hold on to their home, where his diaries were safely kept until 1976. The building is now a museum operated by the National Park Service.

Today, Johnson's diaries provide important historical documentation of the experience of free Southern antebellum Blacks. William Johnson was not unique. We know the names and histories of many successful Black barbers serving both Black and white communities dating back to colonial America.

Mastering Hidden Constraints

In some societies, working with tools that could hurt or injure you was considered servile. Understanding the subtleties of what constitutes servile work is important but challenging. In antebellum America, what was viewed as servile differed between the industrial North and the agricultural South. Henry Boyd had to discover that for himself. Born a slave in Kentucky in 1802, Boyd was taught carpentry as a teen. This was a skill that slave owners considered lowly and servile. Boyd's skill and speed at woodworking were noticed by his master and other white locals. Boyd's owner granted requests from neighbors to let Boyd work for them. As was sometimes the case with slave masters throughout history, the teenager was allowed to keep some of what his owner was paid for these services. By twenty-four, Boyd had bought his freedom and moved across the Ohio River to settle in a place where slavery was outlawed. However, Boyd discovered to his chagrin that nobody in "free" Cincinnati would hire a Black carpenter because carpentry was considered a working-class man's job in the North. Boyd would have to overcome this hidden constraint as well.

For several years, Boyd worked odd jobs. Then a carpenter hired by a shopkeeper he worked for as a janitor showed up drunk. Boyd offered to step in and quickly built a new counter so beautiful that it immediately drew attention from other whites in town. Outsider entrepreneurs have almost always had to demonstrate a greater mastery of their skills to overcome the constraints their cultures impose on them. Boyd's impromptu counter resulted in more carpentry jobs from both his boss and others, eventually allowing him to save enough to buy the freedom of his brother and sister. Only then did he begin to save toward his own workshop.

The quality of Boyd's work, coupled with the speed with which he worked, enabled him to quickly grow his business. He came to be known throughout the North for his bedsteads. To produce beds that didn't wobble, he invented a process using both right- and left-handed wooden screws. Unfortunately, Boyd's attempt to patent this process was rejected, most likely due to the color of his skin, as a white cabinetmaker was issued a patent for the same process a few years later. Regardless, Boyd's business steadily expanded to four discrete buildings employing dozens of workers, both Black and white. By 1844, Boyd was producing a thousand beds a year. Eleven years later, he opened a showroom to display what included a complete range of parlor furniture. Of course, by this point entrepreneurs and other businesspeople were copying his designs.

While Boyd was challenged to keep up with demand, his biggest problem was arson. People kept trying to burn down his factories. Three times they succeeded, at which point no insurer would cover Boyd's business. In 1862, he'd had enough, closing his factories and showroom for good. Henry Boyd retired to live off his wealth while focusing on his second profession: conductor on the Underground Railroad.

William Johnson and Henry Boyd are emblematic leaders of two of the more prominent Black entrepreneurial swarms in pre–Civil War America: barbers and skilled artisans. Many American Blacks in the North and South were entrepreneurs who supported themselves and their families despite the countless societal constraints they faced. There were half a million free Blacks in the United States by the start of the Civil War. One in five lived in the South, and the greatest number of them were entrepreneurs or members of families headed by an entrepreneur.

Religiously Enabled

Because of religious proscriptions, moneylending was often left to heathen minorities in Christian and Muslim countries. The Jews in Europe and the Armenians in the Ottoman Empire were minorities who dominated moneylending. The Raskolniki were another group excluded from more traditional professional pursuits for religious reasons. A highly doctrinaire Orthodox Christian sect in Russia that refused to accept religious reforms unifying the Greek and Russian Orthodox churches in 1655, the Raskolniki were ostracized from urban society and commerce by the social and religious elite. These outsiders focused on trading wheat, a lowly but essential commodity associated with serfs, among their fellow believers who lived in settlements along the Volga River. The Raskolniki then used the wealth generated from this trade to create Russia's first large-scale manufacturing enterprises, this being another arena that the urban merchant class of the time considered beneath them.

Establishing personal service, craft, or trading businesses avoided by members of the middle class represents a time-tested strategy for poor and highly constrained outsiders to become self-directed and wealthy. Other than moneylending, most of these businesses are quickly cash-flow positive, which further alleviates the need to find members of the majority willing to offer lines of credit for their businesses, let alone invest capital. Despite such limitations, the wealth accumulated by these entrepreneurs can be considerable when the founder is skilled, ambitious, and solicitous. This strategy, however, has one major and unavoidable flaw. When the success of outsiders challenges the prosperity or social position of the privileged, reprisals ensue, like those endured by Henry Boyd and countless others. Once the privileged majority feels that its fundamental superiority is challenged, there are few immediate actions outsiders can take to prevent reprisals.

Band Together

Ethnic neighborhoods have always been nucleation sites for entrepreneurial businesses. Two and a half millennia ago, most metics—the foreign workers and entrepreneurs of Athens—lived in close proximity. Minorities and immigrants have many reasons to cluster. Immigrants, on entering a new territory, often don't understand the spoken language or local culture. The xenophobic resentments of the majority are not felt as strongly in minority and immigrant enclaves. Servicing the culturally unique needs of your own ethnic minority is another classic strategy for outsider entrepreneurs that can lead to financial independence. The outsider entrepreneurs in ethnic enclaves, such as Chinatowns, Little Italies, or societally enforced ghettos, seize opportunities to serve the high-density presence of similar needs and desires.

The first wave of immigrant entrepreneurs in an ethnic enclave sets up the restaurants, specialty markets, and import-export businesses necessary for meeting the unique demands of their fellow immigrants. In some enclaves, these successful first-generation entrepreneurs try to keep their wealth within their families, including those still living back home. In this case, the entrepreneurial energy within an enclave dissipates as the accumulating wealth is not reinvested back into the enclave. For example, because many Chinese immigrants aspired to make some gold—literally, in the case of the California Gold Rush—before returning home, the establishment of Chinatowns in San Francisco and New York quickly led to a first generation of wealthy entrepreneurs but were much slower in fostering wealth in subsequent generations.

In other cases, in aspiring to create a community with permanence, the first cohort of successful entrepreneurs lends or invests its accumulating wealth with nonfamily members, which leads to a broadening of the economic base and overall well-being. Subsequent cohorts of enclave entrepreneurs eventually start businesses targeted at both their brethren and the majority outside of the community.

Durham, North Carolina, is such an enclave for Black workers and entrepreneurs who immigrated into a region that was completely rural. It is historically relevant because Black Americans living in the South during the Jim Crow era were one of the most constrained minorities in history. They were prevented from voting and from using white-controlled infrastructures, whites would not do business with them, and they were relegated to prescribed neighborhoods where they had to create their own apolitical self-sustaining social and economic ecosystems.

It would have been impossible to predict that Durham would become an economically important town, as it did not even exist before the Civil War. The area was agricultural, a region where the soil and climate were ideal for producing tobacco that was both high-yielding and tasty to chew or smoke. Tobacco products became a post–Civil War fashion in the United States, which led to a swarm of workshops being founded by white entrepreneurs in and around the tobacco-growing region to produce snuff, chewing tobacco, and cigarettes. An ex-Confederate soldier and ex-subsistence farmer named Washington Duke was one of the members of the swarm. He lived near what would become Durham, accumulating a fortune over two decades making and selling cigarettes. Duke brought his sons into his business, handing it over to them a few years before the 1884 invention of the high-speed cigarette-rolling machine.

Washington's ambitious younger son, John Buchanan Duke, quickly made an exclusive deal to use the machines to produce large quantities of low-cost cigarettes. He then aggressively advertised his cigarette brands around the country, which further increased his volume of production and cost advantages. Studying the strategy of John D. Rockefeller, J. B. Duke used similarly aggressive tactics to buy up his competitors, creating a mammoth cigarette monopoly called American Tobacco. In less than thirty years, thanks to the rapidly growing popularity of tobacco products and the aggressive entrepreneurial ambitions of the Duke family, Durham grew from a patch of land into a vibrant, white-dominated entrepreneurial ecosystem. (As would be expected, based on the entrepreneurial innovation cycle, other entrepreneurs watchful of the needs of the fast-growing tobacco industry offered products to make running a tobacco business easier. For example, the Durham Cotton Manufacturing Company was founded shortly after the Civil War to produce cotton cloth for tobacco bags, which in turn created expertise that led to the formation of the successful Durham Hosiery Mill in 1894.)

The growth and prosperity of Durham attracted Black families from around the South in search of employment and, for some, in starting up businesses. In Durham, that included the dirty job of cleaning tobacco leaves before they were processed into cigarettes. By the mid-1880s, two Black churches were able to build houses of worship to serve as places where the community could gather, pray, and plan. Black entrepreneurs flocked to the city, offering personal services like barbershops for the white community as well as serving the needs of the growing Black community with shops, saloons, and undertakers. What set Durham's minority enclave apart was a first generation of successful Black entrepreneurs who helped the next generation expand their prosperity. This spark was set off by a successful barber.

John Merrick was six when the Civil War ended and his family was freed, enabling him to attend school. His schooling ended at the age of twelve, when he went to work in a brickyard to help support his family; Merrick claimed to have learned his basic math and business skills in that job. To earn extra money, John practiced barbering in his off-hours. He eventually moved to Raleigh, North Carolina, where he worked for a prominent entrepreneurial barber. In 1880, Merrick moved to the boomtown of Durham to work for another entrepreneurial Black barber.

By 1892, Merrick was able to buy that barber's business and start expanding it, opening branches in both the Black and white communities. Merrick spent most of his time cutting hair at his branch that served white business leaders. Because of his warmth and charisma, his wealthy white clients felt comfortable around him. In 1898, as local lore has it, Merrick was solicited for a donation to help pay for the funeral of a member of the Black community. At that moment, he was cutting the hair of tobacco entrepreneur Washington Duke, who suggested to Merrick that he found an insurance company to address such situations. Merrick quickly called together the most successful and prominent members of Durham's Black community to discuss the idea. While everyone was enthusiastic, only one other member of the group—the community's doctor, Aaron Moore—offered to help start the company.

The precursor to the North Carolina Mutual Life Insurance Company began operating that year in a corner of Dr. Moore's office, starting with $300 in assets. In 1900, Merrick (see figure 3.6)

3.6 Portrait of John Merrick.

Source: From R. McCants Andrews, *John Merrick: A Biographical Sketch* (1920), courtesy of The Internet Archive.

and Moore reorganized to bring in a third partner, Charles Spaulding, the young and ambitious owner of the community's most successful grocery store. From there, the business grew steadily, focusing first on the residents of Durham's Black community and then on other Black communities in North Carolina, and finally on Black communities in South Carolina, Virginia, Arkansas, Washington, D.C., and beyond.

Despite bank runs, wars, and depressions, the insurance business grew steadily in assets and outstanding policies. By 1939, North Carolina Mutual Life Insurance Company employed hundreds of Blacks in Durham and was paying out over $18.3 million annually in benefits to policyholders and their beneficiaries. The company continues in business to this day, serving a large number of Black policyholders. As important is the fact that the success of North Carolina Mutual launched a swarm of Black insurance entrepreneurs in Durham: the Bankers Fire Insurance Company, Mutual Building and Loan Association, Union Insurance and Realty Company, and Southern Fidelity Mutual Insurance Company, among more than a dozen others.

With the successful establishment of an insurance company, community leaders discussed the possibility of opening a bank. Merrick again offered to help, this time accepting a position as vice president, serving under Richard Fitzgerald as president. Fitzgerald was even wealthier than Merrick. His business made all the bricks needed for the expanding community, Fitzgerald having learned the trade from his father. The quality of Fitzgerald's bricks enabled his company to win contracts for even white-owned factories and buildings. Merchant and Farmer Bank, which Fitzgerald and Merrick formed in 1907, also survives and prospers to this day serving Durham's Black community.

Led by Merrick, Moore, Spaulding, and Fitzgerald, many of the Black entrepreneurs of Durham prioritized community wealth generation over individual wealth accumulation. These four entrepreneurs went on to cofound a third cohort of businesses, mentoring and helping yet another generation of Black Durham entrepreneurs. The Merrick-Moore-Spaulding Real Estate Company was formed in 1910 to provide real estate insurance, something that had previously been unavailable to the local Black community. Moore founded Lincoln Hospital (as well as the local library). Merrick founded Bull City Drug Company, whose mission included training a new generation of Black pharmacists. He also started two drugstores, which he sold to the cofounders. Fitzgerald founded Durham Real Estate, Mercantile, and Manufacturing Company with the explicit mission of helping Black entrepreneurs establish those types of businesses, similar to what we would consider a regional venture capital entity.

An initial cohort of minority or immigrant entrepreneurs can create a culture of entrepreneurial renewable growth for their community. The key is for each new generation of successful entrepreneurs to invest in younger entrepreneurial cohorts. Similar examples can be found with the Cuban community of Miami, the Irish neighborhoods of New York City, Old World Jewish ghettos, and Chinese enclaves in Southeast Asia, among others. Very few other enclaves have been as initially constrained as Black ones in the Jim Crow South, given that they were forced to do business and create wealth entirely within their own communities. There were many such communities, and most of them did not suffer the tragic, racially inspired reprisal that befell Tulsa, Oklahoma, in 1921. Entrepreneurial businesses within minority enclaves are typically allowed to grow large and wealthy without retribution, provided they do not directly compete with firms owned by the dominant ethnic or religious group.

Constraint Breakers

It's one thing to start a business doing what nobody wants to do. It's another thing to start a business nobody else dares to do. Many outsider entrepreneurs are willing, if not eager, to assume great social risks beyond the normal entrepreneurial risks of losing money and wasting time and energy. "Constraint-breaker" entrepreneurs are outsiders who risk their social standing with the male majority to satisfy their ambitions to be self-directed and master skills of their own choosing.

Ummidia Quadratilla lived in Rome at the end of the first century and into the early years of the second century AD. Depending on your perspective, she was very interesting, incredibly eccentric, or both. Regardless, she was a person to know, and many did know of her in her time; Pliny the Younger even wrote a lengthy character sketch. You can feel the energy of this "sturdy compact" woman from Pliny's description. She came from a distinguished but not noble Italian (i.e., non-Roman) family and, after being widowed, could have lived comfortably off the bounty of the Ummidii estates. Indeed, her status came with the expectation that she would remain pampered in the privacy of her own home and be seen in public only in the company of adult male members of her immediate family. The widow Quadratilla wanted more, something she could not get in any way other than by creating her own enterprise.

Society in Rome during Quadratilla's time was conservative, repelled by the excesses displayed by recent Julian and Claudian rulers. Quadratilla, however, was a connoisseur of the classic Roman ribald pantomime, the performances of which no women of status would dare to be seen watching in public. Pantomime had long been the most popular form of Roman theater, enjoyed by patrician men and plebs of both sexes. It usually involved male actors donning sexually explicit props and costumes. Its actors were famous throughout the empire and commanded huge sums for their performances. When Quadratilla decided to invest her income and wealth in producing pantomimes for festivals and private in-home performances sponsored by the elite and politically connected, it constituted a minor scandal. To strengthen her competitive position, she established a school for actors, who, if they became famous, were obliged to give her a cut of their fees. Her new business had the added benefit of connecting her directly to the politically ambitious, who hired her troupes to perform at the festivals they sponsored to win favor with voters. Quadratilla's actions were considered as outrageous as the performances of the actors she trained, but nobody wanted to stop her because her troupe was the best.

One of the most successful entrepreneurs to overcome constraints against both women and immigrants has yet to be given her due, although we all know her name. The daughter of a widowed maidservant, Marie Grosholz's prospects were bleak. Marie's mother worked as the housekeeper of a successful entrepreneur in Paris, who put the child to work in his workshop from a young age. That entrepreneur was Philippe Curtius. A trained physician from Switzerland, Curtius became fascinated with anatomy and learned the skill of wax modeling to augment his detailed understanding of the human body.

Wax models of people and body parts date from at least Roman times and perhaps as far back as ancient Egypt. Wax is an easy medium to work with and color, and it can retain its form indefinitely. In mid-eighteenth-century Europe, a swarm of wax model entrepreneurs plied their trade, offering custom sculpting services and paid admissions to their studios. Nobles of the time bought wax sculptures of their prestigious relatives for display in their homes. The middle class and commoners paid modest sums to visit the salons of wax artisans to see life-sized models of famous figures and—for educational purposes—anatomically correct models of naked women. Patrons who could afford to pay a higher admission fee could get close enough to touch and examine figures in detail.

Curtius's first salon, in Berne, Switzerland, contained a high-quality collection of models that attracted the attention of the estranged cousin of Louis XV, the Prince de Conti, who, in 1767, enticed Curtius to exhibit in Paris. Conti introduced the physician to the prominent figures of the day, and Curtius used this access to invite them to sit and be sculpted in wax. His life-sized models of Voltaire and Rousseau and his tableau of Marie Antoinette and the royal family at dinner attracted throngs of visitors to his salon. Curtius loved the attention, and Paris loved his wax models, which included a "Cabinet of Curiosities" featuring life-size models of Egyptian mummies and notorious murderers. Curtius's success enabled him to construct a large building devoted to the theatrical displays of wax sculptures, with living quarters above the public space and a workshop in the basement. This was where young Marie Grosholz grew up, among the wax models in various states of construction, repair, and display.

Marie became Curtius's apprentice, eventually sculpting accurate and lifelike models for display. During the tumultuous French Revolution, she played a critical role in maintaining the business while Curtius played various small roles in the fast-moving and dangerous politics of the time. He commanded a small group of militia guardsmen assembled from the neighborhood, and he and his men were present when the Bastille fell. When the governor of the Bastille surrendered and was beheaded, Curtius ensured that the severed head was quickly delivered to Marie, who immediately made a wax model. As other French officials were captured by mobs and beheaded, Marie continued making models of the pillaged heads. Curtius's connections with revolutionary leaders enabled him to obtain a steady stream of heads of previously famous men and women for Marie to mold into wax. The wax heads, along with the (complete) figures of living political leaders of the moment, brought large crowds to Curtius's salon. Some heads pushed the boundaries of taste too far, however.

Although Marie sculpted the heads of the guillotined king and queen, they weren't displayed until decades later. Marie's most famous wax sculpture of the revolution was of the murdered Marat in his bath. Marat had been a friend of Curtius. When news of his assassination reached Marie, she hurried to the crime scene and created a death mask before the body was taken away. Marie then used the mask to create a full wax tableau of the gruesome scene she'd witnessed. It was that tableau, and not the real scene, that Jacques-Louis David painted, an image that came to symbolize the French Reign of Terror.

In 1794, Curtius died of natural causes. Having never married, he had no heirs, so he left his business and property to Marie, "my pupil in my art." She was soon forced to defend her right to the inheritance, and even with that hurdle overcome, the tumultuous last years of the revolution required her to take a substantial mortgage to pay rent. Within a year, Marie married François Tussaud, eight years her junior. In a move that was highly unusual at the time, their marriage contract specified that the new Madame Tussaud retained control of her property (figure 3.7). Over the next five years, Marie bore three children while François ran the business. The first, a girl, died in infancy; the other two were boys. François tried expanding into the theater, but he was a terrible manager, and the theater he built was immediately condemned for shoddy construction. The wax business was neglected during these years, and Marie had to take out another loan to keep it open. In 1801, business brightened as Josephine, Napoleon's wife, commissioned Madame Tussaud to sculpt the emperor. Tussaud astutely made a second sculpture that she could later show.

3.7 Marie Tussaud, wax self-portrait.

Source: Hulton Archive/Getty Images.

Clearly unhappy, Madame Tussaud took advantage of a tem-
porary peace between France and England in 1802 to flaunt all
social expectations and constraints, abandoning her husband and
younger son to take her older son and her most important wax
pieces to England to establish a new life. Before leaving, she had
a solicitor draw up documents renouncing her ownership of her
French property and business, giving full control to François. To
start an independent new life in England as both a woman and an
immigrant who spoke not a word of the language, she accepted
an offer from a one-time friend of Philippe Curtius to show her
wax pieces in a London theater. She agreed to split whatever profits this generated. Although Madame Tussaud's wax figures proved

popular with Londoners anxious to see victims of the French Revolution and look their enemy Napoleon in the eye, the fifty-fifty
profit split left Marie with little to support her and her son. It took
her more than a year to extract herself from this partnership, then
earn enough to tour as well as construct new wax figures to keep
her show current with the public's fascinations.

Even if she'd had second thoughts, Marie could not have gone
back to France, as war with England had again broken out. In 1803,
she moved her show and five-year-old son to Edinburgh, Scotland.
In Britain, Madame Tussaud began to claim that she had lived for
a time at Versailles as a close friend of Louis XV's sister. There is no
record of her having lived at the palace, but she may have visited
there to tutor the princess Madame Élisabeth, who did actually
sculpt wax effigies of religious figures.

For the next thirty years, Tussaud and her son toured throughout Britain and Ireland with an ever-evolving collection of wax
figures. They moved on average twice a year. Madame Tussaud
presided over her business from the door, collecting the entrance
fees from everyone—no exceptions—and tallying up the receipts
and expenses every night. When news brought a new person to
public attention, she would collect drawings, prints, and firsthand
descriptions to make a wax likeness to display. She even arranged
for a catalog of her show to be printed and sold. British royals and
their mistresses and lovers were added to the collection, as were
notorious English murderers. Reconciling and reuniting with her
younger son in England twenty years after she'd left him behind,
she now leveraged both sons to expand hours and gather documents from around Britain and the Continent.

By this point, Tussaud's touring show extended exhibition hours
to the after-dinner time favored by the elite. An orchestra was hired
to play in the evenings, and more figures were shown grouped
in tableaux to imply stories, as with a fictional meeting between

Napoleon and Wellington, or with fully imagined coronations of Napoleon or the English monarch. After decades of nonstop touring and her list of royal patrons, real and imagined, growing with successive editions of her catalog, Madame Tussaud became enamored with the potential of the railroads to deliver customers without needing to set up in a new city every six months. In 1836, she signed a long-term lease for a second-floor space on Baker Street in London, a short distance from three new train stations that would bring hordes of new visitors to the capital. There, Tussaud focused on wax tableaus of Queen Victoria, Albert, and other members of the nobility to let the public get closer to the royal family than they ever could have imagined. Queen Victoria and Albert themselves visited the space on more than one occasion, further adding to the notoriety of Madame Tussaud.

Tussaud's brand has proven timeless, and Madame Tussauds remains a global institution today. After Tussaud herself passed away in 1850, the business remained in her family for two generations, until a grandson chose not to follow his grandmother's strict dictates about watching the books every day and got into financial trouble. Tussaud made her mark as an immigrant from an enemy nation who was also a single mother with a young son and no other means of support. She had an artisanal skill, wax sculpting, and chose to gamble everything she had to embrace a life of constant movement and very long hours virtually every day of the year. She even had to put her young son to work. She also had to make herself socially tolerable, concocting a fantasy life at Versailles that intrigued the public and continuing to embellish her story as royals on both sides of the channel passed away and were no longer able to refute her outlandish claims. Madame Tussaud worked ceaselessly to sidestep the existing social and legal constraints on working women and immigrants.

Madame Tussaud's story is similar to that of many outsider entrepreneurs who created and then ran their businesses in ways considered socially stigmatizing or too demanding. I could have chosen from hundreds of other examples, super-famous or just well known in their time. Madame CJ Walker is an example many talk about today. She was purposely conspicuous—in ways previously considered undignified for a woman—in marketing her hair care products and in her publicly conspicuous consumption. Esteé Lauder, born Josephine Estella Mentzer to immigrant parents, changed her name and built a cosmetics empire based on a myth of being related to European nobility after she was insulted for being a hair salon employee.

Lasting Legacies

A crucial variation on the strategy of brazenly flaunting constraints is that of emigrating to a less-constrained location to escape social, legal, and entrepreneurial constraints. Entrepreneurial emigrants boldly leave friends and family behind to found businesses where opportunities are greater. Many of these people emigrate to established immigrant enclaves; some found new enclaves absent of any support but instigate entire new swarms.

Outsider entrepreneurs have changed the societies in which they learned how to prosper, loosening existing constraints and opening new possibilities for subsequent generations of outsiders. Outsider entrepreneurs also introduce new skills and products around the world, a force that increases the geographic scale of swarms, further amplifying the entrepreneurial innovation cycle. Outsiders diffuse understanding, know-how, and cumulative impact faster and more broadly than privileged male entrepreneurs who are fortunate enough to find themselves proximate to new and commercially important innovations.

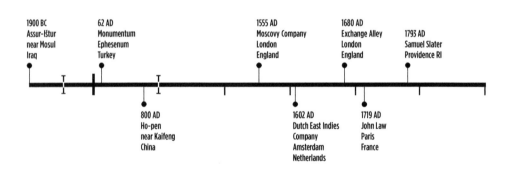

Exchange Alley
London England

London
England

Paris France

Providence RI

Amsterdam
Netherlands

Ephesus
Turkey

Hop-pen
near Kaifeng
China

Assur
(near Mosul)
Iraq

1900 BC
Assur-Ištur
near Mosul
Iraq

62 AD
Monumentum
Ephesenum
Turkey

1555 AD
Moscovy Company
London
England

1680 AD
Exchange Alley
London
England

1793 AD
Samuel Slater
Providence RI

800 AD
Ho-pen
near Kaifeng
China

1602 AD
Dutch East Indies
Company
Amsterdam
Netherlands

1719 AD
John Law
Paris
France

CHAPTER 4

Fuel to Fire

As for him who invests money on a long term and multiplies a shekel
  for two
It is pleasing to Shamash, and he (the investor) prolongs (his) life

—Lines 105 and 106, "The Shamash Hymn of Old Babylonia," before 1900 BC.
(Shamash was the Babylonian Sun god and god of justice.)

T he entrepreneurial innovation cycle is exciting. It sparks massive change. It inspires society-shaking innovations coveted by masses of people. It fosters the creation of enormous amounts of value. Entrepreneurial swarms form and then change direction rapidly as each member tries desperately to stay competitive. Often a highly specialized swarm materializes around these frantic entrepreneurial swarms, one that promises to accelerate their pace. This specialized meta-swarm offers resources to help members of entrepreneurial swarms exploit EIC innovations faster than their competitors and capture greater value—all for their mutual benefit.

This chapter focuses on these highly specialized entrepreneurs. Today we call them venture capitalists, but this kind of entrepreneur appears early in the historical record and in almost all economic systems, so "venture investor" might be the more historically accurate term. That said, I will use "venture capitalist" here to emphasize the direct link between ancient practices and those of today.

Resources invested in scaling supply, demand, or simplicity can yield big returns. Increasing supply—when there is unmet demand—leads to economies of scale, accelerating the accumulation of profit. Scaling demand leads to higher prices and more product being sold, which also accelerates the growth of profits. And an entrepreneur whose methods simplify their operations grows faster than competitors and uses fewer resources, which means they enjoy greater economies of scale than others in the swarm. Thus the EIC yields significant advantages to entrepreneurs who lead in supply, demand, and simplification innovations.

Scaling cannot happen without investing resources, which requires money or some money equivalent. Ambitious entrepreneurs within quickly evolving swarms therefore often want to partner with people or organizations willing to give or lend them resources to grow their businesses, either based on their own innovations or by aggressively copying the innovations of others. They willingly or unwillingly tolerate the increased stress inherent in accepting the terms imposed on them to get added resources. For the past four thousand years, venture capitalists have played a critical role in speeding up many EICs, financing certain members of the swarm whom they feel can scale faster than others using their resources, thereby generating greater wealth for both.

VC BC

There was almost certainly a celebration on the day around 1900 BC when a certain cuneiform tablet constituting a legal document was scribed and witnessed by seven individuals. The agreement bound at least fourteen people to invest gold in an enterprise that would be run by Amur-Ištar. (There may have been a few others, but we cannot read the next few lines of the tablet.) He was given full authority to invest more than thirty minas of gold (approximately fifteen kilograms) as needed to establish a long-distance trading enterprise. Signing a deal like this today would merit as much celebration as it very likely did four millennia ago.

Amur-Ištar lived in Assur in Upper Mesopotamia. He was a member of a trading family and would have listened to many discussions about the challenges of forming and managing caravans. He would have learned the prices paid for products exported to Turkey. He likely would have accompanied the caravans that traveled the six weeks to Kanesh, a major trading depot permanently populated by hundreds of traders from Assur. He also would have watched many animated negotiations over tin, textiles, and other exotic and valuable goods in both Assur and Kanesh. He may even have led a few of the caravans himself by the time this deal was done.

Amur was finally ready to set up his own independent trading firm, and he needed funds to buy dozens of specially bred donkeys, their harnesses, and the products he would export on his first trading journey. At the time, the trade of tin and textiles between Assur and Anatolia (modern-day Turkey) was thriving, limited only by working capital (be'ulātum in Old Assyrian), availability of donkeys, and experienced caravan entrepreneurs to lead expeditions. The community of experienced traders in Assur encouraged and trained relatives and others they had come to trust to become independent entrepreneurs because they could then share in their profits. When an individual felt he or, in some cases, she was ready to manage a trade enterprise, family and friends as well as other prominent citizens could be asked to invest in the venture.

Businesses with limited partners (i.e., partners who cannot lose more than the value of their investment) were called naruqqum, derived from the word for "sack," as in "a sack of valuables." In

Assur, these partnerships were formed for terms of around ten years; Amur-Ištar formed his for twelve. Following the listing of witnesses and investors, the cuneiform tablet explicitly states that Amur will receive a third of the profits for running the fund, provided total profits of his limited partners exceed a specified fraction of their investment, we think two-thirds. The final three lines of the tablet declare that if any investor asks for their investment to be returned before the end of the twelve years, they will forfeit their share of the profits.

The structure of these partnerships was similar in many Mesopotamian city-states. Durations could be shorter, and the number of limited partners sometimes exceeded fifty. The partnership dissolved if the entrepreneur running the fund died. Investments in naruqqum could be inherited, which meant they survived the death of an investor. Such partnerships were popular among the wealthy merchants of Assur. We know, for example, that when his assets were divided among his children, a prominent merchant named Pušu-ken had investments in at least eight naruqqum.

The similarities between naruqqum and the venture capital funds of today is striking. In our time, a typical VC fund is formed by a general partner, a modern-day Amur-Ištar, who is responsible for investing the funds of its limited partners for ten years. General partners are typically entitled to 20 percent of their fund's profits, provided the limited partners receive a prescribed minimum return. General partners also earn 2 percent annually for expenses for the ten-year life of the fund, which equates to capturing almost the same third of the payout for funds that double their money.

A big difference is that in ancient Mesopotamia, the general manager directly ran the firms in his portfolio. Today, general partners usually get somebody else to take charge of the startups they incubate; VCs try not to be distracted by the minutiae of their various moneymaking schemes. In Mesopotamia, an investment fund manager like Amur-Ištar would be very hands-on, freeing limited partners like Pušu-ken from worrying about the day-to-day issues.

Entrepreneurs in Mesopotamia could also raise funds through interest-bearing loans. They used these loans to raise working capital, buy more products to export, or cover short-term cash flow needs. Interest rates were high, typically 20 percent or more, so entrepreneurs couldn't afford loans to start ventures that would last more than a year or so. Entrepreneurs have avoided relying on high-interest loans to start businesses since the beginning of the historical record. Major traders and merchants for the past four thousand years have always preferred long-term equity investments to fund their enterprises, all the way up to the millions of limited-liability partnerships created by entrepreneurs around the globe that exist today.

Fungible Partners

Two thousand years after Amur-Ištar, the Romans decided to update the partnership laws that had survived from Mesopotamian times. Rome wanted its entrepreneurs to be able to take on more expensive long-term projects than ever before, such as the running of tax collection systems. The business of tax farming—privately collecting taxes on behalf of rulers and governments—had existed as far back as ancient Mesopotamia. Many civilizations have relied on tax farmers, and they are still used today. For example, collecting taxes on cars is often contracted out to private businesses. Tax-farming leases are highly sought after—big sums are involved—but they require a large capital base to have any chance of winning the business, even if you have friends in high places. Tax-farming entrepreneurs pay a large fraction of what they plan to collect up front to the state. They must also bear all the costs and risks associated with collecting that tax. They profit from the value they collect in excess of what they paid for the lease, but they also lose any shortfall. To succeed, tax farmers must implement time- and resource-intensive processes to collect the taxes owed by large numbers of people. Because entrepreneurs must invest so much up front, tax-farming leases frequently extend over many years. Rome auctioned its leases to maximize its take, which meant it was motivated to support entrepreneurs in their efforts to raise ever-larger amounts of money.

Because tax-farming entrepreneurs were responsible for a large fraction of Rome's income, lawmakers granted them special status and flexibility. We know the details of these special laws only by accident. During a 1976 excavation of the ancient port of Ephesus in present-day Turkey, a large stone used as a dais in an ancient Catholic church was moved, revealing a faint inscription on its obverse. The inscription, from 62 AD, contains a law that had been in place for over a hundred years (see figure 4.1). It laid out the rights and obligations of tax-farming enterprises that collected import and export taxes at the port. Now known as the *Monumentum Ephesenum*, the stone is studied by one set of scholars interested in Roman law and taxation and by another interested in the origins of the modern corporation.

The law contains three important provisions beyond the general and long-standing Roman laws governing partnerships. First, tax-farming enterprises did not need to dissolve if the general partner died; the existence of the enterprise was not tied to any specific person. Investors could assign responsibility to whomever they wanted. Second, individuals designated by the enterprise could act on its behalf as if the enterprise were an independent entity. Up to this point, the general partner was responsible both to the investors and for directly deploying funds. Only agreements made directly with him would have been honored in the courts.

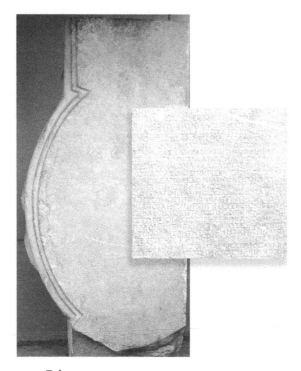

4.1 Monumentum Ephesenum.

Source: Courtesy of the Ephesus Archaeological Museum, used with permission of the General Directorate of Cultural Heritage and Museums of the Ministry of Culture and Tourism (Turkey).

Roman courts now honored agreements made by someone acting on behalf of the general partner. Third, investors could buy and sell their share of the profits without dissolving the enterprise or withdrawing any of the initial capital.

These special exceptions to the laws governing partnerships parallel most of the attributes of modern corporations. This law appears to have worked well, as many wealthy Roman citizens established organizations that collected vast sums on behalf of the government. We suspect that similar laws governed other capital-intensive entrepreneurial enterprises, like those that constructed large buildings.

Medieval Chinese law also enabled investors to sell their "share" of the profits without dissolving an enterprise. These firms were called *ho-pen*. They likely first appeared in the Tang dynasty but became commonplace only in the Song dynasty. By the end of the Tang, Chinese entrepreneurs and businessmen had a sophisticated sense of the role of money and capital. This was near the time when paper money began to circulate widely. The Qingming scroll, described in the introduction, depicts two enterprises that may have been *ho-pen*: the multistory inn and tavern on the main street and the Silk Road import-export business where four camels are setting out with goods near the city gate. When societies encourage and support large long-term enterprises, partnerships evolve into enterprises resembling corporations.

Anyone Can Invest

The wealthy merchants of England were not a merry bunch in 1552. A prominent one at the time, Thomas Edge, wrote, "[Merchants are] incited with the fame of the great masse of riches which the Portugals and Spaniards brought home yeerely from both the Inidies."

Beyond sheer jealousy, English merchants were also hurting because their major export market had just collapsed: wool exports were down 36 percent relative to two years earlier. Merchants wanted government help, but the current ruler, Edward VI, was just a boy. The Privy Council was concerned enough that they replaced the king's regent with the more assertive John Dudley, First Earl of Warwick. Dudley had been Lord Admiral under Henry VIII. He hoped the English merchant class would become leaders in the long-distance maritime trade then monopolized by the two Iberian kingdoms.

4.2 Sebastian Cabot.

Source: Wikipedia, https://en.wikipedia.org/wiki/Sebastian_Cabot_(explorer)

To that end, Dudley recruited Sebastian Cabot (figure 4.2), Spain's pilot major and one of the most experienced and knowledgeable seamen alive, to move to England. Cabot oversaw the organization responsible for outfitting Spain's maritime fleet and training its sea captains. Born in Venice to the well-known sea captain John Cabot, Sebastian spent most of his teenage years in England, where his father had been recruited by Henry VII to discover new territories for England. In 1497, John Cabot claimed Newfoundland for England. His son was probably along for that voyage.

Sebastian aspired to become an even more famous explorer than his father (after John Cabot's death, Sebastian claimed full credit for the discovery of Newfoundland), but Henry VIII wasn't interested in exploration. In 1512, Ferdinand II offered Sebastian the position of Spain's pilot major. Ferdinand was impressed by Cabot's knowledge of the rich fishing waters off "codfish island" in the North Atlantic. Without a second thought, the ambitious young man left England, only to return thirty-six years later when the politics in Spain no longer favored him.

With the collapse of the woolen cloth market, several prominent merchants of England approached Cabot about pooling the merchants' resources to form a "company" that would leverage his expertise and leadership to find the fabled northern passage to the Indies. They proposed what constituted the most ambitious startup ever to be formed and offered Cabot the chance to run it. Although Spain and Portugal commanded trading fleets with dozens of ships, those vessels were owned and provisioned by the crown. Everything brought back from Asia or America belonged to the monarch and not any one merchant. The kings auctioned off their spoils at the end of each voyage. The English merchants were suggesting a private enterprise of international scope, and Cabot jumped at the offer.

Companies were a well-established concept in Europe at the time. Rulers or governments granted rights over valuable property (like mines) or trading monopolies to organizations that agreed to manage the rights in the best interest of the ruler (which usually involved loaning the monarch money on top of paying substantial ongoing taxes). English companies operated as large partnerships in which each member of the corporation acted independently, subject to rules established by the company's governing body. Because of the scale of the enterprise, Cabot and his backers agreed to form this new company differently. They felt it needed to operate as a unified body with jointly owned assets—that is, a *joint-stock* company. For the company to operate as a singular entity, its members would need to assign operating responsibility to people who would manage it in the best interests of all the members. Members exerted control of the company through a general assembly, which operated like a shareholders' meeting. An elected court of assistants would then act as a board of directors. The people with operating responsibility could be either investors or "servants"—essentially, paid employees. This joint-stock system meant that investors owned a specified fraction of the assets. For the first time, this made it straightforward to buy and sell partial ownership in an enterprise with large numbers of investors.

Cabot recruited a respected general and England's most knowledgeable navigator, Richard Chancellor, and quickly outfitted and provisioned three ships. So anxious were they to depart, they didn't wait for King Edward's signature on the royal charter. As it happened, young Edward died before signing that charter. Per the late king's wishes, John Dudley put Edward's cousin Lady Jane Grey on the throne over Edward's half-sister, Mary. Mary deposed Jane after nine days, and Dudley, the sponsor of Cabot's endeavor, was executed. But Cabot's troubles didn't end there. Chancellor's ship lost contact with the other two, making it as far as present-day Archangel, Russia, before winter set in. The other two boats wound up off the coast of Lapland when the ice set in, and their crews perished.

In Russia, Chancellor made contact with local villagers, who sent news of the visitors to Tsar Ivan IV, known as Ivan the Terrible. Chancellor arrived at a propitious time, as Russia was surrounded by unfriendly states, making trade with Europe difficult, especially when it came to armaments. Ivan invited Chancellor to visit him in Moscow and expressed his willingness to allow "free marte with all free liberties" to English merchants throughout Russia.

In return, Ivan wanted cannons and swords. As soon as the ice retreated, Chancellor raced back to England, no longer interested in a direct northern route to the East Indies. On his return, Chancellor learned that the charter had never been signed, the company's chief supporter had been executed, and the banished Mary had returned as queen.

Cabot, an experienced navigator of both oceans and politics, was not implicated in any of the problems that led to Dudley's downfall. In 1555, he and Chancellor were able to negotiate a new royal charter, with Mary granting their company a monopoly over all trade north of Scandinavia. They agreed to name their company "marchants adventurers of England, for the discovery of lands, territories, iles, dominions, and seignories unknowen, and not before that late adventure or enterprise by sea or navigation, commonly frequented."

Everyone called it the Russia Company or the Muscovy Company. With one hundred ninety-nine male and two female members, and Cabot as governor for life, it represented a larger and more diverse group of investors than any commercial enterprise to date. Several privy counselors were charter members, as were other members of the nobility. These nonmerchants invested purely as speculators; they had nothing to trade with Russia themselves. This was unprecedented. Politicians accepting "gifts" from entrepreneurs had been standard practice since the first urban entrepreneurs, but inviting them to explicitly risk their money as part of an entrepreneurial syndicate was new. The attitude toward startups now changed. With a joint-stock structure, investors were no longer expected to actually invest their time in making a venture profitable, something politicians were never interested in doing. The participatory nature of entrepreneurship had become optional. It was no longer a requirement that a business be managed by its investors.

Money from Strangers

As expected, a swarm formed around entrepreneurs who were found-ing maritime trading ventures. The swarm concentrated in the port towns of England and across the channel in the ports of the newly independent Dutch Republic. The English ventures usually used the joint-stock structure pioneered by the Russia Company and sought royal charters and trading monopolies. The Dutch mostly used partnerships without official charters or monopoly privileges. Successful Dutch members of the swarm, such as the Long Dis-tance Company and the New Brabant Company, demonstrated that entrepreneurial merchants could trade profitably with Asia and America if they could avoid the Spanish and Portuguese. More aggressive English entrepreneurs, like Sir Francis Drake and Sir Walter Raleigh, demonstrated that they could overpower Spanish and Portuguese flotillas, bring home their treasures, and give their investors huge returns. Drake's voyage yielded nearly a fifty-fold return on investment. After the defeat of the Spanish Armada, even more privateers sought the permission of Queen Elizabeth to sail to the East and West Indies in search of Spanish and Portuguese boats filled with gold, silver, and spice.

The swarming Dutch and English maritime entrepreneurs kept track of one another's successes and failures. By 1602, the merchant-friendly leaders of the Dutch Republic feared their independently financed maritime entrepreneurs trading in the East Indies would be at a disadvantage when competing with the royally chartered English East Indies Company. The leaders also worried that the increasingly aggressive tactics being used to secure enough of the limited number of available skilled crew and boatbuilders would weaken the country's ability to compete.

In 1602, the republic's top official called together the Dutch maritime entrepreneurs who were trading in the Far East and convinced them to combine efforts as a single trading company. As an inducement, this new company would have a monopoly on trade with the East Indies for twenty-one years. The Vereenigde Oostindische Compagnie would be known outside of Holland as the Dutch East Indies Company, or the VOC. This new entity was set up as a joint-stock company. To give it enough capital to compete with both the English and the Portuguese, the company was allowed to accept investments from "all residents of these lands." No minimum or maximum investment was required. As a result of this open policy, 1,143 people from all walks of life invested in the new, government-sponsored company.

The VOC was not founded or run by a self-directed individual. It was never an entrepreneurial enterprise by our definition. Its success, however, set a precedent. It showed that the general public represented a good source of funds for joint-stock startups. This innovation was not lost on the entrepreneurs of the time, and it inspired a new swarm of entrepreneurs who helped other entrepreneurs raise money from the public. It also showed investors that companies could be good investments.

Let Me Help You Invest in a Startup

By the end of the seventeenth century, English entrepreneurs had figured out how to form joint-stock companies without Parliament's permission. Aside from those who needed Parliamentary charters for a royal monopoly in trade or manufacture, entrepreneurs simply drew up what we would consider a prospectus describing their company and sold shares to anyone with capital to invest. Key to this shift was a swarm of entrepreneurs that formed to facilitate the buying and selling of shares in joint-stock companies. In England they were called "jobbers," a term for someone who "purchases and resells." Because buying and selling stock was not considered an established trade, jobbers were prohibited from buying and selling shares on the grounds of the new Royal Exchange. Instead, they congregated across the street, doing business in two coffeehouses, Jonathan's and Garraway's, in what became known as Exchange Alley. Exchange Alley isn't an alley as much as a warren of passageways and dead ends. In some places, it's barely wide enough for seven people to stand shoulder to shoulder. Humble as it is physically—it still exists today, renamed Change Alley—it was the locus of a seismic shift in how entrepreneurs raised money for their startups.

In an age when a 5 percent return on investment was considered acceptable, the chance at a spectacular increase in the value of one's savings enticed many to visit Exchange Alley to learn about the latest startups. Personal assets were growing among an expanding merchant class as well as the ranks of professionals such as clerks, lawyers, and doctors. People with newfound savings wanted to invest in assets other than land or government bonds issued by the recently founded Bank of England. Many had heard how Sir William Phips's West Indies trading company had paid dividends nearly five hundred times the original price of the stock. The jobbers of Exchange Alley knew the latest share prices of all the joint-stock companies and were happy to share the latest rumors with those seeking to invest.

Leveraging the optimistic mood of these investors, entrepreneurs swarmed to form startups. The British colonies in the Caribbean and North America were doing well and needed provisions of all sorts. Coal-fired furnaces were revolutionizing the production of staples ranging from glass to beer. The population was on the rise in England, and many second and third sons were provisioning new farms, homes, and shops. Rising populations also meant more funerals, inspiring some entrepreneurs to begin offering funeral home services. Real estate speculators and agents formed companies and sold shares to develop property on a large scale. Pawnbrokers and shipwreck salvage companies were particularly prosperous at the time, attracting many investors.

Other entrepreneurs followed the same formula that tech entrepreneurs do today: getting a patent and then raising money to produce the invention. Startups formed to produce Savery's steam pump, Tyzack's burglar alarm, Puckle's machine gun, Austin's musket-proof chariot, and Sutton's waterproofs, among dozens of other innovations brought to market. Founding entrepreneurs were called "projectors" since they sold their projects to others. Aided by jobbers, projectors convinced thousands of people that investing in a startup was an exciting opportunity, with rewards that outweighed the risks.

As the number of startups continued to climb, jobbers grew their enterprises by hiring clerks. The crowds in Exchange Alley were packed so tightly that pickpockets flourished. People started to refer to startups as "bubbles" because of their ability to form and grow quickly (not in the later, derogatory sense related to a bubble's tendency to pop). Hairdressing shops and tea parlors opened nearby to cater to female investors. The mood was exuberant, almost delusional. One prospectus described a "company for carrying on an undertaking of great advantage, but nobody to know what it is." It sought an investment of half a million pounds by offering five thousand shares at one hundred pounds each. The annual dividend on each share was projected to be 100 percent of the share price. Investors were required to make an initial deposit of two pounds and pay the rest over the course of the year. Despite the vagueness of the proposition, one thousand deposits were received on the first day. The following day, the office was closed. The adventurer had sailed to the Continent the previous evening. Though this was an extreme example, most of the startups of the day went out of business, and many who lost money in them felt duped to one extent or another.

In 1697, a parliamentary committee condemned the "pernicious" actions of jobbers. But MPs were well-to-do individuals who also wanted the opportunity to make more than 5 percent on their money. They didn't want to stop the flow of new shares completely. Instead, they enacted a law requiring jobbers to register with the government, limiting their number. This made jobber entrepreneurs even more powerful, as they no longer needed to fear competition for new business. Registered jobbers also enjoyed increased legitimacy, which made investors more comfortable. Entrepreneurs were ecstatic. Legitimized jobbers helped to maintain a robust market for their shares. By the start of the eighteenth century, England's product and financial innovations had become benchmarks that others in Europe aspired but failed to emulate. At the end of the first decade of the 1700s, paper money was in circulation only in Britain (England had just merged with Scotland), Holland, Sweden, Venice and Genoa, Italy. Everywhere else, anything valuable was purchased with coin. European entrepreneurs had catching up to do.

The VC of France

The Scotsman John Law adamantly believed other countries could be even more financially innovative than England. The son of a successful goldsmith and moneylender in an age when precious metals were the standard units of currency, Law developed an unusually clear understanding of the complex nature of value. Mathematically precocious, Law mastered algebra as a teenager at a time when most studied it as an advanced subject at university. Reaching the age of inheritance with no interest in carrying on his father's business, Law moved to London to live the life of a gentleman. He quickly developed a reputation for being "nicely expert in all manners of debaucheries."

In the last decades of the 1600s, gambling was the favorite pastime of the wealthy throughout Europe. Good-looking, genial, and willing to bet large sums, Law was invited to game with England's young elite (figure 4.3). Combining drink, women, and gambling with a carefree attitude quickly led to his spending and losing the full amount of his inheritance, requiring him to call on his widowed mother to keep him out of debtor's prison. This personal humiliation led to a transformation in Law's behavior. Neither wanting to lose what little money he had left nor giving up gambling and the good life, Law seized on an entrepreneurial approach. He dove into the study of gambling. His mathematical talents made learning the new and little-known field of probability both interesting

4.3 John Law portrait by Casimir Balthazar.

Source: Wikipedia, https://en.wikipedia.org/wiki/John_Law_(economist).

and rewarding. As he now knew the odds while those he played with did not, his bank account grew back quickly.

This was an economically volatile time. Parliament debated various schemes for reducing the country's war debt. Law was fascinated by the debates on lotteries and other theories of how banks could help economies grow by offering credit. In 1694, the Bank of England was chartered as a joint-stock company with a monopoly on issuing banknotes backed by the royal treasury. Law, paying close attention, noticed an immediate increase in London's economic activity as the bank's notes—equivalent to what we think of as paper money—eased the previously constrained money supply.

Law's life took an unexpected direction in 1695 when he killed a young gentleman in a duel. The victim was so well connected that the usual commutation of the death sentence of the surviving dueler was not granted by the king. Law's own well-connected friends saved him by arranging for him to escape from jail and flee to the Continent.

In Europe, this good-looking, genial, big-stakes gambler quickly made friends with the gambling elite who had diplomatic ties, freeing him to travel widely. His visits to Amsterdam, Genoa, Paris, and Venice gave him firsthand knowledge of the economic conditions in countries with very different monetary philosophies. His elite connections also enabled him to discuss these policies directly with government and banking officials.

Over two decades, Law accumulated a fortune in both winnings and economic knowledge. Over time he refined his "system" for increasing economic prosperity. It revolved around establishing banks that issued notes backed by gold at a fixed ratio. Law believed that a government issuing notes worth as much as four times the gold on hand would still leave noteholders with the sense that their notes were as good as gold. The notes would replace personal IOUs and would circulate freely without anyone questioning or discounting their value. With more gold-backed notes in circulation, people would feel more prosperous and, as a result, spend more. Law was one of the first to understand the relationship between credit and banking reserves, which he described in several pamphlets that he sent to economic ministers around Europe. Government officials credited Law for the novelty of his ideas but rejected them as too bold to implement. Most economic ministers of the time focused less on overall economic well-being than on financing lavish royal lifestyles.

In 1715, Law's system finally captured the attention of someone with influence: the nephew of King Louis XIV of France, the Duke d'Orleans. Louis's death that year made d'Orleans the regent for the late king's infant great-grandson, leaving him to deal with France's nearly empty treasury. The regent tried but failed to get his council of ministers to accept Law's proposal to form a Bank of France. Ever the entrepreneurial risk-taker, Law offered to form a bank backed by his own personal fortune to eliminate any basis for objection. France accepted his offer.

The Bank Générale opened quickly, located on the ground floor of Law's home (on what is now the Place Vendôme). France's cynical newspapers and gossips predicted Law's imminent economic ruin, but the bank's notes proved to be the least risky and time-consuming way to pay for anything of significant value. Seeing the government accept the notes at full face value without question, merchants and taxpayers began to accept them as payment for bills. They also began to deposit their gold and silver with the bank. Within a year even the skeptics admitted that Law's bank increased the circulation of money and boosted overall economic activity.

While Law's bank put French merchants in a better mood, it did not relieve the staggering royal debt. At the end of 1715, Law proposed an ambitious plan to entice the public to invest in France's entrepreneurial future. The country's economic conditions had made its entrepreneurs risk-averse and underfunded relative to their English and Dutch competitors. Law predicted that the public's investment in the growth of French entrepreneurial enterprises would lead to fabulous national prosperity. To entice the skeptical French population to invest in startups, he proposed accepting devalued bonds of the near-bankrupt government as payment for shares at face value. This move, he predicted, would entice France's middle class to invest in future growth while drastically reducing the country's interest burden (because his startups would accept significantly lower interest rates on the debt they would soon own). The regent approved the plan over the objections of jealous ministers and members of the powerless Parliament.

To move forward with his venture fund idea, Law took ownership of a charter that Louis XIV had originally given to adventurers to explore and exploit the wealth of the Mississippi River and its environs. No meaningful revenues had been generated by three different owners of the charter. Law felt sure great wealth waited to be exploited, similar to the wealth being generated by the English, Spanish, and Portuguese from their American landholdings. He forced the owner to sell, reconstituted the charter, and formed it as a joint-stock company: the Company of the West. The public took to calling it the Mississippi Company. To finance the Mississippi Company's growth, Law proposed selling 200,000 shares at 500 livres, for a total of 100 million livres, a staggering capitalization for any company of the age (one livre equaled a pound of silver and could pay for a year's worth of unskilled labor). Not used to investing in shares and joint-stock companies, the skeptical public bought only 30 percent of the available shares.

To consolidate his political and economic power, in 1718, Law successfully proposed selling his bank to the royal treasury, where it was renamed the Banque Royale. As a government bank, it could now print the notes used to compensate him "royally" for the sale. The bank could then use the remaining gold in France's treasury as a reserve, expanding the gold's economic impact. Law remained the bank's leader and therefore became an official member of government. The sale enabled Law to spend more of his time aggressively growing the one company in his venture portfolio. He needed to make owning Mississippi Company shares more appealing to the public. This fixation diverted his attention from diversifying his portfolio of companies and reducing its risk. As a skilled gambler, Law understood the benefits of diversifying risks. Whether he considered the Mississippi Company a sure thing or deliberately chose to ignore best practices, it turned out to be a bad call.

To make the Mississippi Company's shares more alluring, Law went on a buying spree. He quickly purchased the monopoly rights to buying products and slaves in Senegal and sending them to French colonies in return for tobacco to sell in France. He then purchased the failed French East Indies Company to secure monopoly rights on virtually all of France's trade to both the East and West Indies, sparse though it was. To finance further expansion, he audaciously announced the sale of an additional 50,000 shares to the public at 500 livres apiece, even as existing shares were trading below that price. The new shares could be purchased only with notes or coins, not discounted royal bonds. The financial community sneered, again predicting imminent ruin. Law announced the final details of his offer when shares went on sale: investors could buy shares with a 10 percent down payment, paying the rest in installments. In essence, anyone could borrow 90 percent of the price of these shares with zero interest! They could even sell the shares before paying the second installment. The catch was that they could buy only four of these new "daughter" shares for every original "mother" share they owned. Finally, the public took notice.

In just a few months, the price rose to 1,000 livres, and the value of the Mississippi Company grew to over 300 million Livres.

Theoretically, both France and Law himself could have gone on to prosper had the regent and Law conservatively managed the royal bank and the Mississippi Company. But both were greedy for more. Why not, when everything was going so well? While Law remained head of the Banque Royale, he no longer watched over it as the bank's owner, tightly controlling the printing of banknotes to ensure that the value of the outstanding notes stayed below four times the gold reserves. With interest in buying shares soaring, the public raced to raise cash. Encouraging the overall increase in credit, Law and the regent allowed existing and potential investors to borrow money on the appreciated value of their shares. The Banque Royale was happy to support all this newfound wealth by printing money faster than the gold deposits could justify. As long as the public had confidence in both the bank and the Mississippi Company, the stock could keep on appreciating while more and more notes were printed.

To entice the public to buy even more shares, Law then bought the royal mint and the tax-farming contract for all of France. The Mississippi Company now controlled France's monetary supply chain along with its long-distance trade. The price of shares rose faster, allowing people to borrow more to buy more shares, along with jewels, property, and all forms of finery. The Mississippi Company commissioned the building and outfitting of the largest fleet of merchant ships on the planet. At that point, however, rumors began to circulate that there were no additional cargoes coming from America or the Indies to fill these ships. Some of these rumors were initiated by the actions of Law's friend and partner, Richard Cantillon, an Irish-French banker (mentioned earlier as the person who coined the word "entrepreneur"). Cantillon's brother had been dispatched to find the rumored riches of the Mississippi Valley and to found a French colony. Months later he reported back of death and militant indigenous populations. Cantillon sold his shares near the peak value of 10,000 livres, earning himself a fortune but shaking the confidence of every other investor.

As investors lost confidence in the Mississippi Company, its shares started to fall. Thousands of investors of all social statuses who had borrowed money to invest in the company were wiped out. As people withdrew gold from the bank to pay debts, its reserves plummeted. Law frantically outlawed the ownership of gold and silver, destroying any remaining confidence in the bank and its paper money. It also made the public hostile enough to try to lynch him. Law ultimately fled France, with the regent's help, but his wife and daughter were prevented from following him and never saw him again. Emotionally crushed, Law died alone in Venice eight years later.

France went back to using gold as its only form of money and banned the formation of joint-stock companies. The public would not trust banknotes or paper money, or invest in startups, for another hundred years. Law left France's economy in even worse shape than it had been under Louis XIV.

Law understood reserve deposits and credit, but he did not understand investing in value creation. He coveted the idea of using the Mississippi Company as an all-purpose investment fund, but he did not understand how to enhance the value of its assets other than by building more ships. Naively, he gambled everything on France's American holdings quickly yielding trade as valuable as those of its rivals, rivals who had been in the game much longer and understood the situation much better. Law's failure scared the Continent's economic ministers and investors away from further attempts to leverage the innovative and value-creating potential of entrepreneurs to spur economic growth. In fact, much of Europe remained skeptical of entrepreneurship through the twentieth century. Entrepreneurs continued to exist in Europe, and many thrived, but they did so on a much smaller scale than in the United States, usually raising money from family, friends, and others in a tight social circle.

Money Looking for Strangers

A more successful experiment in venture investing took place seventy years after Law's downfall, in the newly independent United States. The Browns were a large, established New England whaling and merchant family who supported their new generations in setting up independent businesses. In many ways, older-generation Browns became venture investors in younger-generation Browns. In this way, by the end of the 1780s, family members had created successful whale candle, pig-iron, cod-fishing, and distillery businesses. The Browns indoctrinated their younger generations in sound fiscal management, objective decision-making, and the importance of proper training.

In 1789, an elder Brown invested money in two cousins-in-law whose firm, Brown & Almy, aspired to build and operate America's first cotton mill. They wanted to copy Richard Arkwright's very profitable high-volume cotton textile factories in England. They purchased some locally made copies of Arkwright's water frames, but the machines could not be made to work properly. The Browns realized they did not have the knowledge to start or run such a business. Rather than admit failure and move on, they decided to invest in someone who did. Brown & Almy put out a request among their extended family to help locate someone with the necessary skills.

By the end of the year, they received a letter from a twenty-one-year-old English immigrant, Samuel Slater (figure 4.4), who had spent eight years working for Arkwright and his partner, Strutt. Almy & Brown (the firm had renamed itself) wrote back offering to

4.4 Samuel Slater.

Source: Wikimedia Commons, https://commons.wikimedia.org/wiki
/File:Samuel_Slater_industrialist.jpg.

fund Slater for up to six months to demonstrate his skills in building and operating a water frame. They further intimated that if they
"[found] the business profitable, we can enlarge it." Slater moved
to Providence, Rhode Island, and in two months built a working
machine that demonstrated unprecedented speed in spinning yarn.
The stranger proved himself as skilled as he had claimed.

In April 1790, Almy, Brown, and Slater worked out what we
would recognize as an investment contract. Almy, Brown, and their
investors would fund the building, outfitting, and managing of a
high-volume, low-cost cotton mill. While Slater would receive "full
and adequate compensation for his whole time and services," he
would also receive half of the profits. He was, however, required
to reinvest his portion of the profits to pay back a loan Almy &
Brown had given him to buy his half of the assets. This structure
amounted to having the founder's stock ownership vest over time.
Slater also agreed that building and running the mill would be his

one and only job. Slater built his mill near Providence and had it fully operational by 1793 (figure 4.5). Although he and the Brown family frequently wrote sniping and complaining letters to one another, the mill proved a great success, and Slater died fabulously wealthy in 1835. His success touched off an American swarm of cotton mill copycat entrepreneurs. In less than twenty years, there were fifty-three textile factories in New England.

From this point, all the elements are in place for the emergence of what we now think of as our contemporary forms of entrepreneurship. The entrepreneurially inclined and newly independent United States, devoid of European prejudices against joint-stock companies, was fertile territory for the formation of new highly competitive, innovative entrepreneurial swarms. The actions of and reactions to these new types of swarms require their own chapter to tell.

4.5 Slater's Mill still stands today.

Source: Wikimedia Commons, https://upload.wikimedia.org/wikipedia/commons/5/5c/Slater
_and_Wilkinson_Mills_-_exterior_%26_water_power_systems.jpg

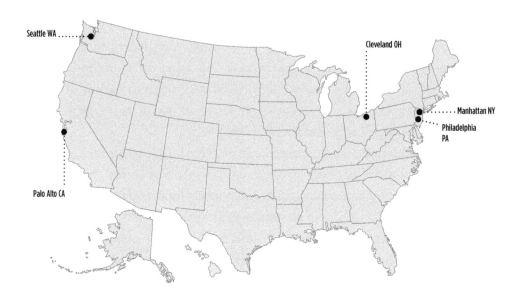

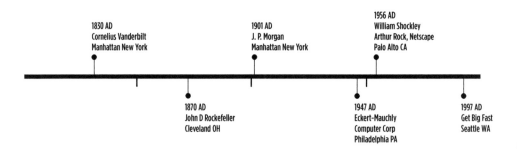

Seattle WA

Cleveland OH

Manhattan NY

Philadelphia
PA

Palo Alto CA

1830 AD
Cornelius Vanderbilt
Manhattan New York

1901 AD
J. P. Morgan
Manhattan New York

1956 AD
William Shockley
Arthur Rock, Netscape
Palo Alto CA

1870 AD
John D Rockefeller
Cleveland OH

1947 AD
Eckert-Mauchly
Computer Corp
Philadelphia PA

1997 AD
Get Big Fast
Seattle WA

CHAPTER 5

Entrepreneur Versus Entrepreneur

Money, which represents the prose of life, and which is hardly spoken of in parlors without an apology, is, in its effects and laws, as beautiful as roses.

—Ralph Waldo Emerson, 1844

The battle to control the creation of new wealth associated with starting new businesses increased in sophistication, frenzy, and fractiousness in the hundred years after the formation of the United States. Entrepreneurs, more than any other constituency, had established the new country, having left England to build lives free of a culture that made them feel constrained. These settlers had been self-directed, highly skilled in creating value, and experienced in commerce. More than half the signers of the Declaration of Independence were merchants or first-generation large-scale farmers.

The framers of the Constitution purposefully structured a federal government that wouldn't interfere with commerce, keeping interstate commerce free and encouraging ingenuity and ambition through the issuance of patents. States were free to regulate commerce within their domains, but individual state constitutions added few commercial constraints. They, too, had been drafted by and with the help of merchants, large-scale farmers, and plantation owners. The American experiment was, above all, an entrepreneurial one. And American entrepreneurs would make their own rules.

America's fiercely independent new culture became a breeding ground for aggressive and determined individuals who wanted to engage in the creation and exchange of value without constraint. It spawned a generation of masterful entrepreneurs who developed new skills for capturing value and wealth. These fully American entrepreneurs were also intent on defending what they'd built from their eager competitors. As the first generation of native-born entrepreneurs amassed great wealth in a relatively unregulated environment, they sparred with one another over what the tacit rules of American competition would become and how they would be collectively enforced. As entrepreneurs themselves, each knew just how rapacious and ingenious their peers could be.

By the second half of the nineteenth century, heightened competition brought forth a new form of enterprise that, while entrepreneurial in origin, quickly evolved into a structure that no longer responded to the founder's desires: the corporation. By the early twentieth century, the modern corporation, managed by salaried specialists and controlled by stockholders, became the most potent way of organizing a business. Founder- and family-dominated corporations remained, but the professionally managed corporation, created to protect the wealth generated by entrepreneurs like Cornelius Vanderbilt, John D. Rockefeller, and J. P. Morgan, dominated by protecting investors from risk. As an unforeseen consequence, the entrepreneur-designed modern corporation made entrepreneurial ventures harder to fund for three generations.

Golden Rules

The most successful of America's first home-grown generation of entrepreneurs was Cornelius Vanderbilt, Jr. (figure 5.1). The world knew him as the Commodore because he controlled much of the shipping in New York Harbor. Vanderbilt felt that much of his success derived from his ironclad adherence to agreements. He was a man of his word and punished anyone who reneged on a deal, whether written or by handshake. In late December 1866, a long-time enemy of the Commodore was elected president of the New York Central Railroad and abruptly canceled several contracts with railroads controlled by Vanderbilt. Vanderbilt's response to this betrayal was swift, public, and ruinous, carrying the clear

5.1 Cornelius Vanderbilt.

Source: Wikipedia, https://en.wikipedia.org/wiki/Cornelius_Vanderbilt.

message that any competitor risked their entire business by failing to fulfill a bargain with him. The scope of his retaliation during the brutal winter of 1867 confirmed Vanderbilt's position as the most feared entrepreneur of his age, bringing businesses stretching from Chicago to New York City to their knees—along with many innocent bystanders.

At the time, the New York Central Railroad controlled much of the freight traffic between the Great Lakes, Chicago, and New York. It vied with the Pennsylvania Central Railroad as the largest corporation in the world. Corporations at that time could do business only within the state in which they were incorporated, so New York's line began in Buffalo, where it connected to other railroads whose tracks penetrated into the Great Lakes area. The New York Central line ran from Buffalo to Albany, where freight and passengers going to Manhattan were transferred to steamboats or one of two railroads. Both of those railroad lines had recently come under the control of the Commodore. He and the previous New York Central president had agreed to increase the percentage of freight and passengers that would travel to Manhattan by rail rather than steamboat. When Vanderbilt's rival took advantage of his new position to abruptly cancel those preexisting agreements, Vanderbilt knew that his reputation was at stake. Without delay, he ordered his railroad cars to stop picking up New York Central passengers and freight in Albany. Chaos ensued; steamboats couldn't operate in the winter months, so Vanderbilt's two railroads were the only option. While passengers could lug their heavy suitcases across the icy bridge spanning the Hudson to buy their own tickets, the owners of the in-transit freight could not immediately negotiate the removal of their goods from the New York Central freight cars for transport across the bridge, let alone negotiate their passage onward to the city. Therefore, the freight remained frozen.

News of Vanderbilt's blockade spread quickly via telegraph, and much of New York Central's business instantly shifted to the Erie and Pennsylvania Railroads. New York Central would go bankrupt if it didn't capitulate. The newly elected president and the close-knit board of directors that supported him dumped their New York Central shares, which had plummeted in value. (They were likely required to sell their shares because the shares had been purchased with borrowed money.) Seizing the opportunity, Vanderbilt and his friends bought up those shares. By the end of the year, the Commodore had replaced his nemesis as president of the New York Central Railroad.

The brazen blockade of New York was widely deplored in the press, a familiar experience for Vanderbilt. Shocked by stories of mothers with children making their way across the Hudson in freezing conditions, not to mention crucial freight remaining undelivered, a New York State Senate committee convened to recommend changes to the laws to prevent the public's being held as entrepreneurial hostages. Vanderbilt told the committee, "The law, as I view it, goes too slow for me when I have the remedy in my own hands." In his view, entrepreneurs—using the limited liability afforded to corporations as shields for the consequences of their aggressive moves—were far more effective at curbing other entrepreneurs than any law could ever be. Since the nation was embroiled in a presidential impeachment battle at the time, the furor died down quickly. Neither Congress nor any state took up Vanderbilt's challenge. Clearly, it would be easier to let entrepreneurs deal with one another.

Almost all cultures have a sense of what constitutes fair play. Prior to Vanderbilt, entrepreneurs in almost all cultures deferred to those who had entered the market first. You needed to find your own niche to fill or risk being shunned by your peers. Vanderbilt didn't care what his peers thought. He believed money was the only measure of power and justice. This high-profile episode of entrepreneurial retribution solidified his strategy of financially destroying any competitor who stood in his way. Also, it became the template for other high-profile entrepreneurs.

Vanderbilt's strategy favors the entrepreneur with the largest cash reserves, not necessarily the largest corporation. Businesspeople today refer to this style of competition as "The Golden Rule," that is, the one with the most gold rules. It adds to the overall risk of being an entrepreneur. Not only do entrepreneurs assume the risk that their company might not attract enough customers, or the risk of external economic or political disruptions, now they face the very real possibility that a wealthier competitor could aggressively smother their business at any time.

An American Entrepreneur

Born in 1794, when George Washington was still president of a newly independent United States, Cornelius Vanderbilt, Jr., had a uniquely American upbringing. His father, Vanderbilt Sr., like almost everyone in the Dutch community on Staten Island, was a farmer. Seeing an opportunity in selling crops across the bay in Manhattan, where they would fetch a higher price, he built himself a boat and was soon earning more than his neighbors. Next, the elder Vanderbilt offered, for a price, to transport their produce to Manhattan as well, creating a supplementary income that cushioned the family through bad weather and wars. Meanwhile, Vanderbilt Sr.'s wife, Phebe, kept the money she earned from her sewing and vegetable garden in the bottom of the family's grandfather clock and lent out sums, with interest, to family and neighbors. Serious about collecting on her debts, she even foreclosed on her own daughter's mortgage.

Education was not a priority in the Vanderbilt family, and Cornelius Jr. received little of it. Money was what mattered. Earning money was synonymous with earning the love and respect of his parents. By the age of eleven, Cornelius Jr.'s diligence in doing his chores had earned him the right to sail his father's boat alone to Manhattan to deliver bales of hay. When he was sixteen, his father lent him a boat to captain and gave him a cut of the profits. Cornelius Jr. quickly earned a reputation for being tough, reliable, and completely committed to making money.

By the age of twenty-three, Cornelius Jr. was part owner of several other small boats working in New York Harbor and along the coast as far south as Virginia. Leaving the captaining of his boats to others, he captained for Thomas Gibbons, one of the wealthiest men in the country. Gibbons owned a notorious steamship nicknamed *The Mouse*. Gibbons hoped to use *The Mouse* to break a steamboat monopoly held by Aaron Ogden, former governor of New Jersey. While governor, Ogden had secured exclusive rights to operate steamboats between New Jersey and Manhattan. With Vanderbilt at the helm of *The Mouse*, Gibbons hoped to challenge that monopoly. Gibbons's crusade had been instigated by a personal feud with his former business partner and neighbor. When Ogden refused to duel Gibbons to resolve the feud—perhaps because Alexander Hamilton had recently died in a duel with Ogden's friend Aaron Burr—full-scale commercial warfare was Gibbons's only viable option.

Captaining *The Mouse* drew Cornelius into an epic, high-profile battle of great concern to the entire aristocratic community of the day. American elites were mostly self-made or directly descended from successful entrepreneurs. They didn't want this squabble to upset the prevailing equilibrium of gentlemanly competition. The most lucrative charters to incorporate businesses of the day— banks, turnpikes, and steamboats—were monopolies granted to established families with political connections. Monopolies were profitable, making it possible for entrepreneurs to appropriately invest in a business without worrying about competition. Monopolies made economic sense in a new country with so many unmet needs. Vanderbilt, Jr., as someone who was not a member of a family with any political ties, heartily supported Gibbons's perspective, feeling that state-granted monopolies were unfair to ambitious but unconnected entrepreneurs like himself.

For more than a decade, Vanderbilt cunningly confounded bailiffs who tried to impound Gibbons's boat whenever it entered New York waters. He also supervised the building of faster and faster steamboats in order to attract the most customers. When speed didn't draw enough customers to fill his ferries, Vanderbilt, with Gibbons's backing, cut fares to below expenses, causing large financial losses for Ogden. Twelve years after the battle began, the U.S. Supreme Court decided in *Ogden v. Gibbons* that states had no rights to grant monopolies that restricted interstate commerce. The license Ogden held was rendered worthless. Combined with the financial losses Gibbons and Vanderbilt had inflicted, he was forced to declare bankruptcy. (Aaron Burr had to intercede to help Ogden avoid debtor's prison.) Steamboat monopolies were booming in America in the mid-1820s, and the epic Supreme Court ruling freed Cornelius to break them. He set out to do just that.

At first, Vanderbilt focused on expanding Gibbons's steamboat business, but Gibbons passed away within a few years and his son decided to dissolve the business. Having shrewdly saved his share of Gibbons's profits—a lesson he learned from his thrifty mother—Cornelius sold his shares in the sailboats that he controlled to start his own steamship company. He began with the fastest steamboat afloat, the *Citizen*. New York City, flourishing after the opening of the Erie Canal, had a harbor swarming with monopolistic steamboat owners. Without a doubt, this was the best place for an aggressive monopoly-busting steamboat entrepreneur to operate.

Vanderbilt's strategy was to weaken inefficient monopolists with superior steamboats and bruising fare battles with the goal of buying their assets and claiming their monopolies for himself or, at the very least, forcing them to buy him out at a hefty return, paying, in effect, protection money. Being frugal meant he could weather fare battles better than most. He had a special knack for spotting inefficiencies and malingerers, which he called "saving of the expenditures." Each time Vanderbilt knocked out a competitor and captured its profits, he would use the additional wealth to do it all over again on a bigger scale.

Vanderbilt's ceaseless aggression was unprecedented in entrepreneurial history. In this book we'll meet other hugely successful entrepreneurs, but every one of them in just about every major civilization up to that point had pursued entrepreneurship as a means to an end. Ultimately, entrepreneurs sought to become members of the elite of the land themselves. Once they had amassed enough wealth, they no longer wanted to focus on growth or the daily supervision of commercial dealings. Entrepreneurship was a way to acquire wealth and improve social standing, not to prove you could be the toughest competitor. That kind of thinking was crass and would get you shunned. But Vanderbilt never aspired to put on gentlemanly airs—he spent his money on what he wanted—not to impress anyone else. Careless of his social status and the opinions of his peers, he relentlessly grew his steamship businesses, eventually dominating his national and then his international competitors, forcing them all to accept a change in the rules. Now, anyone could "oppose" (the word of that day for "compete") anyone else and drive them out of business if they were able. After the 1867 blockade, no entrepreneur would think otherwise.

Winner Takes All

Almost two generations younger than Vanderbilt, John D. Rockefeller was a great admirer of the Commodore. That said, he felt he knew better, and, more important, God was on his side, believing "God gave me my money." By the time he was twenty-five, he'd seen how open and free competition in the new oil industry had ruined opportunities for everyone in that business. This experience convinced him that each industry needed to be orchestrated by a single entrepreneur to ensure a just distribution of profits. Rockefeller, a devoutly religious and thrifty Baptist who recorded every expenditure in a notebook, felt ideally suited to orchestrate the nascent oil business in this way.

Rockefeller set out with the same ambition as Vanderbilt—to make as much money as possible—but with a very different motivation. He hoped to do God's work by charitably redistributing the largess. His father, a traveling patent medicine huckster, abandoned the family for years at a time, leaving them to support themselves and leaving John with an outsized sense of responsibility and a passion for order, frugality, and piety. As a Baptist, John felt a duty of charity toward those in need. At six, he'd given part of the money he'd earned from odd jobs, like picking potatoes, to other children who were more needy. As diligent in learning accounting as he was charitable, he was made partner in a wholesale produce business by the age of twenty-three.

Oil was a major new entrepreneurial opportunity at the time. During the Civil War, Rockefeller (figure 5.2) found himself fortuitously well positioned to participate in the nascent oil business. An English chemist living in Cleveland came to the already prosperous twenty-four-year-old looking for a venture investment to commercialize his process for turning recently discovered crude oil

5.2 John D. Rockefeller in 1885.

into clean-burning kerosene. Rockefeller and his wholesale produce partner each invested $4,000 in the refinery startup.

The refinery, though profitable, demanded Rockefeller's constant attention because the price of the standard forty-two-gallon barrel of oil fluctuated wildly, between $4 and $12 in 1864. Rockefeller understood how to benefit from these wild swings and wanted to borrow money to expand, but his partner did not. Never scared to borrow as much money as he felt he needed, Rockefeller obtained enough to buy out his partner. Within a year he borrowed even more to build a second refinery, making him the largest Cleveland refinery operator of the time, all by the age of twenty-six.

Even with profits pouring in, Rockefeller wanted to drive them higher, so he got creative. He dried the lumber used for barrels while it was still in the forest to reduce the weight of the wood and therefore the cost of transportation to his own cooperage. He figured out how to sell refinery by-products to producers of petroleum jelly and fertilizer. He bought his oil directly from the men who pumped it, cutting out the middleman. To tap the growing foreign demand for kerosene, he sent his brother, William, to New York City to start an exporting business. He also tapped William to find banks willing to finance further expansion. John's immaculate and detailed account books impressed bankers, giving them the confidence to lend more money to this twenty-six-year-old businessman than they would anyone else.

As has been true for all booming new businesses in history, the growth of the oil business attracted swarms of entrepreneurs. Many of them set up refineries. In fact, many refinery employees, having learned the necessary skills, left their jobs to set up their own operations, further expanding supply. Pittsburgh, New York, Baltimore, Philadelphia, and the oil region of western Pennsylvania developed into refining centers in competition with Cleveland, which itself had fifty refineries within three years of Rockefeller's taking control of his first.

Supply exceeding demand, the price of kerosene dropped. By the late 1860s, most refiners were struggling to stay solvent. Rockefeller, however, remained clear-headed under pressure, proudly declaring that he was good at "seeing opportunity in every disaster." He felt confident that God had put him in this position to tame the industry and eliminate the "ruinous competition"—the swarms of entrepreneurs driving costs down.

Since he operated the largest and most profitable refinery operations in Cleveland, Rockefeller decided to leverage his size and cash flow together with Cleveland's strategic location at the nexus of all three of the railroad trunk lines to get a better freight deal. (One of the railroads was Vanderbilt's New York Central, another was Jay Gould's Erie, and the third was the Pennsylvania Railroad, run by the first professional manager of a major corporation, John Thomson.) With the help of Henry Flagler, a junior partner and the son of a major Cleveland investor, Rockefeller secretly negotiated the lowest shipping rates of anyone in the industry, at first with Gould's Erie Railroad. Now Rockefeller was even more profitable than any of his competitors. Using the newly liberal rules of incorporation in Ohio to become a corporation rather than a partnership, Standard Oil, unlike any other refinery operation, had become profitable and stable enough to raise money by selling shares. Rockefeller sold $2 million worth of shares, mostly to prominent members of Cleveland's business elite (although $50,000 worth wound up under the control of the Commodore). He now had a war chest to wage a new kind of war with his competitors.

In January 1872, just five years after the Commodore's blockade, John D. Rockefeller implemented a new strategy for keeping competitors at bay and under control: consolidation. Cornelius Vanderbilt, Jr., inadvertently helped trigger this new era. Both the Commodore and John Thomson at the Pennsylvania Railroad wanted to stop costly rate wars between the major railroads. Previous attempts to form a cartel to regulate freight pricing had fallen apart when one or more of the participants cheated. It isn't clear who instigated the creation of the Southern Improvement Corporation (SIC), but Rockefeller was clearly near the center of it. The SIC was a covert agreement to form a freight cartel with Rockefeller as the "honest broker" ensuring that each railroad wound up with its fair share of freight at the right price. With Rockefeller being the largest freight customer in the country by a wide margin, the railroads felt they could trust him, and the deal was spectacular for both sides. The participating railroads kept prices where they wanted them while Standard Oil of Ohio (and any other refiners it invited to join the SIC) received a 50 percent rebate on the higher freight rates the railroads would simultaneously publish—in addition to a bounty of forty cents on every barrel of oil shipped to Cleveland by any competitor not in the deal.

Over the time it took to negotiate and sign the SIC deal, Rockefeller cajoled, bullied, or bribed twenty-two of his remaining twenty-six Cleveland refining competitors to capitulate to a buy-out, with the explicit threat that they would be wiped out (thanks to the SIC) if they didn't accept his terms. Rockefeller considered himself generous in offering the option of cash on the spot or the equivalent value in Standard Oil shares. (Few accepted the shares, but those that did and kept them eventually became wealthy.) He was so effective in describing how he'd run each of his competitors out of business that he was able to buy out up to three a day. The period would eventually be known as the Cleveland Massacre.

The massacre came to an end when the SIC collapsed before it was ever implemented. When news of the deal leaked, it caused such an uproar among oilmen, the press, and even the Pennsylvania legislature (a body that usually rubber-stamped any deal requested by the Pennsylvania Railroad) that the SIC's charter was revoked. By that point, however, Rockefeller had already consolidated 90 percent of Cleveland's refining capacity.

Rockefeller later described his strategy as having been "forced" on him. "We had to do it in self-defense," he argued. "The oil business was in confusion and daily growing worse. Someone had to make a stand." Just as Vanderbilt had brazenly challenged the notion that laws could mediate entrepreneurial competition, Rockefeller repudiated the idea that laissez-faire capitalism mediated by entrepreneurs could lead to rational economies. Historically, economic "confusion" like that surrounding the oil industry had been contained by entrepreneurs forming guilds or associations. Monopolies and pricing cartels had never been illegal. Since ancient times, entrepreneurs had sensed it was in their collective best interests to minimize price competition. The SIC was among several attempts around 1870 to control pricing (others were in more staid businesses such as salt, rope, and whiskey).

But cartels break down in fast-growing businesses or when entrepreneurs are not in a tight social circle. America itself was a fast-growing business, and Vanderbilt had made social circles irrelevant to entrepreneurial competition. Once he'd made it clear that every entrepreneur would have to fight to keep every bit of business they had, the cartel model no longer worked. The SIC was an attempt to construct a more complex cartel adapted to the rapidly evolving and interdependent oil and railroad industries, one that involved an honest-broker customer. It failed. A new era of unbridled, winner-take-all entrepreneurial competition had begun.

Rockefeller did not stop at controlling refining in Cleveland. His brilliance at organizing, simplifying, and delegating enabled the unprecedented financial and geographical scale of his enterprise. Undeterred by the collapse of the SIC, he negotiated even larger secret rebates, further increasing his profits, which enabled him to borrow even more money to buy even more refiners in other cities. Once he had consolidated almost all the refiners in the country, he moved to control oil distributors, and then the new business of oil pipelines, eventually making Standard Oil the first entrepreneurially created vertically integrated monopoly.

Before 1880, most states prevented or made it very difficult for corporations to own property or operate in other states. This constraint created challenges for Standard Oil to own refiners outside Ohio. In response, Rockefeller used the recent legal innovation of a trust to enable the coordinated action of the directors of different legal entities. Then, when New Jersey, wanting to attract large corporations, amended its laws to allow interstate holdings, Rockefeller created Standard Oil of New Jersey as his ultimate holding company.

It's telling that Standard Oil, in creating a national and partly international monopoly, was able to smooth out—though never eliminate—the boom and bust cycles that plagued businesses in the Gilded Age. Because of its absolute control of the kerosene business, Standard Oil employees never experienced layoffs or reduced wages. Consequently, they never unionized. Rockefeller was certain that God had led him to an improved form of business and that the refiners and distributors who complained about his business practices were fools for not joining him. He believed that competition was detrimental and that cooperation would end egotism and materialism, both of which he and his fellow Baptists abhorred.

Although Rockefeller always held that his own actions in this crusade met his Christian ethical standards, he did not feel compelled to set similar moral requirements for his lieutenants. If internal correspondence were in code, deals were kept secret, and legislators were bribed, he didn't need to know about any of it—although memos have surfaced over the years suggesting he knew more than he ever let on.

The unintended consequence of both Vanderbilt's blockade and the SIC was that Rockefeller was able to form a real monopoly, one with more economic power than any of the railroads. They had created a beast they could no longer control. Rockefeller's strategy worked so effectively that he surpassed even Vanderbilt in wealth. Standard Oil of New Jersey became the most powerful and profitable corporation the world had ever seen. Less than fifteen years after Vanderbilt ignored all constraints on competition, Rockefeller demonstrated that a strategy of winner takes all was even more effective in this new age.

Rockefeller's strategy was often copied over the last decades of the nineteenth century by other entrepreneurs, including John B. Duke of American Tobacco, whose entrepreneurial father played such a big role in the creation of the metropolis around Durham, North Carolina. But it was the entrepreneurial financier J. P. Morgan who demonstrated how, by dominating finance, he could create strategies that dominated even winner takes all, provided entrepreneurs left the scene.

Corporate Man + Finance Man > Entrepreneur

John Pierpont Morgan (figure 5.3) was the only son of the successful American financier Junius Spencer Morgan, who managed the prosperous London-based bank Peabody, Morgan & Company.

5.3 John Pierpont Morgan.

Junius arranged for his son to apprentice at several financial firms. In 1860, he supported J. P. in setting up his own firm to act as his father's agent in the United States.

Although the success and stability of J. Pierpont Morgan & Company was ensured by the work it did for his father, J. P. independently sought his own business in New York City. The railroads were expanding rapidly and getting most of their financing from wealthy Europeans. J. P. saw an opportunity there. He looked for clients who demonstrated the same aggressive pursuit of growth and profit that Vanderbilt had demonstrated as essential qualities of American-style entrepreneurship. After refinancing some struggling railroads, however, he decided companies like these were best led by professional managers in the mold of John Thomson of the Pennsylvania Railroad, not by founder-entrepreneurs such as Vanderbilt and Rockefeller or by stock speculators like Jay Gould. Also, he came to insist on using Rockefeller's corporate trust structure for the companies he helped to finance. This ensured he could maintain control of each company that he brought back to life.

Neither Vanderbilt nor Rockefeller had needed Wall Street to finance their empires because both were profitable enough to finance their own growth. (Rockefeller was respected enough by Cleveland's business community that he could raise $2 million from them without the need of any middlepersons.) They also distrusted bankers. J. P. Morgan aspired to create even more dominant and valuable trusts, and for that he would leverage his unparalleled ability to raise money. He began to arrange financing of unprecedented scale to acquire large competitors and then install professional managers. Morgan used Thomson as the role model of a big corporation chief executive. Within the newly merged competitors, professional managers would be expected to increase profits by coordinating activities and operations and improving productivity, achieving what is now referred to as economies of scale.

Professional managers, Morgan believed, would not become distracted by personal projects or stock manipulations. He was never interested in "speculating," what he called raising money for entrepreneurs and new companies. That was too risky. He purposely let other Wall Street firms he considered inferior, such as Goldman Sachs and Lehman Brothers, work with smaller companies directly run by entrepreneurs.

In 1901, Morgan convinced Andrew Carnegie to sell him Carnegie Steel Works. Joining it with Consolidated Steel and Wire Company and eight other companies under his control, Morgan created U.S. Steel, the first firm to be worth more than $1 billion. The *New York Times* reported that the new company's "advantage is found in the fact that it brings under a central, and presumably scientific, management, a large number of the best-equipped iron and steel plants in the world." Morgan similarly formed General Electric by consolidating Thomas Edison's companies under one management structure and then merging that entity with the Thomas-Houston Electric Company, which specialized in electric generators and arc lighting. J. P. also created International Harvester when he combined the McCormick Harvesting Machine Company with the Deering Harvester Company.

J. P. Morgan demonstrated to investors that financiers rather than individual entrepreneurs could create larger and more profitable corporations in an era when no market was safe from Vanderbilt-like competition applied in a Rockefeller-like winner-takes-all fashion. Salaried professional managers were more reliable than founders in improving productivity and staying focused on their duties to shareholders. As a consequence, a new dogma emerged that it was best for successful entrepreneurs to sell their enterprises to become part of larger monopolistic enterprises rather than fight such institutions to keep a business under personal control and in the family.

The Wright Brothers, for example, sold their business within seven years of its founding to a properly financed and professionally managed corporation focused on consolidating competition. Henry Ford was ultimately surpassed when General Motors's largest shareholder, Pierre S. du Pont, replaced its founder William Durant with professional management in the person of Alfred P. Sloan. Ford's first automotive startup went bankrupt and he was kicked out of his second, the Henry Ford Company, by his financial backers. (The company was subsequently renamed Cadillac Automobile Company.) Not even the unprecedented, back-to-back innovations of the Model T and assembly-line production could ensure Ford's entrepreneurial preeminence over his well-financed, professionally managed rival.

Vanderbilt, Rockefeller, and Morgan, in learning how to make it hard for other entrepreneurs to survive in the markets they went after, unintentionally created an exceptionally difficult environment for entrepreneurs to visualize success in major markets. As a result, fewer and fewer attempted to bring their ideas to market as individuals. Newly huge enterprises such as U.S. Steel, AT&T, General Electric, International Harvester, and IBM neither tolerated competition nor wanted the help of entrepreneurs as they sought to vertically integrate their supply chains. Their managers dealt whenever they could with other large, professionally managed enterprises. They invested in engineers and laboratories that increased their patent protection and kept a steady stream of incrementally improved products flowing to their customers. (By 1929, there were a thousand laboratories in the United States operated by major corporations.) They solidified industry dominance by creating well-financed distribution networks under their complete control. Many professionally managed corporations actively fought to prevent entrepreneurial innovations from entering their markets, as was the case with FM radio, penicillin (drug companies initially rejected commercializing penicillin as being uneconomical), and document copying.

The U.S. government, having instigated a growing list of regulations and regulatory agencies created in the first decades of the twentieth century to oversee big business, now also favored doing business with larger professionally managed companies. Characteristic of this favoritism was the government's role in the creation of RCA as the dominant firm in early radio broadcast and manufacture. The U.S. Navy, fearful of foreign control of wireless communications, asked the well-financed and professionally managed General Electric to take over the U.S. subsidiary of the English Marconi Wireless Telegraph Company. The government could very well have supported Marconi's American subsidiary in its independence from its English/Italian entrepreneur-inventor and English shareholders but, influenced by naval commanders, chose GE to be the government's sponsor.

Because of its clout and government support, General Electric was able to consolidate wireless technologies owned by AT&T, Westinghouse, and United Fruit to create an insurmountable patent portfolio. GE later made the division an independent company, Radio Corporation of America (RCA), to avoid antitrust prosecution. For the next three generations, entrepreneurs had a very difficult time challenging RCA and the large corporations it licensed in any area related to broadcast equipment, radio receivers, and commercial radio broadcasting. In fact, the military and its concerns played a recurring role in this era of ever greater consolidation. Through the hot and cold wars of the twentieth century, the government continued to favor large, professionally managed corporations with contracts that spurred the creation of major new businesses with military relevance, such as jet aircraft, radar, penicillin (the U.S. government initiated and led the project to commercialize the drug), and computers.

Witnessing this rise of industrial champions in the United States, foreign governments feared for the competitiveness of their local businesses, intervening to create national winner-takes-all "champions" on their own soil. These governments used lucrative contracts, financing, protectionist tariffs, nationalization, and regulations to ensure that politically supportive local entrepreneurs (willing to bring in professional management) could grow large enough to control their national market and compete in export markets. A major component of pre–World War II fascism in Germany, Italy, and Japan specifically revolved around government formation and support of business cartels to stimulate economic activity, particularly in exports. Local entrepreneurs in cartelized markets were pushed out or forced into niches deemed too small to warrant government involvement.

Even though the attention and support of governments shifted away from entrepreneurs throughout the first half of the twentieth century, entrepreneurship still dominated growth in smaller, less aggressive, less capital-intensive, regional, niche, or bedrock businesses. Not all new businesses formed between 1900 and 1970 came to be dominated by large, Wall Street–financed, professionally managed corporations. Unlike professionally managed corporations, entrepreneur-run companies felt comfortable with other entrepreneurs in their supply chains. For example, Sears, Roebuck and Company offered Upton Brothers' washing machine as the first electric model in their catalog. (The company ultimately changed its name to Whirlpool, with Louis Upton remaining on its board until 1975.) Entrepreneurial swarms in clothing, retail, specialized machines, personal services, distribution, sales companies, as well as car and machinery dealerships all thrived during this time based on the older rules of entrepreneurial competition. The scale of their operations and their inherent profitability limited the need for venture investment; loans from banks became these entrepreneurs' preferred way to finance working capital for growth.

For much of the twentieth century, Vanderbilt-style Golden Rule aggression coupled with Morgan-style financier-led consolidation limited the scale of many entrepreneurial aspirations. During this period scaling became the fixation of professionally managed Wall Street–backed enterprises. Innovation instigated by entrepreneurial innovation cycles was typically replaced by inventions by technical employees of large corporations. Innovations that sprang from invention of new electrical devices, materials, and controls did not happen as quickly under the control of large corporations as innovations incubated within an EIC.

Out from Under Corporations Again

During World War II, new technologies—particularly in the fields of electronics, materials, and controls—were developed in government laboratories and at universities under contract. After the war, many of the engineers who had been engaged in that work contemplated starting companies to commercialize those technologies. But it remained difficult for these entrepreneurs to compete with larger, professionally managed corporations that copied their ideas and possessed enormous sales forces eager to sell new products. For example, after the completion of the University of Pennsylvania's government contract to develop the ENIAC computer during the war, the two project leaders, John Mauchly and J. Presper Eckert, formed the Eckert-Mauchly Computer Corporation. As a small business in an environment still distinctly unfriendly to entrepreneurship, they struggled to design, fund, apply for, and contest patents—while trying to sell the next-generation computer they wanted to build. After four years, they sold their company to the Remington Rand corporation, a diversified manufacturer of weapons, typewriters, electric razors, adding machines, and punch card sorters. Two years later, Remington Rand acquired another struggling computer company, Engineering Research Associates, and succeeded in commercializing UNIVAC, a computer that developed a reputation for performance at the expense of reliability. IBM followed with an inferior computer that was sold by the best sales force in the world at the time. UNIVAC was marginalized, and IBM captured a dominant position in the nascent computer industry, maintaining its dominance in business equipment until semiconductor, personal computer, and internet entrepreneurs changed the rules of competition again.

An Entrepreneurial Disaster Leads to a New Paradigm

The failure of William Shockley (figure 5.4), an engineering genius working at AT&T's Bell Labs, to launch a transistor-manufacturing company ultimately led to a new set of paradigms of entrepreneurial

5.4 William Shockley.

Source: Wikipedia, https://en.wikipedia.org
/wiki/William_Shockley.

competition and venture investing, which dominate the world today. Shockley was coinventor of the transistor, an invention widely heralded at the time as revolutionary and a harbinger of an electronics revolution. In giving birth to modern electronics, Shockley wanted the transistor to be his legacy and took a different entrepreneurial route than Eckert and Mauchly. He did what most entrepreneurs throughout history did: he secured funding from a successful entrepreneur he knew. Arnold Beckman was a fellow Cal Tech alum who had founded a successful specialized laboratory equipment company. Shockley received a de facto blank check to found an independent division of Beckman Instruments, called Shockley Semiconductor Laboratories (figure 5.5), to produce transistors and related devices. Beckman was so excited to support Shockley, soon to win the Nobel Prize with his coinventors Bardeen and Brittan, that he didn't even require the new division to be located near his headquarters in Southern California. Instead, Shockley set up shop in Palo Alto, California, to be close to his mother. (Yes, this is the real reason for the location of Silicon Valley.)

5.5 Photo of the original building where Shockley Semiconductor Laboratory opened in 1956.

Source: Chemical Heritage Foundation Collections.

To staff the new division, Shockley sought potential team members from a list of the smartest technical talent he could identify. Nine engineers working for large companies, none of them aspiring entrepreneurs, were lured to California based on Shockley's reputation and the acknowledged importance of the transistor. Unfortunately, Shockley was a terrible leader—so bad, in fact, that after only a year, seven of the nine engineers started looking for new jobs. Because they enjoyed working together, they decided to find a company that would hire them as a team. They contacted a small Wall Street investment banking firm known to the father of one of them to ask for advice. Two bankers, Bud Coyle and Arthur Rock, took on the challenge of contacting thirty-five stock exchange–listed companies to sponsor the scientists, now eight in number (figure 5.6), in forming an independent semiconductor

5.6 Photo of the "Traitorous Eight." From left to right: Gordon Moore, C. Sheldon Roberts, Eugene Kleiner, Robert Noyce, Victor Grinich, Julius Blank, Jean Hoerni, and Jay Last (1960).

Photo by Wayne Miller, courtesy of Magnum Photos.

division. None of the companies even wanted to meet them. As a last attempt, Coyle decided to contact Sherman Fairchild, an inventor-entrepreneur who not only owned or controlled multiple companies focused on his own inventions and interests but was also IBM's largest shareholder (as sole heir of IBM's first president).

Fairchild was already looking for ways to play in this new market, and he wasn't burdened with the same bias against ideas generated outside professionally managed large corporations. He jumped at the opportunity to create the Fairchild Semiconductor Corporation. Though the eight engineers owned about a third of the stock, ownership was set up as a trust so that Fairchild Camera and Instrument voted everyone's shares, including being able to buy them out after three years, which it did. Within days of founding Fairchild Semiconductor, the Soviets launched the first satellite, Sputnik, into Earth's orbit, and the rapid growth of the nascent semiconductor business was assured.

Over the next decade, Fairchild Semiconductor prospered as it invented many new devices and techniques, including the integrated circuit. It was nevertheless continuously under intense pressure from the challenges of manufacturing larger and larger quantities of technologically sophisticated products and from rapidly intensifying competition, a mix of a swarm of entrepreneurs and established companies. Several of the most important competitors were created by one or more of the founders of Fairchild Semiconductor. After the parent company took complete control of their semiconductor division, there was no longer a major financial incentive for them to stay. The established reporting structure left little room for advancement for the ambitious engineers and salespeople who had developed unique and valuable skills.

Arthur Rock (figure 5.7), the banker who brokered the original Fairchild Semiconductor deal, became an entrepreneur himself and moved to San Francisco in 1961 with $5 million from East Coast

5.7 Arthur Rock.

Source: Wikimedia Commons, https://commons.wikimedia.org/wiki/File:Arthur_Rock.jpg.
Photograph by Christopher Michel, Wikipedia.

investors and a few of the Fairchild founders. He wanted to invest in many of these new companies, and he succeeded in amassing an unprecedented fortune for his investors. Rock's fund ended in 1968, having made more than $100 million.

Several other venture capital firms then formed, which made funding electronics startups straightforward for people with semiconductor experience and a vision for a new product. That year was a frenzied time for startups, with the announcement of about one new semiconductor company a month. That same year, the remaining two founders of Fairchild Semiconductor, Robert Noyce and Gordon Moore, left the company at last to start their own semiconductor company, Intel. They did it by calling Arthur Rock.

Large, professionally managed corporations tried but failed to dominate the semiconductor business. Fueled by growing amounts of venture capital, the semiconductor EIC yielded innovation at a pace too fast for their glacial large-company decision-making processes. New entrepreneurial swarms developed that led to new products like hand-held calculators and faster, cheaper computers, which further accelerated semiconductor adoption and drove down prices before large corporations could introduce equivalent devices. Competition in the ensuing new markets—personal computers, software, and gaming—would be a race to determine who could master both the development and delivery of technically sophisticated products. Venture capitalists competed to finance experienced entrepreneurs with the boldest ideas. The entrepreneurial genie was back out of the bottle, at least in the vicinity of Palo Alto.

Growth Over Profits

Realizing its commercial potential was far greater than any military advantage it could deliver, in 1990 the U.S. government decommissioned ARPANET, a global computer network that it had developed over the previous two decades with the help of university researchers. The government first allowed academics and then commercial firms to copy the network's protocols and infrastructure, giving rise to an internet owned by no one. Academics were the first to experiment with the global communications network, developing technologies like HTTP, the code that renders web pages, and the first web browsers. Sensing these innovations could be widely adopted, entrepreneurs and their venture capital backers rushed to exploit the new technologies. They mimicked strategies that had worked for the founders of Apple and Microsoft: be the first to develop and provide reliable support in a new product area. A new swarm formed to leverage the new internet for commercial gain, who would test a new strategy for entrepreneurs and their investors in an environment where everyone in the world could copy ideas the instant they were introduced.

The company that became Netscape was founded in April 1994 and released its Navigator web browser that October. By year end several million people had downloaded and were using it. One of the two founders, Jim Clark, had cofounded a successful computer company, Silicon Graphics, and knew most of the successful computer entrepreneurs and venture capitalists in Silicon Valley. The other was a twenty-three-year-old recent college graduate named Marc Andreesen, who didn't sleep much and had helped code a noncommercial web browser while in college. To help recruit and keep everyone organized despite the unprecedented pace of Navigator's adoption, the two founders agreed to bring an experienced third person, Jim Barksdale, to the company to be its CEO. Barksdale had already helped two other ambitious startups grow to be worth billions. With him on board, Clark and his VC investor, John Doer of the pioneering Silicon Valley firm Kleiner Perkins, sensed the moment was right to do what hadn't been done before: take a not-yet-profitable, barely eighteen-month-old company public. Netscape's $2.9 billion IPO was a sensation, as the stock shot up from $28 a share to over $71 in the first minutes of trading. Investors, both professional and amateur individuals, did not want to miss investing in such a fast-growing company, many openly comparing Netscape to Apple and Microsoft when they had gone public (even though both companies had been older and profitable at the time of their IPOs). Stock analysts, seeking to justify the unprofitable Netscape's unprecedented valuation, pointed to its growth and profit potential.

Growth now became *the* primary valuation metric. The primary metric for the previous six thousand years of venture investing—profit—was no longer the critical criterion for valuing the shares of fast-growing companies. Savvy VCs instantly started looking to invest in entrepreneurs who could describe how they planned to grow fast. This new paradigm of venture investing did not change despite Netscape's losing its dominant position to Bill Gates and Microsoft's free Internet Explorer browser. Even though the U.S. government sued Microsoft for antitrust, Gates had successfully imposed Vanderbilt's Golden Rule.

Get Big Fast

A year before the Netscape IPO, Wall Street hedge fund executive Jeff Bezos analyzed the commercial opportunities provided by a free internet and concluded that it would enable significant economies of scale in retailing by cutting out brick-and-mortar stores, particularly for a commodity product like books. Bezos left Wall Street and its large cash bonuses to prove that customers would wait two days for a book to arrive in the mail in return for lower prices (enabled by lower overhead) and greater selection. Over the next two years, using mostly his own funds, Bezos proved to his own satisfaction that his business model could work. Noting the shift in investor sentiment toward growth after Netscape, Bezos adopted a strategy he described as "get big fast." He reasoned that he was in a Rockefeller winner-take-all race to achieve the economies of scale inherent in a business that needed brick-and-mortar stores. Having proven that consumers would flock to his online store, he was now in a race to raise as much money as quickly as possible from VCs and investors focused on growth—not profit.

The get big fast (GBF) strategy almost killed Amazon. Its growth depended on how much money it could raise and then spend on productively creating advantage over the countless e-commerce competitors that were inspired to copy them. When the dot-com bubble burst, almost every e-commerce competitor with a low bank balance was wiped out, regardless of the growth strategy it pursued. Amazon survived the bubble because its astute CFO borrowed

$678 million just before the crash. Amazon's survival and eventual dominance was not pure luck, but it was also not proof of the dominance of a more robust entrepreneurial strategy. Many VCs and their limited-partner investors nonetheless embrace GBF, using the success of Amazon—post dot-com crash—as a role model, ignoring the role that the strategy played in almost killing the company.

At present, an "arms race" is playing itself out in the VC community. Larger and larger sums are raised to invest in startups hoping to dominate their markets before they can be outspent. Companies like Uber, Airbnb, Juul, and WeWork all sought to acquire unprecedented levels of funding in the hopes of dominating their markets. VCs like Masayoshi Son, the general manager of the $100 billion venture capital Vision Fund, have offered huge investments at unprecedented valuations to entrepreneurs aspiring to use technology to get big fast in large markets. But the survival of GBF companies depends on their ability to continue to find investors who are willing to bet big regardless of changing economic conditions. As those conditions grow more volatile, it is not clear whether this strategy will remain viable.

A Change in Perspective

The structure of entrepreneurship has not changed much over sixty-five hundred years. Entrepreneurs swarm and must innovate to succeed and stay competitive. And no matter how many constraints are imposed, successful entrepreneurs of all genders, ethnicities, and social classes—even slaves—figure out ways to be self-directed, offer innovative products (even if innovative only to small groups), and entice customers to gladly give them something more valuable in return. The dynamics of swarming and the need to keep innovating to stay competitive creates an entrepreneurial innovation cycle that drives change—and *forces* change—on everyone around. In the next three chapters we'll examine how scaling supply, demand, and simplicity alter how we live, love, work, and relax as well as how and when we feel stressed and become sick. They have also scaled to the extent that they endanger the very existence of our planet.

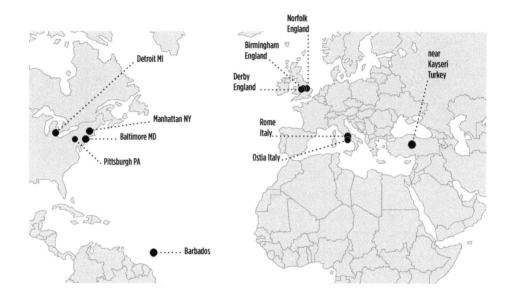

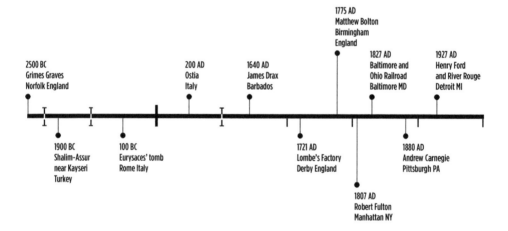

2500 BC
Grimes Graves
Norfolk England

1900 BC
Shalim-Assur
near Kayseri
Turkey

100 BC
Eurysaces' tomb
Rome Italy

200 AD
Ostia
Italy

1640 AD
James Drax
Barbados

1721 AD
Lombe's Factory
Derby England

1775 AD
Matthew Bolton
Birmingham
England

1807 AD
Robert Fulton
Manhattan NY

1827 AD
Baltimore and
Ohio Railroad
Baltimore MD

1880 AD
Andrew Carnegie
Pittsburgh PA

1927 AD
Henry Ford
and River Rouge
Detroit MI

CHAPTER 6

Scaling Supply

Wherever hope for profit calls, fleets will follow.

—Juvenal, *Satires*, 14.267–78, early second century AD

Entrepreneurs with unique and highly desirable skills have always been under pressure to produce more. Since entrepreneurs are self-directed, it's their choice to respond to the pressure or not. Most choose to make or deliver only as much product or service as necessary to get enough value in return to satisfy their own personal needs and desires. Content with making do, they leave it to other entrepreneurs to produce equivalent products to satisfy demand.

Some entrepreneurs, however, seek to dominate the supply of what they produce. Once they establish that society wants more of it, they are motivated to produce as much as they can. These are the entrepreneurs who show up most frequently in the archeological record. The greatest scale results in the most artifacts.

This keen desire to scale up the supply of a product induces these ambitious entrepreneurs to innovate. They seek to sidestep whatever constraints are limiting them from producing more: insufficient material, space, time, energy, or people, or inability to get their product into the hands of eager customers. The ingenious methods they develop are then copied by other entrepreneurs. This process of imitation is an important conduit for the diffusion of innovation. The spread of entrepreneurial innovations from scaling supply has changed the course of history.

Sweetness and Barbary

As can be said of most successful entrepreneurs, James Drax did not invent anything himself. Instead, he imitated others at larger scale and with more control. By 1645, Drax owned the largest, most efficient, and lowest-cost producer of the most desired product on the planet: sugar. As generations since have relied on the techniques he perfected, they are now considered mundane, their origins obscure. In reality, Drax's efforts were an essential step toward the Industrial Revolution. The techniques and strategies he assembled for controlling the finicky process of sugar production and clearing the bottlenecks that had previously constrained the effective use of labor and machines became the basis for many production processes still in use today. Drax-inspired process control and organizational structure have been essential to scaling output ever since.

James Drax (sorry, no picture) dreamed of adventure and wealth, so he wasn't particularly excited at his prospects as the second son of a small-town English vicar. In 1627, at the age of eighteen, he set sail with forty-nine other men to settle the uninhabited island of Barbados. Located in the southern Caribbean, the island had recently been claimed for England by a pirate blown off course during a storm. Barbados is small enough that you can walk end to end or side to side in less than a day. Drax and his fellow settlers were sent there with several months of provisions in the hopes that they could grow tropical cash crops that the Courteen Company, the entrepreneurial trading company that owned the ship, could sell in England.

Drax and the passengers who did not die in route were discharged on a sandy beach bordering the impenetrable forest that dominated the island. They arrived completely unprepared for the burning sun, high winds, torrential rains, relentless insects, and stiflingly hot and humid air. At first, the settlers lived in a cave by the beach.

Most of the settlers failed to eke out a living and became too weak to fight off infections and other ailments and died. But a few succeeded, Drax among them, in producing tobacco. Unfortunately, the soil wasn't very well suited for tobacco. The quality of what they grew was poor compared with what the colonists in Virginia could produce. As a result, the small population of the island barely subsisted for the first ten years.

Drax, an ambitious, practical man of action, was unafraid of change. He was widely admired by his fellow settlers. Those who knew him said he had an "ingenious spirit." He was diligent in producing as much as possible on the acreage he was given, using any production in excess of his fundamental needs to buy land from a growing population of failed settlers. By the mid-1630s, with the help of Dutch merchants and financing from London, Drax and other successful settlers began to switch to cotton. Cotton made for a higher-quality export, and the increased revenues improved the living standards of Drax and a few of the other original settlers.

By 1640, Drax was still unsatisfied with his profits despite having the second-largest holding on the island, with nearly four hundred acres and more than twenty slaves. Cotton prices were falling. He aspired to an even larger-scale operation with an even higher-value product. Boarding a passing boat heading for the Dutch outpost at Recife, on the western tip of Brazil, Drax went on a quest to master the production of sugar.

Sugar is a product, not a crop. It is derived from juices extracted from sugar cane that are then purified and crystalized in a series of refining processes. These steps must be performed in close succession, as the sugars in cane juice sour quickly. Temperatures must be precisely controlled, as does the timing of the entire purification sequence. After the initial refining, the resulting brown sugar cakes must be packed in clay and drained for weeks or months depending on the climate and quality of the cane. The production of even limited quantities of crystalline sugar requires specialized equipment, tight production control, and the mastery of multiple unique skills.

The Dutch, fighting for their independence from Spanish rule, had recently taken control of a large sugar-producing region of Portugal-controlled Brazil (Spain and Portugal shared the same king at the time). The Dutch West Indies Company explicitly coveted trade in sugar and the extra profits they could make from further refining barrels of brown plantation sugar. Since they weren't interested in the planting and initial production, the Dutch merchants in control of Recife were happy to show Drax how to produce sugar that they could then export to Europe.

Although Brazil at the time produced more sugar than the rest of the world combined, its methods were similar to the ones the Crusaders had learned from Muslims five hundred years before. Throughout the Holy Land, sugar had been produced on large landholdings where the owner constructed a mill for crushing the cane with a nearby boiling house and drying shed. The mills were powered by humans, animals, and sometimes water. In Brazil the cane was grown by tenant farmers living on small leased parcels nearby, sometimes supported by a slave or two. Each tenant had a specific day to deliver cane to the mill, which the owner would quickly process into crude brown sugar and molasses. This was the state of the art Drax learned in Recife.

Back in Barbados, Drax spent the next several years improving on every aspect of the process he'd learned, from growing the sugar cane through to the logistics of shipping the final product. Through experimentation and dedication, he developed the world's largest and most efficient sugar production process. He started by placing his mill on the top of a hill, with adjacent boiling houses at a slightly lower elevation so that gravity could move the juice into culverts that ran directly into waiting hot cauldrons to begin the refining process. Cauldrons of successively smaller sizes for subsequent refining also had gravity-fed culverts connecting them in sequence. Drax likely added the other refining steps, though we find no prior evidence of his six-step refining setup in Brazil. Refining using a larger number of copper cauldrons in decreasing sizes resulted in heat being applied more precisely at each step. This gave Drax's sugar a reputation for consistently high quality. Quoting Richard Ligon, who lived briefly on Barbados and in 1657 wrote *The True and Exact History of the Island of Barbadoes*, "And those that use this care, have such credit with the Buyer, as they scarce open the Cask to make a trial; so well they are assured of the goodness of the Sugars they make, as of Collonel James Drax."

Drax's most important decision was to hire a Dutch engineer to oversee the construction of a windmill, a skill in which the Dutch had gained mastery. Since Barbados has no rivers, animals were the only option for providing power, and Drax's unobstructed windmill on the island delivered five times more energy. This meant he could feed his mill five times more cane than anyone ever had before. Rather than rely on the Brazilian practice of engaging tenant farmers, Drax maintained control of the planting and harvesting of his four hundred acres to ensure a continuous supply of sugar cane for his windmill. He also sequenced planting so that the acreage of crops that would ripen each week would equal his mill capacity. Drax scaled the boiling and refining operations to operate twenty-four hours a day, six days a week, perhaps the first round-the-clock operation ever at this scale (figures 6.1 and 6.2).

The scale of Drax's production required hundreds of additional slaves just to plant, weed, and harvest the cane, as well as to work dozens of cauldrons around the clock, in addition to storing and packing the dozens of tons of sugar produced each day. Drax contracted with Dutch slave traders to bring him entire boatloads of people, bringing the slave population on his holdings to over five hundred. He worked them relentlessly in dreadful conditions. The work involved cutting with sharp blades, feeding unstoppable presses that crushed hands as well as cane, and boiling sugar for twelve-hour shifts in stifling boiling houses. Drax needed dozens of new slaves each year to replace those who died or were maimed. (More on the consequences of entrepreneurs scaling the slave trade in a subsequent chapter.)

The scale of Drax's operations was complex enough to require the first-ever three-tiered business management hierarchy. There was an overseer as well as separate supervisors for the fieldworkers, mill, boiling house, drying house, packing house, the shipping warehouse at the port, and the donkey- and horse-cart traffic required to haul many tons of material from place to place. In a separate building near the port, Drax operated a "still-house," which fermented skimmed-off sugar froth into "kill-devil," a powerful rum. Finally, there was a team of clerks under a senior clerk; they negotiated sales with the local agents of English and Dutch sugar merchants, paid taxes, and arranged for the importation of required materials and slaves. The senior clerk and the overseer reported directly to Drax. Supervisors and other individuals with responsibility reported to each of them.

6.1 Slaves cutting sugarcane on the Caribbean island of Antigua, aquatint from *Ten Views of the Island of Antigua* by William Clark, 1832. Sugar plantations throughout the world followed Drax's methods until emancipation.

6.2 Slaves using a windmill to crush cane after harvesting it on the Caribbean island of Antigua, aquatint from *Ten Views of the Island of Antigua* by William Clark, 1832.

Whereas Roman armies had multiple levels of hierarchy of assigned specialists, entrepreneurs prior to Drax's enterprise had chosen to minimize direct costs and maintain direct control by scaling up through renting space to individuals who took responsibility for their own production. Drax knew Brazilian sugar producers used tenant farmers to grow cane, but he boldly took on the challenge of controlling all aspects of both large-scale farming and large-scale production. This required more complex organizational structures and tighter process controls, resulting in his trilevel management hierarchy.

Within five years of Drax's switch from cotton to sugar production, his methods were being copied all around Barbados, transforming the island into a prosperous and bustling enclave that would soon be England's richest overseas colony. When Richard Ligon arrived in 1647, he described his surprise at the level of activity in the port: "[We] found riding at Anchor, 22 good ships, with boats plying to and fro, with Sails and Oars, which carried commodities from place to place: so quick stirring, and numerous, as I have seen it below the bridge at London."

In his previously noted book, Ligon describes in great detail the operations of a sugar plantation owned and operated by Drax's friend and fellow original settler and cave dweller, William Hilliard, who copied Drax's "ingenious" techniques. Ligon's book was widely read and went into a second printing. His section describing the operations of sugar plantations was copied almost verbatim in multiple manuals on how to run plantations that were published over the next two hundred years. By 1660, Drax's system was in wide use throughout the Caribbean; he had set the standard for large-scale production of all kinds. By 1750, swarms of entrepreneurs had made sugar the most important trade commodity in Europe.

Everyone noticed the scale of sugar production—and wealth generation—particularly entrepreneurs in other swarms. In 1721, brothers and silk merchants Thomas and John Lombe designed and constructed the first mechanized factory to produce silk thread (figure 6.3). As textile merchants specifically seeking to implement the best production techniques known, they would surely have been aware of Drax's system of plantation management. Prior to the Lombes, textile production was home-based, whereby a family would invest in a spinning wheel and a local textile merchant entrepreneur would drop off raw materials at dozens of homes for each household to spin (or weave), to return days later to pick up the finished thread (or woven cloth). This "letting-out" system had worked fine for centuries, just as sugar mill owners prior to Drax had contracted out the growing of sugar cane to small landowners.

Responding to rumors of a new silk machine in Italy, John Lombe made a visit there and observed a multiple-spindle silk-spinning machine. He was able to reproduce the machine when he returned

6.3 The Lombe silk factory.

Source: Revolutionary Players, https://www.revolutionaryplayers.org.uk/thomas-lombe-1685-1739/.

to England and proceeded to organize textile production in a radically different way. The Lombes' simple five-story building gave every machine access to the power generated by the attached twenty-three-foot-high waterwheel. Every floor was filled with regularly spaced spinning machines worked mostly by children. The regimented production was simple to supervise, and the raw materials and finished thread were easy to distribute and collect. An important added benefit was that it also made it harder for competitors to see what was happening.

Of course, other entrepreneurs found out about the factory, and the Lombes's concepts were subsequently copied by Wedgwood and then Arkwright, key instigators of the Industrial Revolution. Today, every factory is designed to ensure that production progresses in an uninterrupted flow from start to finish, with dedicated specialists repetitively performing key tasks at an established cadence.

Drax was the spark—albeit a brutal one—for entrepreneurs and managers aspiring to scale production on a much larger scale than ever to meet increased public demand. After Drax, entrepreneurs became confident in massing hundreds of workers along with layers of supervision to maintain quality and keep materials steadily flowing in and out of special-purpose buildings with special-purpose equipment.

Again and Again

Grimes Graves is an eerie place to visit. Local Anglo-Saxon tribes had described it, a field of nearly a hundred acres surrounded by forest and pockmarked with unnatural indentations in the soil, as belonging to their masked god, Grim. Nineteenth-century historians tried to make sense of the terrain by claiming it was the site of an ancient battle between the Saxons and Danes. It was unusual enough that it attracted some of the earliest archeological excavations outside Egypt, Greece, and Rome. Not until the 1970s was it identified conclusively as a neolithic flint factory.

Flint tools were in great demand and widely traded in neolithic times and after. They were produced throughout the world wherever flint was found. Around six thousand years ago, we find people desiring flint badly enough to get it from challenging locations like the sides of cliffs or dozens of feet underground. Around 4000 BC, flint knapping technology matured to the point that an experienced knapper could produce durable cutting surfaces in a variety of shapes and sizes—axes, arrowheads, awls, knives, and more—in minutes. Our customer extraordinaire Ötzi, whom we met in chapter 1, had a collection of skillfully knapped flint blades on him when he was murdered fifty-three hundred years ago. Starting around Ötzi's time, we start to find sites where small groups would take control over an area rich in high-quality flint to establish large-scale mining and flint tool production operations. Grimes Graves is one of those sites, and it remains easily accessible today. You can even go into one of the pits if you're not afraid of descending a ladder forty feet into darkness and then crawling on your belly through rock galleries barely large enough to squeeze through. I don't plan on doing it a second time.

The tribe that controlled Grimes Grave produced many thousands of tools a year. These have been found around England and as far away as present-day Marseilles. They used cattle shoulder blades as shovels and antlers as their digging picks; red deer antlers are much harder than flint. With these tools twenty people could dig a pit thirty feet deep in about three months. They dug through thick layers of chalk to reach veins of flint in lumps slightly bigger and heavier than a rugby ball. These flint modules were very pure, created by natural forces three hundred million years earlier.

They were ideal for large, high-quality axes. To get to the pure layer, the group at Grimes Graves had to dig through two layers of poorer-quality flint, good for smaller tools like arrowheads and knives. As they dug deeper, they constructed wooden ladders and scaffolding to facilitate mining the two flint layers they'd dug through. The pits were made about thirty feet wide at the surface to provide enough light to work forty feet below. When they reached the pure flint, they would follow the veins of modules by digging tiny narrow galleries off the main pit, leaving columns every six to eight feet to avoid cave-ins; the miners at Grimes Graves had a good understanding of its geology.

The tribal leader of this group acted independently of other tribes and likely did not coerce members to do their prescribed jobs. The tribe had members who were highly skilled in mining and knapping. The tools they produced were of the highest quality in both workmanship and material. The quantities they produced far exceeded their personal or gift-giving needs. They met the great demand for the product by digging a new pit as soon as the previous pit's yield of the highest-quality flint had been exhausted. At that point, the depleted pit would serve to store the rubble excavated out of the new one. To achieve all this, the tribe developed repeatable processes facilitated with specialized tools (i.e., red deer antlers, wooden ladders, scaffolding). Thus we see that since neolithic times, entrepreneurs have scaled up their supply by devising an efficient system and then repeating it.

More and More

Close to four thousand years ago, an entrepreneur named Shalim-Assur decided exactly what to do with his latest shipment of textiles. Several copies of his instructions were made on cuneiform tablets. One copy went with the caravan, and another went ahead with a courier. According to the instructions, the shipment contained the following (figure 6.4):

714 bolts of textiles, of various types and specified quality levels
20 talents of tin under seal (approximately 600 kilos), plus extra tin for paying expenses along the way
34 donkeys and their harnesses
1 talent of scrap metal
600 nails
37½ liters of oil of two different grades of quality
22 shekels of carnelian stones (approximately 175 grams)
100 gemstones
60 liters of saffron
14 kilos of cedar fragrance
Other smaller items

6.4 Cuneiform tablet with caravan accounts, Kanesh, ca. 1800 BC.

Source: Metropolitan Museum of Art, https://www.metmuseum.org/art/collection/search/325851.

According to Shalim-Assur's instructions, 181 bolts of textiles would be smuggled into the town of Timelkiya; apparently his long-time caravan manager would know how to go about doing that. The rest of the shipment would be taken to Kanesh, where it was to be cleared properly at the custom house, including the 5 percent tax on textiles and the 3 percent tax on tin. His two sons living in Kanesh, Ennam-Assur and Ali-ahum, would take the remaining goods and sell them in three other prosperous Anatolian towns, where they would fetch higher prices than in Kanesh. Shalim-Assur explicitly instructed that these goods should be sold only for silver, the currency of the day, and not for credit under any circumstances.

Shalim-Assur was just one successful long-distance trader of thousands who conducted similar trading at the time. All major Mesopotamian cities and towns established at the nexus of trading routes were home to traders. He lived in Assur, a town situated about forty miles south of present-day Mosul, Iraq. At the time, Assur was the gateway to central Anatolia, a region hungry for textiles and gems, as well as for tin to combine with its ample supply of copper to make bronze. Anatolia also had large silver deposits, which is what made it such a good destination for Shalim-Assur's goods.

To expand the variety of goods to trade with Anatolia, the city-state of Assur attracted traders from southern Mesopotamia to bring woolen textiles and baskets to exchange for the silver and copper that traders of Assur had so much of. From the east came traders with tin as well as gems, such as the much-coveted deep blue lapis lazuli. Assur's king established and maintained a trading treaty with the local Anatolian ruler that controlled the region around Kanesh. Assur's king also had treaties with other local rulers that enabled safe passage for traders along the seven-hundred-mile caravan route between Assur and Kanesh. With this support, Assur's entrepreneurial citizens established an extensive trading colony at

Kanesh as an effective strategy for dominating the lucrative silver trade in Mesopotamia.

There was a large incentive for the traders of Assur to scale up the export of textiles, tin, and gemstones. They made a profit of about 50 percent on each caravan. These entrepreneurs became the masters of caravanning. They developed techniques and technologies that vastly increased the quantities of silver and textiles that they could transport at one time. Each donkey was outfitted with a leather harness, two saddlebags, and a top-pack, with a total carrying capacity of around 160 pounds. A caravan of twenty to thirty donkeys required only one experienced caravan manager supported by a handful of assistants; they did not appear to need armed escort due to the safe-passage treaties their king had put in place. This gave the traders of Assur a major advantage in the scale of trade they could facilitate with Anatolia.

Because the silver that traders brought back from Kanesh weighed less than the textiles they exported, most of the donkeys and their harnesses were sold off in Anatolia, spurring entrepreneurs living around Assur to breed caravan donkeys while other, smaller-scale entrepreneurs produced the required leather harnesses and bags. Assur had a population of between five and seven thousand at the time, so a large fraction of the households were headed by an independent entrepreneur with a connection to long-distance trading. The entire community focused on developing donkey caravan technologies and techniques to improve their trading advantages and increase trade. As mentioned, the successful entrepreneurs of Assur formed limited-liability partnerships to fund new traders, so there was a steady stream of talent to help the city maintain its advantage. It was a model of a prosperous entrepreneurial community with a specialty.

Assur's commerce was ruled by a city council made up of traders. The council made rules, set taxes, and adjudicated disputes. To attract traders from other parts of Mesopotamia to exchange their goods in the town square of Assur, the city-state wrote letters to other city-states proclaiming that it had the lowest import and export taxes in the region. Although Assur had a king, he is not mentioned much in the thousands of tablets that have been recovered and translated. We see him mentioned only for having negotiated trade treaties with other city-states. Apparently, he left the oversight of commerce and trade to the city council.

These entrepreneurs used the word "profit" and realized they would make larger profits if they specialized. This specialization gave them insights and expertise that enabled them to develop new techniques for delivering more product each time they traded. By being part of a specialist community that they themselves led, they maintained their competitive advantage and could be confident of the support they would receive for being the best at what they did relative to the thousands of other traders who swarmed Mesopotamia. For hundreds of years, they thrived while others aspired to copy their model.

For at least the past four thousand years, entrepreneurs have scaled by forming communities of specialists, each independently developing or implementing methods to improve the overall prosperity of the community. Whether on Barbados, in Renaissance Florence, or in Silicon Valley, when the community is largely governed by the specialists who live there, they operate at a distinct regional advantage.

Millions and Millions

Entrepreneurial scaling of supply was essential for the survival of Rome. At the peak of its power, the empire had a population of at least sixty-five million, one million of whom lived in the city itself. All those people required food, clothing, utilitarian goods like lamps and plates, and housing. While government administrators oversaw the importation of grain to feed Rome and critical infrastructure such as roads and ports, most of the empire's actual production, logistics, and commerce were left to entrepreneurs.

One of the best-preserved Roman towns is Ostia, located at the mouth of the Tiber River, thirty miles downriver from the capital. Once Emperor Claudius built a port complex to make it easier and safer for boats to unload large quantities of supplies headed to Rome, Ostia grew rapidly. Entrepreneurs came to dominate its daily life. They owned the apartment buildings where most people rented living space. They also operated the shops catering to the residents as well as the seamen and traders who did business in the town. They owned the warehouses, food stands where people could grab a quick meal, and servicepeople like cleaners and couriers.

For more than a quarter of a mile, the road in and out of Ostia was lined with *tabernas*, the Roman word for a shop accessible from the street. There were hundreds of them, each supplying something to the bustling town and its visitors. Tabernas were small-scale entrepreneurial operations, but Ostia was also home to large ones. Bread was the staple of the Roman diet. To scale its supply, the largest bakery in town operated ten mule-powered grain mills and five animal-powered dough-mixing machines. The layout enabled materials to move efficiently from one end of the building to the other and back again. Eurysaces, an extremely successful baker in Rome, was so proud of his cylinder-shaped dough-making machines that he had his funeral monument designed to look like one. To this day, Eurysaces's three-story-tall cylindrical monument stands right outside Rome's city wall (figure 6.5), next to one of the major routes in and out of the city. The baker wanted it known for all time just how successful he had been in producing large quantities of bread.

6.5 Eurysace's tomb outside the Porta Maggiore in Rome.

Source: Wikipedia, https://en.wikipedia.org/wiki/Tomb_of_Eurysaces_the_Baker.

Behind Ostia's large theater there is an open, tree-shaded plaza of several acres known as the Piazzale delle Corporazioni. Sixty-one offices open on to it around the periphery. In the sidewalk in front of most of the offices are mosaics depicting the nature of the services offered: imported grain from Tunisia, fish oil from Spain, even exotic wild animals from Africa. Looking at the site today, you get the sense that in Ostia, entrepreneurs could supply anything anyone with money wanted or needed.

Horrea, two-story Roman warehouses, are found throughout Ostia. They were privately owned, specially designed buildings for storing food and products prior to shipment to Rome or elsewhere throughout the empire. The quantities moving into the city alone each year were immense: over four million amphorae of wine, five million sacks of wheat, and tens of thousands of tons of stone and other building materials. Almost all importing was subcontracted to entrepreneurs, who also produced all the wine, oil, and most of the building materials consumed. Only the wheat and, later, some of the olive oil heading to Rome was controlled by the emperor and his administrators.

Rome is often overlooked or ignored as a place of innovation, yet ambitious Roman entrepreneurs were extremely innovative in their ability to scale up their operations—they had to be, to produce and deliver their products in such massive quantities. Dough-making machinery may not make it onto anyone's list of all-time important innovations, but Rome likely could not have been fed without it, and it was definitely an entrepreneurial baker—perhaps even Eurysaces himself—who was responsible.

The scale of the production facilities that produced amphorae and dishes was also immense. Ambitious provincial landowning entrepreneurs constructed large kilns and workshops where individuals could rent time on pottery wheels and buy clay procured and prepared by the owner to produce standardized objects, which the entrepreneur would then distribute and sell. The largest such factories could produce thirty-five thousand plates per batch in their kilns, the largest in the world to that time, with up to ten such kilns on a single site. With a kiln cycle taking up to two weeks, more than ten million plates could have been produced in a year at a single location. Similar large-scale operations have been excavated that produced standardized bricks, oil lamps, and even marble sarcophagi, each produced cadaver-ready except for the details of the face and hands, which would be chiseled by a local stonemason.

Roman innovations were practical and focused on supply. Large boats with capacities up to a thousand tons, highly efficient winches and pulleys, waterpower, concrete, waterproofing, and large-scale dry storage were crucial for the secure and efficient movement of goods from where they were produced to where they were consumed. Rome's incentive system kept entrepreneurs focused on making more and more stuff available. Although Roman nobility considered work and the responsibility of production beneath them, they were happy to assign slaves to manage the work required for the operation of their estates and prestige businesses like fine winemaking. Slaves who demonstrated high levels of competence sometimes convinced their owners to grant them freedom so they could use their specialized skills to run profitable businesses, with the former owners receiving a share of the profits. These businesses could be so profitable that former owners would even fund the startup capital. Freed slaves such as Eurysaces the baker were proud of their entrepreneurial accomplishments and documented their contributions in hundreds of elaborate funerary monuments and memorials, which survive to this day.

Roman emperors issued laws to incentivize entrepreneurs to supply Rome with wheat, even if the emperor's administrators controlled procurement and distribution. Anyone operating boats that delivered wheat were exempted from most taxes. Former slaves who wanted to start wheat delivery businesses could become full citizens. As discussed in chapter 4, Rome created laws that allowed entrepreneurs to pool their resources to tackle large-scale, capital-intensive projects such as the construction of large private and public buildings. Rome could maintain its status as the world's most successful empire only by encouraging its entrepreneurs to scale their supply to meet its needs.

As already described, the next pivotal contributions to the scaling of supply were instigated by Drax, without fanfare other than the resulting luxurious mansions and estates that he and his fellow sugar barons created. These techniques were copied nearly everywhere, resulting in the creation of factories, management hierarchy, and process controls that set the stage for supplying quantities of product never before imagined.

Supra-Human-Scale Supply

The English manufacturer Matthew Boulton had a great deal to be proud of, including the commercialization of Watt's steam engine, but what topped his personal list of accomplishments was his creation of the first commercial mint. Boulton's mint could produce hundreds of millions of finely engraved coins and medals each year. As he wrote, "Of all the mechanical subjects I ever entered upon, there is none in which I ever engaged with so much ardour as that of bringing to perfection the art of coining."

In the prime of his entrepreneurial career, and armed with superior knowledge of metalworking, Boulton designed and built a steam-powered machine that could stamp one coin per second, all while loading and unloading itself. The machine's coins were far more precise and uniform than what hand-stamping could achieve, and its output was dozens of times faster. Overnight, he displaced what had been the standard method for minting since the sixth century BC.

Supplying product on this scale may never have been contemplated by anyone before Boulton. As is true with all such enterprises, it wasn't just an idea but an entire process that was required to make coins so quickly and uniformly. Boulton had to procure and refine the appropriate purity of copper and then roll it to exactly the right thickness for the sheets to be stamped using specially hardened and designed steel dies, which were held firmly in place in his new high-speed presses. Just as challenging was selling the product. As counterfeiters had been around since production of the very first coins, rulers were skeptical of letting independent entrepreneurs produce their currencies. Fortunately for Boulton, the British East Indies Company needed coins for the new territories that were coming under its control in India, so he had large orders soon after demonstrating the uniformly high quality of his output. Soon his coins were being ordered and used in vast quantities in India, Ireland, Russia, America, the new African colony of Sierra Leone, and, eventually, England itself.

Boulton wasn't just a man of his times; he created his times. Born to a successful craftsperson entrepreneur who specialized in "toys"—small steel objects like buttons, watch chains, and buckles—he took over after his father's death in 1759. Intent on vastly expanding the business, the thirty-one-year-old Boulton set out for London to promote his wares and succeeded in getting a friend to present a sword he had fabricated to Prince Edward. Admiring the sword's extraordinarily well-constructed hilt, Edward's older brother, the future King George, got one for himself, which made Boulton famous among the elite for silver- and steel-working. Having succeeded in creating demand for his wares, Boulton returned to Birmingham to expand "toy" production on a grand scale. With a partner experienced in selling luxury goods throughout Europe, Boulton also started a business making finely wrought candlesticks, wine pitchers, and other luxury items using machine-formed but hand-finished silver plate.

Boulton leased thirteen acres to build a factory large enough to support what were by then several businesses. An important feature of the site was a flowing brook that could provide power to drive the lathes and stamping tools. He insisted on the highest-quality machines, tools, and processes. As a result, the factory and its basic machinery cost five times more than expected, causing Boulton and his partner to borrow heavily. Fortunately, the businesses grew quickly enough to pay off those debts, even if the silver plate business never became a big moneymaker.

Within a few years, Boulton's ability to grow became limited by how much power he could harness from the adjacent stream. His attention turned to the new steam engines being used to pump water out of mines. Boulton reached out to James Watt, who had developed an improved engine. Watt was an inventor without much propensity for business. He had partnered with someone to commercialize his invention, but the partner had run into financial difficulties before achieving much success. In 1775, Boulton, with Watt's approval, bought out that partner and moved Watt to Birmingham to focus full-time on improving the performance of his steam engine. Almost immediately, Boulton saw the need for greater precision in boring the cylinder of Watt's patented condenser. He convinced an ironmaster with expertise in boring cannon barrels to make their condensers, more than doubling the performance of Watt's steam engine. It was now decisively more economical to operate than the established Newcomen steam engine.

With this final innovation, Boulton's and Watt's business of supplying steam engines to coal and copper mines took off. As a result, it wasn't until 1780 that Boulton was able to divert Watt's attention to the problems associated with driving his toy-making machines with steam rather than waterpower. The challenge was not in needing more power from their steam engine but how to turn its natural up-down motion into the constantly powered circular motion needed to turn the wheels that provided continuous motion on most machines of the day. Many had tried and failed to do so with Newcomen engines. It took years of experimentation for Watt, Boulton, and many of their experienced and talented team to develop their power converter (referred to as sun and planet gearing coupled to a centrifugal governor driven by a double-acting cylinder—see figure 6.6). With this further innovation, the steam

6.6 The centrifugal governor on a 1788 Boulton and Watt steam engine.

Source: Wikipedia, https://en.wikipedia.org/wiki/Centrifugal_governor#/media
/File:Boulton_and_Watt_centrifugal_governor-MJ.jpg.

engines now became the preferred power source for factories and Caribbean plantation sugar cane grinding.

At this point, Boulton got the idea to apply this approach to coins. The world would need hundreds of millions of low-denomination coins to pay the newly emerging class of factory workers, as well as to enable people from all classes to buy the cheaper yet superior machine-produced goods that Boulton and other entrepreneurs where quickly bringing to market. Boulton was proud of his accomplishments and happy to let dignitaries and others tour his factory—though not the mint, of course. Such visits disseminated news of his innovations and helped inspire and goad other entrepreneurs to automate their factories. Before Boulton, people designed machines that performed a single step of a process better than a person could. Nobody tried automating multiple steps in sequence, not even Hargreaves or Arkwright, with their recently invented cotton-spinning machines. With Boulton's steam-powered presses, entrepreneurs now saw a machine that could perform several steps: load, stamp, unload. Thereafter, steam-powered machines rapidly increased in complexity and specialization, enriching many mechanically inclined entrepreneurs and further increasing economic productivity.

Until Boulton and Watt developed a steam engine suitable for providing power to machines, entrepreneurs had been limited in the scale of their ambitions. As we've seen in this chapter, entrepreneurs used slaves, draught animals, flowing rivers, and wind to provide sufficient power for scaled-up operations, but all these forms of power were limited. Watt and Boulton themselves were well aware of the significance of their innovation. Watt even patented the idea of a steam-powered carriage in 1782. But he was too busy with powering factories to perfect or commercialize his idea, leaving it to others to unleash steam power on transport.

Improving on several failed attempts by other entrepreneurs to attach Newcomen engines to boats, in 1807, the entrepreneur Robert Fulton attached a Boulton and Watt steam engine to a specially designed paddlewheel boat, *The North River Steamboat*—later renamed *The Clermont*—to create the first commercially viable steamboat service. It ran between New York City and Albany. New York granted Fulton a monopoly on all steamboat service within the state to entice him to scale his business as quickly as possible. As we saw in the last chapter, entrepreneurs subsequently swarmed around the potential of steamships, inspiring new attitudes and strategies for competition.

Miles and Miles

Ultimately, once the steam engine made power a virtually unlimited resource, scaling supply tested the ability of any entrepreneur to maintain control of their own ideas, ambitions, and idiosyncratic methods. The expense and complexity of scaling railroads ultimately demonstrated that idiosyncratic methods wasted time and money compared with the leadership of an entirely new class of worker: the professional manager.

Railroads were much more complicated businesses than anything the world had seen at the time. The big businesses of the time were government-controlled, highly decentralized, and loosely coordinated trading companies like the Dutch and British East Indies Companies. Trading companies handled a great deal of money and employed thousands of people, but they operated on a timescale of months and gave their ship captains and port managers complete autonomy. Textile and sugar mills of the time needed tight supervision to make sure that machines and people worked in synchronization, but everyone was nearby and could be called together to decide and coordinate whatever needed to be done. Canal companies required large investments, but they didn't run boats, they just collected tolls. Unlike any of these large-scale endeavors, railroads needed to coordinate many functions simultaneously: putting down the rails, running the trains, soliciting passengers and freight, hiring and training people to operate expensive and potentially dangerous equipment, as well as synchronizing schedules that inevitably changed because of weather, breakdowns, business conditions, and other unknowns.

No entrepreneur proved up to the challenge of scaling anything more complex than a short-haul railroad. They understood the challenges and hired technically and organizationally astute assistants to plan and scale their operations. Simultaneously, railroad entrepreneurs needed to raise large amounts of money, which meant they needed investments from strangers, requiring that they embrace joint-stock limited-liability corporations as their funding structure. Ultimately, investor strangers lost confidence in the railroad entrepreneurs they had backed and handed control to the technically and organizationally proficient professional managers whom the entrepreneurs had hired to help them. The realization by investors that professional managers can scale up entrepreneurial ideas better than entrepreneurs was triggered by the experience of the Baltimore and Ohio Railroad (the B&O). From that point forward, investors felt emboldened to kick entrepreneurs out of the joint-stock companies they had formed and replace them with professional managers if the entrepreneurs stumbled in their ability to scale supply.

In 1820, the Erie Canal, an audacious project envisioned, funded, and implemented by the state of New York, connected the Hudson River with the Great Lakes and gave the state and its primary port, New York City, major cost advantages for handling freight to and from the rapidly expanding West. The canal represented an existential threat to merchants in the other major port towns of the East Coast. To compete, some lobbied their state legislators to subsidize canal projects to connect their towns with major rivers west of the Appalachians.

Shortly after being appointed commissioner of the nascent Chesapeake and Ohio Canal System, the banker and merchant Philip Thomas became disillusioned with its prospects to help the merchants of Baltimore compete with their brethren in New York City. Having heard how coal entrepreneurs in England used mobile, high-pressure steam engines to haul tons of coal many miles from where it was mined to where it could be loaded onto barges, he and another Baltimore merchant and banker, George Brown, traveled to England in 1826 to understand these innovations. Brown's brother William helped them in their investigation. (Years earlier, William had emigrated to Liverpool to make his own fortune as a merchant and banker. George and William's father, Alex, had come to Baltimore from Ireland to found Alex Brown & Sons with his five sons. William started a branch of the business in Liverpool and then went on to form his own banking firm, Brown, Shipley & Co.) William was well placed to help his brother's locomotive research, since he was a prominent investor in the Liverpool & Manchester Railroad, which, four years after this visit, became the world's first passenger railroad in 1830.

Philip Thomas and George Brown were excited by what they learned about the potential of railroads in England. They returned home and convened a meeting in January 1827 with twenty-five other Baltimore entrepreneurs in the hope of convincing them to create a railroad to connect the city with the Ohio River. There was unanimous agreement among the assembled entrepreneurs to proceed. Within a week, a charter had been drafted giving the proposed corporation appropriate rights-of-way, ownership of adjacent land, and tax-free status. The merchants devised a capital structure whereby $3 million would be raised from shares sold to the public and $1 million would come from both the city of Baltimore and the state of Maryland. Excited by the potential of "bringing an empire to our doors," both Maryland and Virginia quickly granted the right for the Baltimore & Ohio Railroad to incorporate. In the following eleven days, twenty-three thousand people signed up for the then-unprecedented $4,178,000 of shares in the new company, paid in installments. The people of Maryland and Virginia had caught railroad fever.

Following the formation of the B&O Railroad, Thomas was appointed president and Brown, treasurer. Neither had any experience in creating or running an operation of anything at this scale.

They estimated a maximum cost of $20,000 per mile based on a naive extrapolation of the known costs of a short-haul, horse-drawn rail line in Massachusetts. The Liverpool and Manchester Railroad was under construction at the time, with a length of thirty-one miles and traversing an undulating landscape through which canals had long been established.

To reach the Ohio River, the B&O aspired to lay at least ten times as much track, all across the densely forested and rocky Appalachian Mountains. For help, Thomas and Brown turned to the U.S. Army, because West Point trained the only engineers in the country. President John Quincy Adams felt that a railroad crossing the Appalachians was a worthy project and ordered the Army to conduct surveys to determine the best route. The B&O wound up hiring several of the Army's construction and survey officers, but they clashed in style and process with the home-grown, self-trained road-builders the railroad hired to build the bridges and lay down track. These disputes resulted in delays, wasted efforts, massive inefficiencies, and cost overruns that Thomas and Brown did not even attempt to control.

In May 1830, with the company already secretly in financial distress, the B&O officially opened for business: a horse-pulled passenger carriage that traveled thirteen miles to a picturesque spot on the Patapsco River. America's first steam-powered locomotive, the Tom Thumb, took over the route a few months later. To fund construction, the B&O sold additional shares to the state and city, bringing government officials to its board. By 1836, the railroad was running eighty miles across Maryland to Harpers Ferry on the Potomac River, but its route still ended far from the Ohio River.

After nine years of constant crisis, Philip Thomas resigned. Needing money, the board of directors recruited Louis McLane, a former politician and secretary of the treasury under Andrew Jackson, as the new president. McLane was a decisive and experienced administrator who had turned around an ailing canal company. Once on board, he surveyed the B&O operations and various rail-laying projects and declared the company "a wreck," both operationally and financially, with little prospect of completing its main line. His reputation and experience gave the state of Maryland and investors in England the confidence to provide funds to complete the line. McLane had little interest in getting involved with the railroad's operations and projects; he sought to professionalize the running of the railroad. In this he was enthusiastically supported by his chief engineer, Benjamin Latrobe II. (Latrobe's father, Benjamin, was the famous architect who had designed the Washington Monument and had laid out Washington, D.C., after it was burned by the British.)

Over the next decade, McLane and Latrobe formalized the railroad's organizational and reporting structures, splitting it along operational and financial lines. (Recall that Drax split his reporting structure the same way.) They created descriptions for the responsibilities of key positions and departments, with the Board of Directors having no operational role whatsoever. They defined the reports that would be issued by each department weekly, monthly, and quarterly. This was the first formal written description of how a large business would operate and maintain control. By 1848, the B&O's organizational description and operating manual had grown into a four-hundred-page document: *Organization of the Service of the Baltimore & Ohio Railroad*. It made no mention of entrepreneurs and required no self-directed individuals of vision and drive. According to McLane and Latrobe, entrepreneurs were no longer necessary or desirable for growing complex businesses and maximizing profits. Technocrats, well-organized and supervised career professionals with very specialized skills, would serve best. They implicitly made the case that entrepreneurs should be fired from their creations once those enterprises began to scale.

When McLane and Latrobe succeeded in making the B&O profitable and made efficient progress in building track through the mountains, other railroad supervisors noticed. Seven years later, the New York and Erie Railroad's superintendent, Daniel McCallum, expanded on their work with his own manual, one that included the world's first organizational chart (figure 6.7). The board of the

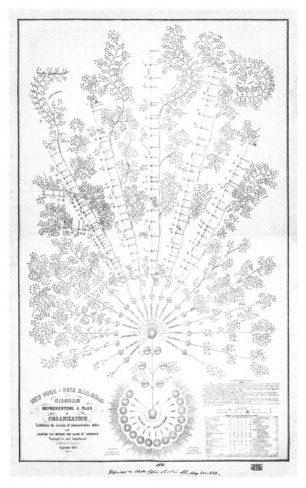

6.7 Daniel McCallum's organizational diagram of the New York and Erie Railroad, 1855.

Pennsylvania Central Railroad, initially created and funded by the state, recruited experienced railroad engineers to lead the organization. The success of the B&O, Erie, and Penn Central railroads led financiers, essential for supplying the capital for railroads to keep scaling, to question the role that founders played in the running of their companies. In the last chapter we saw how J. P. Morgan utilized professional managers to eliminate entrepreneurs from the largest corporations of the day, leading to a precipitous decline in entrepreneurial scale for much of the twentieth century.

Control It All

Many entrepreneurs saw the relevance of the teachings of McLane, Latrobe, and McCallum to their future prosperity and the ability to maintain control of their creations as they increased scale. Andrew Carnegie learned the benefits of good organizational structure by working as the personal assistant of a railroad professional, Thomas Scott. In 1853, Scott was the superintendent on a portion of the expanding Pennsylvania Railroad and would soon become its first vice president. Scott steered opportunities to Carnegie to invest in suppliers of iron, carriages, and services that he knew the railroad would use. While it was not illegal at the time, benefiting from insider knowledge like this was something the railroad executives kept to themselves. Cutting Carnegie in on these deals was a sign of Scott's affection and respect for his abilities.

During the Civil War, Carnegie followed Scott to Washington, D.C., with Scott overseeing the military's railroad operations and Carnegie, its telegraph operations. By the end of the war, Carnegie's various investments had made him wealthy enough to start the Keystone Bridge Company, which built the first steel bridge over the Mississippi. His work with structural steel led him to realize that a newly invented technology, the Bessemer process for converting crude pig iron into steel, could enable the production of vastly more resilient yet affordable rails. Carnegie founded Carnegie Steel and quickly dominated rail production. Having learned, with Scott, the importance of a tightly controlled operation with an organization staffed with skilled department managers, he created the first completely vertically integrated operation of scale, from mining coal and ore through the delivery of finished steel products. Carnegie's vertically integrated, multilevel hierarchy, with daily and sometimes hourly reporting, became the model for ambitious entrepreneurs who sought to maintain control of the companies they had founded.

Henry Ford, always obsessed with control, took large-scale vertical integration to its logical extreme with his River Rouge Complex (figure 6.8). To Carnegie's vision of organizational control and

6.8 Henry Ford's River Rouge Complex, ca. 1927.

Source: https://en.wikipedia.org/wiki/Ford_River_Rouge_Complex.

vertical integration Ford added the assembly line, an idea inspired by large-scale meat processing and proposed by a team of his engineers and production supervisors. The assembly line required a synchronized choreography of people and machines to operate effectively and remains the benchmark for producing physical products at the lowest cost.

Today's largest factories, some with a hundred thousand workers, are owned and controlled by Asian entrepreneurs using the principles of tight organizational controls, high-frequency reporting, vertical integration, and assembly lines pioneered by Drax, Latrobe, Carnegie, and Ford to produce the billions of the affordable smartphones and sneakers we all want.

Terabytes and Terabytes

Today's pioneering entrepreneurs use electronic technologies to achieve unprecedented digital scale, yet they still rely on the strategies discussed in this chapter. They move electrons rather than atoms to create and deliver the information and entertainment we covet. Tech entrepreneurs supply us with terabytes of information, a scale of information beyond any individual's ability to assemble or control. Entrepreneurs are in a race to develop the specialized software applications that enable the creation and consumption of terabytes of information with as little human intervention as possible. The entrepreneurial scaling challenge is now focused on how best to organize the supervision of millions of computers serving tens of millions of users at once, a task of unprecedented complexity.

Entrepreneurs have been dealing with complexity for thousands of years, but only with the help of other entrepreneurs who have created and managed specialized methods to deliver more control and information. With specialization and tools comes increasing complexity. Enabling a single human to maintain control in complex environments is another critical dimension of the story of entrepreneurial innovation, one we'll focus on in chapter 8. First, we need to examine how entrepreneurs have overcome the consequences of being able to produce more product than customers want by innovating ways to get them to want more.

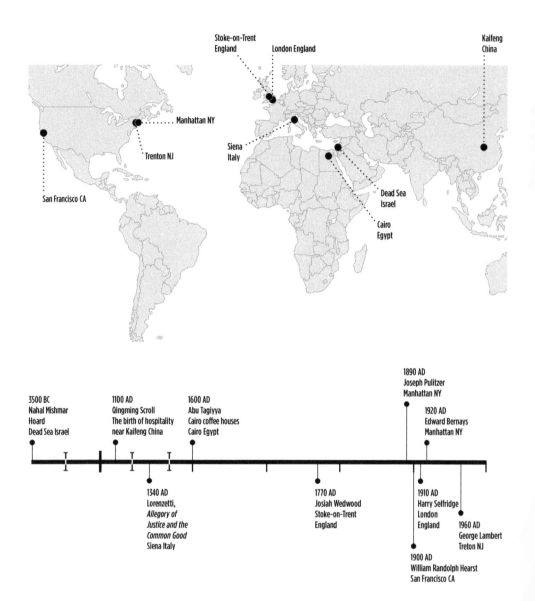

San Francisco CA

Manhattan NY

Trenton NJ

Stoke-on-Trent
England

London England

Siena
Italy

Kaifeng
China

Dead Sea
Israel

Cairo
Egypt

1890 AD
Joseph Pulitzer
Manhattan NY

3500 BC
Nahal Mishmar
Hoard
Dead Sea Israel

1100 AD
Qingming Scroll
The birth of hospitality
near Kaifeng China

1600 AD
Abu Tagiyya
Cairo coffee houses
Cairo Egypt

1920 AD
Edward Bernays
Manhattan NY

1340 AD
Lorenzetti,
*Allegory of
Justice and the
Common Good*
Siena Italy

1770 AD
Josiah Wedwood
Stoke-on-Trent
England

1910 AD
Harry Selfridge
London
England

1960 AD
George Lambert
Treton NJ

1900 AD
William Randolph Hearst
San Francisco CA

CHAPTER 7

Scaling Demand

Supply must actively seek to create its corresponding demand.

—Edward Bernays, *Propaganda*, 1928

There is only so much a human being actually needs for survival: food, water, shelter, and a few articles of clothing for protection from the elements. On the other hand, there is no end of things we might *want*—given the proper nudge. Scaling supply works only so long as there is sufficient demand to meet it. This has always provided a strong incentive for entrepreneurs to figure out how to generate more demand.

The problem you're trying to solve is that people have everything they think they need. The solution? Convince them they want something they didn't *know* they wanted. Or, stranger still, convince them they have a problem they didn't even know they had. That's what George Lambert did when he plucked the obscure term "halitosis" from a nineteenth-century medical textbook to sell more Listerine. The product was originally formulated as a surgical antiseptic, then marketed as a floor cleaner and even a gonorrhea cure before Lambert hit on the idea of mouthwash. While people have tried to remedy bad breath since ancient Egypt, it was Lambert's idea to frame it as a medical condition in and of itself. The angle worked: revenue went from $115,000 to $8 million in under seven years. Scaling demand may be an artificial endeavor, but it is often a profitable one.

Scaling demand proved crucial to the Industrial Revolution. We remember this period as one of colossal business growth, but the fact is, things were off to a rocky start for the entrepreneurs of the day. Beginning in the mid-eighteenth century, a handful of innovative entrepreneurs used new technologies to cheaply mass-produce staples such as belt buckles, textiles, and ceramics. As their methods were copied, competing "manufacturers," as they were then called, raced to capture a piece of the market by lowering prices. Even at lower prices, however, customers were simply unaccustomed to buying more of anything than they strictly needed. Soon, huge quantities of unsold stock piled up, and many of the era's entrepreneurs went bankrupt. Producing more than could be sold became a chronic problem—until an ambitious young potter turned his attention from scaling supply to scaling demand.

The First Brand

Josiah Wedgwood, the sickly twelfth child of his family, was the descendant of a long line of English potters. The Wedgwoods had been pioneers of the trade in Staffordshire, where there was an abundance of good clay. When Josiah was nine, his father died suddenly. The boy, despite a pronounced limp from childhood illnesses, went to work hauling coal to the kilns for his eldest brother, Thomas, who had inherited the family pottery and homestead. At fourteen, Josiah became Thomas's unpaid apprentice, diligently

7.1 Portrait of Josiah Wedgwood at age 50 by George Stubbs.

Source: Wikipedia, https://en.wikipedia.org/wiki/Josiah_Wedgwood.

mastering the family trade and earning a reputation for skill, commitment, and creativity. He went on to work for other potters in the area, steadily acquiring more responsibility and eventually supervising production.

An astute observer, Wedgwood (figure 7.1) took note of how quickly successful innovations were copied, no matter how minor. If one potter's charming cabbage-shaped teapot sold well, dozens of other potters would offer cabbage-shaped pots the following year. The year after that, everyone's warehouse shelves would sag under mountains of unsold clay cabbages. Early lessons like these would inform Wedgwood's strategy as a master innovator himself.

Wedgwood's first break came at twenty-nine, when he managed to convince his successful first cousins, Thomas (another of many

Thomases in the Wedgwood clan) and Long John, to rent him an old, out-of-use pottery. He still had to pay a substantial rent, but young Josiah was confident in the sales potential of the eye-catching tortoiseshell and green glazes he had formulated in his free time. Indeed, he was immediately successful.

Wedgwood's second break came when he convinced another, more distant, cousin of some means to allow him to finally marry the man's daughter. Through this union, Josiah gained a caring wife, Sarah (figure 7.2), who turned out to be an able collaborator in the business, as well as a financial patron who could lend him capital to invest in the latest machinery. Wedgwood used these new machines to more reliably scale production of his popular, cutting-edge creations.

With all of Wedgwood's success, however, the competition remained fierce. There were many potters in England at the time,

7.2 Sarah Wedgwood.

Source: Grace's Guide to British Industrial History, https://www.gracesguide.co.uk /Sarah_Wedgwood.

and several were skilled enough to quickly copy Wedgwood's designs and then offer them at lower prices. The young entrepreneur regularly worked late into the night to invent new glazes and designs, hoping to stay ahead of the market.

Wedgwood's third break came when his work caught the eye of an attendant to Queen Charlotte. The wife of King George III wanted a new tea service. Wedgwood took this opportunity to showcase his new take on creamware popular at the time, a style of pottery featuring a glossy lead glaze. Creamware was usually cream-colored, hence the name, but Wedgwood's new glaze used cobalt to achieve an eye-catching bluish white that was brighter and lighter. The queen had never seen anything like it—she had her new tea service.

For your average potter in those days, the next step would have been to leverage the queen's favor to sell to other members of the nobility. Tradesmen had long spurred elite demand this way. Josiah did this, but he saw a larger opportunity. Thanks to his new machinery and the more efficient production methods he'd developed to match, he could now produce pottery of a quality comparable to that of the queen's own service at a cost that the growing middle class could afford. His real challenge would be to convince these potential customers that they actually needed a tea service worthy of Her Majesty.

Wedgwood implemented a three-pronged strategy to create this new demand. First, he asked the queen if he could name the new style "The Queens ware." She agreed, and this became the first tea service "brand," a royal one at that. Second, Wedgwood and his business partner, Thomas Bentley, opened a shop located in a fashionable area of London just south of Covent Garden. Wedgwood intentionally designed the store to make it appealing to women, both as a place to shop and a social venue (figure 7.3). Third, he arranged for the shop to hold exhibitions of his finest

7.3 Wedgewood's store in St. James's Square, London, 1809.

services, including the queen's own service and one he later made for Catherine the Great. His salespeople used these displays to educate consumers, the vast majority of whom would never be invited to either palace for tea. After all, Wedgwood reasoned, how could people even know they wanted something if they'd never even seen it in person?

Sales exploded. In fact, demand outstripped Wedgwood's newly scaled supply. He could not expand production quickly enough. He even resorted to buying copycat tea services that not long before had been driving him to distraction and selling them as his own. Prosperous people from all over England, and then the rest of Europe, sought to obtain elegant, high-quality Wedgwood tea services—and vases—as a marker of sophistication.

Wedgwood scaled demand like no entrepreneur ever before. He convinced consumers that they wanted something they didn't actually need by educating them about his product. It's important to realize how innovative this approach was. The advertising and signage of the time merely announced the *availability* of a product to those who already wanted it. Wedgwood made the market itself bigger. He also held on to the lion's share of this increased demand through what we would now call "branding." He named his products after famous customers, such as Lord Buckingham or King Henry IV of France. He fostered attention for his business by paying for puff pieces about his products in the press. Over time, it was Wedgwood that people wanted to own, not merely plates, cups, or vases.

Wedgwood's merchandising and branding techniques are studied and copied to this day as prime examples of demand generation in action. Steve Jobs adopted a nearly identical retail strategy— for many of the same strategic reasons—with the creation of the hugely successful Apple Store concept. Today, all major retailers have come to understand how important it is to educate consumers about what they might want instead of waiting for them to realize their preferences on their own.

As Wedgwood's tactics spread beyond ceramics, demand scaled for all kinds of products, finally coming into parity with the new, mechanically amplified supply. Thanks in no small part to Wedgwood, the Industrial Revolution was now well under way. Along the way, "shopping" came into common usage to describe the pleasant pastime of finding things to buy.

Josiah Wedgwood was perhaps the most ambitious entrepreneur of this very ambitious period of innovation and expansion. He pioneered the idea of what we now call a brand; transformed his own name into a universally recognized symbol of quality, taste, and distinction; and gave birth to the modern shopping experience. He passed away at the age of sixty-four as one of the wealthiest people in England.

Objects of Astonishment, Catalysts of Desire

Some of the first entrepreneurs accumulated their wealth by securing what I call "objects of astonishment" from distant lands too remote to be conquered. Those in power could display these objects to proclaim their elevated status. Once a royal owned a certain exotic good, these entrepreneurs were then able to sell similar objects of near-astonishment to the rest of the elites. (These were the first influencer campaigns.)

In 1960, Israel was a new country intent on validating its place in the world. Leaders made it a national priority to find more ancient Judean texts like the recently discovered Dead Sea Scrolls. The Israeli Army worked with archeologists to conduct a systematic search of all the caves around the area. On a hot day in March 1961, archeologist Pessah Bar-Adon descended over a hundred feet of rope to a cliffside cave entrance perched 650 feet above the dry wadi below. A student volunteer and a soldier had discovered metal objects in a pit in the rear of the cave hidden behind a stone propped on its side. Over the next two days, Bar-Adon's team recovered a hoard of more than 430 objects dating from before 3500 BC.

What is now known as the Nahal Mishmar Treasure contained standards, maces, vases, and ivories in its hoard, as well as some metal objects we cannot classify because we've never seen anything like them before (or since). Some are of spectacular workmanship.

Standards and maces denoted power at that time and would have been coveted by people wishing to be respected and feared. These in particular were among the most beautiful and sophisticated that archeologists have ever found from that period (figure 7.4). Analysis indicates that they were made in several locations by multiple artisans who had developed their skills independently of one another. For one thing, a surprising variety of metallurgic processes and copper mixtures were used.

7.4 Examples of objects of astonishment, before 3500 BC, found in Nahal Mishmar, Israel.

Source: Portfolio (in Hebrew), https://www.prtfl.co.il/archives/111898.

These findings indicate that some of the artisans had dedicated themselves to innovating metallurgical techniques at a time when copper production was secretive, specialized, and practiced in only a few places. Some items were made using sophisticated lost-wax casting methods. To produce these pieces, a wax model was packed tightly in sand with a hole at the top and bottom. When molten copper was poured in at the top, the wax melted and dripped out the bottom, leaving a perfect copper duplicate.

Again, analysis hints at no overarching supervision. These innovative artisans worked independently, each experimenting to achieve technological feats that none of their competitors could. In short, we have every reason to believe these were entrepreneurs. Since no copper workshops have been identified near the site, it's reasonable to surmise that at least some of the objects came from Shiqmim (described in chapter 2), located sixty miles to the southwest. Trading called for a skill set very different from metallurgy, so it's unlikely these copper entrepreneurs spent time traveling to entice wealthy people to give them something valuable in return for their astonishing objects. It's also unlikely that the owner of the hoard sent an agent to acquire these items. Independent traders—other entrepreneurs—most likely obtained these objects and then sold them to elite customers along a given route.

We do not know who owned this hoard, but the quantity and quality of the assemblage indicates they were Levantine elite. Whether their wealth came from political, mercantile, or cultish sources we do not know. But they clearly felt the need to invest vast resources in procuring objects of astonishment. Even today, some of these objects take your breath away. Whoever owned them would have commanded serious respect and envy. Just as clearly, learning of the existence of these exquisite objects would have made other elites aspire to own similar marvelous copper creations. Experienced traders knew what these elites wanted and what they were willing to pay to get it. Those early trader-entrepreneurs discovered that demand is infectious—we want what other people with social status have.

Most such objects would have been melted down over the centuries for the copper, but standards and maces dating to the same period have been discovered in other locations in the Near East and eastern Mediterranean. Elites who wanted to display their power and status in the fourth millennium BC needed to either lure an experienced copper artisan to join their extended household or invite an entrepreneur who traded in such objects to visit.

Scaling demand through objects of astonishment became trickier with urbanization. Cities were coalescing in Mesopotamia at this time and soon thereafter in the Indus Valley. In cities of up to fifty thousand, traders knew where the elites lived and what they wanted and were savvy enough to know that only rulers could own true objects of astonishment. Other members of the elite would have to make due with objects of similar design but inferior workmanship and materials. In fact, we know from Mesopotamian cuneiform tablets that in the third millennium BC, traders were expected to offer their finest wares to the ruler of a city-state before anyone else. As we've seen, successful Mesopotamian traders accumulated substantial wealth, but they were still not members of the highest social strata, which comprised the ruler's family and high-ranking temple priests and administrators. Traders living in cities understood that they could not sell the finest objects of astonishment to lesser elite, or keep them for themselves, if they wanted to retain permission to trade.

Because objects of astonishment elevate status, they spur demand. But status doesn't last; it has to be periodically reaffirmed with rituals, marriages, and alliances, each of which requires new objects of astonishment to be given as gifts or displayed as symbols of power. Therefore, demand for these objects grows not just with the number of those who can afford them but also with the number of people they need to impress. This type of demand grows exponentially. Even in ancient times, passion for a product could "go viral."

Of course, rather than depend on entrepreneurs, some elites—particularly rulers of large territories—directly produced the objects of astonishment that they needed to maintain their status and power. The pharaohs of Egypt established extensive workshops and entire villages filled with artisans who were paid to produce objects for tombs as well as gifts for other nobles. Ancient Chinese rulers and heads of powerful clans, required to produce large quantities of funerary bronzes for themselves and their extended families and loyal lords, did the same.

The objects produced in the workshops owned and controlled by ruling elites also display astonishing levels of workmanship and craft; entrepreneurial artisans did not have a monopoly on skill. These elites often put into place "sumptuary laws" intended to prevent anyone under their rule from owning objects that exceeded certain prescribed quality and workmanship standards. In effect, they cornered quality for themselves. Nonetheless, these same elites continued to acquire objects of astonishment from traders offering items their in-house artisans could not yet produce. This ensured that no upstart could equal their status or power.

Using objects of astonishment to induce envy and spur demand among people of wealth is independent of time or geography. Even in early medieval Europe, when feudal and ecclesiastical lords ruled domains that were nearly self-sufficient, objects of astonishment were still coveted. They were the rare objects still being traded during this time of economic stagnation.

The range of astonishing products to display for those who aspired to greater status and power was vast, including weapons, textiles, jewelry, ornamental service objects like plates or containers, ritual vessels, and sculptures of animals or mythical scenes. In fact, objects of astonishment haven't always been objects. Entrepreneurs have long earned profits from trade in astonishing living beings, whether exotic, finely bred, and highly trained animals to slaves of exceptional strength or beauty.

Objects of astonishment from all points in human history can be found in museums and the private collections of the present-day elite. Not all were the product of artisanal entrepreneurship or bartered from entrepreneurial merchants, but a great many are entrepreneurial in origin. Entrepreneurial painters made portraits into objects of astonishment starting in the mid-fifteenth century, and what did they place alongside the subjects they painted? More objects of astonishment.

The Lure of Hospitality

Another advance in scaling demand is exemplified in the Qingming shanghe tu scroll, described in the introduction. The number and variety of the depicted wine shops and restaurants make the scroll truly notable in the history of entrepreneurship. Hospitality—offering food, alcohol, comfort, and entertainment in a relaxed setting—proved a breakthrough idea for getting people of all kinds to spend money on something they did not need. Chinese entrepreneurs understood the demand-scaling power of positive emotions.

Hospitality as practiced in Song-era China and depicted in the Qingming scroll targeted the full range of classes: from commoners to "scholars" (people studying for civil service exams or tutoring others to pass the exams) and even prosperous landowners and merchants. Some restaurants, particularly the less formal ones, appeal to a range of classes, while the fancier ones, located in extravagant, multistoried structures, are clearly intended only for wealthier clientele. That said, all classes enjoy their free time spending what money they have to spare on food, drink, and entertainment. From the number of stacked empty plates, some of these customers have been eating for longer and spending more money than necessary to satisfy any degree of hunger (figure 7.5).

Leaving your home to leisurely indulge in pleasurable pursuits was not possible, let alone socially acceptable, until around this time. China in the Song dynasty and the Tang dynasty preceding it benefited from new agricultural techniques that made more terrain

7.5 Detail from the Qingming scroll. Note the stack of plates by the customer in the restaurant at the base of the bridge on the right.

Source: From Valerie Hansen, "The Beijing Qingming Scroll and Its Significance for the Study of Chinese History," *Journal of Sung-Yuan Studies* (1996): sec. 14.

suitable for growing rice, lowering the cost of food and adding to the wealth of many small landowners. Having more food to sell spurred Chinese entrepreneurs to innovate ways to get customers to buy more food and drink.

Commoners, more secure in their ability to keep their families fed and clothed, earned extra money by weaving cloth and making other artisanal products that they could sell. All these commoners with money to spend led Chinese entrepreneurs to create places designed to encourage the enjoyment of food and wine. Emboldened and enriched by more customers eating and drinking more food and wine, competitors vied to build the most lavish and appealing hospitality establishments. Eventually, even elites could entertain their guests better by going to a restaurant than staying in their own prosperous homes.

In Roman times, offering hospitality to nonelite strangers was highly constrained. Many lower-class Romans had limited access to a kitchen and bought most of their meals at local food stalls, stigmatizing the practice for the elite. Saying you had seen a member of the Senate or imperial family eating out was a slur on their reputation. (Claudius, however, admitted to frequenting *popinae*—wine bars—in his youth.) Some stalls had tables and benches where you could sit and eat with strangers, but you paid extra for the right to sit down, and when you were finished you were expected to leave, unless you paid to move to the back room to gamble or fraternize with the women upstairs.

These Roman eating establishments were not built to serve people in a relaxing atmosphere; only the elite did that in the privacy of their own homes. Thus, hospitality did not catch on in Europe until long after it did in China. An analogous painting to the Qingming scroll can be found in Siena, in the meeting hall of the Nine, the city's rulers. Painted by Ambrogio Lorenzetti between 1337 and 1340, the *Allegory of Justice and the Common Good* (figure 7.6) depicts a scene of life in the city: donkeys laden with sacks of goods, artisans and merchants working in stalls and shops—but no restaurants or people buying what they don't need. Siena had inns, but we don't see them depicted, because they were exclusively for out-of-town visitors. Innkeepers of the time provided traveling merchants and court petitioners with

7.6 Ambrogio Lorenzetti, detail from *Effects of Good Government on the City Life*, between 1337 and 1340.

Source: Art in Tuscany, http://www.travelingintuscany.com/art/ambrogiolorenzetti /goodandbadgovernment.htm.

food, drink, and a place to sleep, but they did not tempt locals from their homes.

In a castle in northern Italy, a fresco dating from around 1500 depicts a tavern where a few locals appear to be passing the time (figure 7.7). While a few men play backgammon and cards on one end of a long table, the other end features a prostitute attacking a man with a knife. Another man stands ready to strike with a metal tankard—we can't tell if he's aiming at the prostitute or her target. Situated within the castle so guards and servants would pass it frequently, the fresco may have been intended as a warning about the trouble to be found at taverns.

In the late sixteenth century, Islamic merchants, perhaps inspired by traders who had visited China, began offering hospitality to spur demand for their wares. Coffee became popular in the Islamic world in the early 1500s, when Sufis started using it to stay awake

7.7 Anonymous, Guardroom, Castello Challant, Issogne, ca. 1500.

Source: Web Gallery of Art, https://www.wga.hu/frames-e.html?/html/m/master
/xunk_it/xunk_it3a/index.html.

during meditation and prayers. Since the beans were harvested in nearby Yemen and Ethiopia, they were an affordable indulgence in Cairo. Coffee merchants, to scale demand for the growing supply, opened comfortable and convenient coffeehouses where men could meet and relax. The wealthiest entrepreneur in Cairo around 1600, Isma'il Abu Taqiyya, imported coffee and owned numerous popular coffeehouses.

Europeans traveling to Cairo in the early seventeenth century adopted the new practice of drinking coffee. Some of the more entrepreneurially minded returned to England and Europe with a supply of beans to open their own coffeehouses. Seeing the wisdom in hospitality, they tried to make their establishments as welcoming as those they had enjoyed in Cairo. European coffeehouses in the 1700s became places to buy shares in joint-stock companies or discuss the new ideas that were fermenting into what became the

Enlightenment. It was only after European entrepreneurs learned how to be hospitable that commoners started to spend money and consume products they wouldn't have otherwise.

Shopping and Hospitality Combined

Josiah Wedgwood gave birth to much of the modern shopping experience, but it was Harry Selfridge (figure 7.8) who codified the hospitality that completed this evolution. At a time when new "department stores" competed globally over metrics like largest space or broadest offering of products, Selfridge, who opened his London store in 1909, focused on the customer experience.

7.8 Harry Selfridge, ca. 1910.

Source: Wikipedia, https://en.wikipedia.org/wiki/Harry_Gordon_Selfridge.

Selfridge knew from twenty-five years spent working at Marshall Field in Chicago that the decision to buy something discretionary, like a silk scarf, was entirely subjective and emotional. If the urge to buy could be instilled somehow, the potential for demand would be vast. Convinced of the potential effectiveness of this unique approach, he moved to London to open a store that would prove his point.

Commissioning demographic reports, Selfridge learned that new jobs had drawn large numbers of people to London in the prior half-century. These reports revealed where they lived, what they read, and where they spent their limited free time. To scale demand for his vast supply of products, he would have to seduce these new shoppers, whet appetites they didn't yet know they had.

This process of seduction started at the ground floor. Selfridge bought the largest glass plates available for twelve of the windows facing passersby. Then, rather than simply displaying products as his competitors did, he hired a dedicated display manager to design scenes for each window. These elegant still-life (although sometimes Selfridge used live models) were vignettes about how a product could improve a customer's life. They were intended to create positive emotions that would then become associated with the products within each scene.

As shoppers entered the store, Selfridge put his finest products directly within their reach (figure 7.9). They were able to handle items, to luxuriate in the texture of silk or the scent of a perfume for the very first time. These were things they could not have known they'd wanted until that moment of newly discovered pleasure. To complement this tactile shopping experience, Selfridge's salespeople were extensively trained to assist and inform customers rather than explicitly sell to them. Selfridge understood that the desire had to come first.

7.9 The perfume department at Selfridge's Department Store, ca. 1910.

Source: Alamy, https://www.alamy.com/perfume-department-selfridges-oxford-street
-london-date-circa-1910-image183031079.html.

Hospitality is about people catering to the desires of others for the purpose of associating a product or service with strong positive feelings. Although corporations that focus on hospitality have scaled through consolidation—think Hilton and Marriot in hotels—entrepreneurs remain the innovating force in hospitality as a category. Because the experience of hospitality is ultimately so personal, so subjective, it is entrepreneurs who innovate new hospitality experiences—from dining to accommodations to retail—and create complementary sites and services like Yelp to review experiences and Instagram to share them.

Today, some of the aspects of hospitality that Wedgwood and Selfridge introduced to retail are slipping away as new entrepreneurs zealously automate the shopping experience. Automation is a classic entrepreneurial technique that we'll discuss in the next chapter. In the case of retail, however, this approach has disconnected hospitality from the shopping experience, setting up opportunities for a generation of entrepreneurs to come. Even today, formerly online-only brands like Warby Parker and Glossier have come around to the value of the real-life shopping experience pioneered by these entrepreneurs.

Objects of Mass Desire

Before the time of Joseph Pulitzer and William Randolph Hearst, newspapers were for the literate and educated. Spurred by inexpensive newsprint and printing technology that brought costs down significantly, Pulitzer and Hearst sought to expand demand far beyond the traditional paper-reading demographic.

First, they made newspapers more accessible by having articles illustrated for those who possessed only basic literacy. Second, they created special-interest sections to lure readers to buy an entire newspaper even if only to read one particularly compelling section. Affordable yet thick Sunday editions bursting with coverage of politics, art, entertainment, and comic strips provided hours of leisure-time entertainment for an entire family. As a consequence of these innovations, daily readership boomed, reaching over half a million for some publications.

Around this time an entirely new business category—public relations—sprang up to help other businesses generate more demand for their products by changing public perception of those products through mass media like newspapers. Edward Bernays was a pioneer in PR—in fact, he coined the term. Bernays spent a formative time working with the U.S. Committee on Public Information crafting propaganda campaigns during World War I. "What could be done for a nation at war," he realized, "could be done for organizations and people in a nation of peace." Thus, war propaganda evolved into modern public relations. After the war Bernays founded his own firm, one that became legendary for spurring consumer desires to scale demand.

Early on, Bernays was hired by the Beechnut Packing Company to increase demand for its bacon. Polling physicians about healthy eating habits, Bernays latched on to the fact that many reported a belief in the salutary benefits of eating a hearty breakfast. He framed the results of his informal inquiry as a full-fledged medical recommendation for bacon and eggs every morning, which Beechnut went on to advertise. Business boomed, and bacon has been a staple of American breakfast ever since.

American Tobacco approached Bernays to help them stimulate demand among women for cigarettes. Smoking was considered masculine at the time. If they could get women to light up, too, demand would double. Bernays created a campaign called "Reach for a Lucky Instead of a Sweet," fostering the impression that smoking aided weight loss. The campaign featured images of slender women smoking cigarettes (figure 7.10). Much to the detriment of

7.10 Advertisement for Lucky cigarettes, 1930.

Source: Getty Images.

public health for a century to come, demand for cigarettes surged among women.

Bernays wasn't done with tobacco yet. A prominent psychoanalyst advised him that some women were starting to view cigarettes as symbols of freedom. Consequently, he arranged for ten prominent debutantes to simultaneously light cigarettes in front of the press area for the Easter Day Parade up New York's Fifth Avenue. When asked by the journalists what they were doing, the debutantes said they were lighting their "torches of freedom" to protest women's inequality. The stunt created a firestorm of debate, immediately legitimizing women's smoking as an act of political defiance. For years Bernays boasted about how he'd gotten "women across the country to light up in public." Late in life, however, he publicly regretted the widespread health problems that his efforts had magnified.

Bernays wasn't bashful about calling his entrepreneurial pursuits propaganda or acknowledging their manipulative nature. His techniques to associate products with good looks, euphoric feelings, and sexual desire have been studied, replicated, and amplified ever since. Most advertising now tells a story of how a particular product will make our lives more pleasurable and successful. This ceaseless desire for "more and better" is Bernays's true legacy.

From Demand to Addiction

The latest surge of demand creation has been spurred by a corresponding abundance of computing power. Today's entrepreneurs work feverishly to make their digital products more desirable, to make them—using behavioral psychology and sophisticated design derived from the gambling industry—as addictive as possible.

Game entrepreneurs develop algorithms to make their creations more compelling; for example, determining when to give players a "reward"—making it to a new level, earning a virtual prize—at the moment most would have otherwise stopped playing the game. These algorithms are trade secrets, not openly discussed, but the business need for them is undeniable. Manipulating gamers to invest enough time to master a game ensures that they will buy the next version or stay subscribed to an online service. In fact, a staggering majority of game profits comes from new versions of existing games. In a little over a decade, gaming became a larger form of entertainment than movies. Some video games are popular enough to draw tens of thousands of fans to live competitions. A stadium full of people studying every subtle movement of a group of seated professional gamers is a profound indication of the power these games now have.

Similar technologies have been deployed to increase "engagement" (a euphemism for level of addiction) with social media. Digital technology has also been deployed by entrepreneurs to display the products we are most likely to be interested in buying when we browse online. Advertising technology companies track every aspect of our lives, online and off—Google even tracks your physical location with your phone to see whether a digital ad spurred a visit to a retail location. Algorithms assign a probability of getting a person with a specific viewing history to buy a product depending on when, where, and how it is advertised. Based on these probabilities, marketers instantaneously bid for the opportunity to place their digital ads where and when they are most likely to get a customer to click on it.

The jury is still out on whether ad tracking and placement substantially increases demand or just enables one brand to capture a customer who was already intent on buying a new pair of shoes. After all, the ads that follow you around the internet were usually triggered by clicks that showed an interest in shoes in the first place.

One way or the other, however, it's clear that new technologies will continue to enable entrepreneurs—using techniques pioneered by Pulitzer, Hearst, Bernays, and other innovators—to make us want even more stuff that we don't really need.

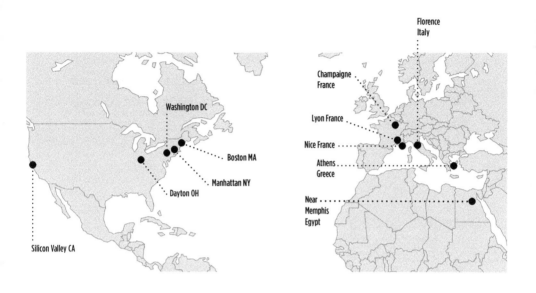

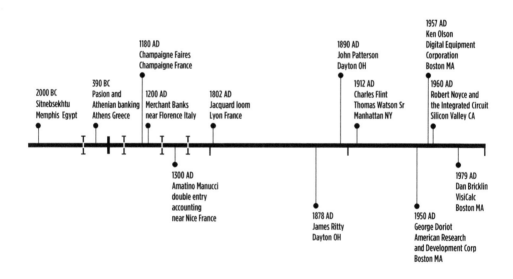

1957 AD
Ken Olson
Digital Equipment
Corporation
Boston MA

1890 AD
John Patterson
Dayton OH

1180 AD
Champaigne Faires
Champaigne France

390 BC
Pasion and
Athenian banking
Athens Greece

2000 BC
Sitnebsekhtu
Memphis Egypt

1200 AD
Merchant Banks
near Florence Italy

1802 AD
Jacquard loom
Lyon France

1912 AD
Charles Flint
Thomas Watson Sr
Manhattan NY

1960 AD
Robert Noyce and
the Integrated Circuit
Silicon Valley CA

1300 AD
Amatino Manucci
double entry
accounting
near Nice France

1979 AD
Dan Bricklin
VisiCalc
Boston MA

1878 AD
James Ritty
Dayton OH

1950 AD
George Doriot
American Research
and Development Corp
Boston MA

CHAPTER 8

Scaling Simplicity

Success is probably the worst problem for an entrepreneur.

—Ken Olsen, founder, Digital Equipment Corporation

E ntrepreneurs love to scale. It feels satisfying to produce more of a product or deliver a service to ever-larger numbers of people. It doesn't hurt that profit and wealth scale as well, often coupled with prestige and power. Competitive entrepreneurs aspire to have or achieve more than anyone else, and they feel dissatisfied when they aren't getting or achieving as much as they think they should. This hunger for scale can drive an entrepreneur to new heights of innovation. We've seen how ambitious entrepreneurs have scaled up supply to deliver massive quantities of products and services. We've also seen them innovate ways to expand their markets by getting people to buy what they do not need. Ambitious entrepreneurs are always searching for ways to scale further using whatever technologies are available.

There is a tension here, however. Ambition must be weighed against the pressures that accumulate from overseeing larger enterprises.

Throughout time we find entrepreneurs starting to wonder: is scale worth the trouble? Why not be satisfied with the success I already have? This is why making scale easier to manage has been an opportunity for other entrepreneurs throughout history. B2B is very BC. There have always been products and services intended to reduce the time and effort required to manage more people and complex processes, or to perform difficult tasks beyond the capabilities of any individual. Making it easier for other entrepreneurs to scale supply and demand can be thought of as scaling simplicity. This is the third major driver of entrepreneurial innovation.

Anticipating the Next Move

An entrepreneur's natural inclination is often to try to make things easier, first by producing more with fewer materials and less labor. For this they developed tools. The first such tools were relatively simple—specialty cutting tools and jigs, for example—and specifics of the origins of the earliest tools and fixtures are lost to time. Over time, entrepreneurs developed machines to help their work or make them more productive. Simple machines and tools that provide mechanical advantages have been produced long before they were documented. Carts and irrigation levers are examples of machines that were in use by entrepreneurs before writing. Many machines have been developed since then by entrepreneurs wishing to scale and improve their profits.

As a machine gets more complex to operate and supervise, it adds complexity to processes. Complex machines require operators with special skills and training and repairs by specialists. They require added steps and new processes, such as having to add specialized lubricants to keep moving parts from freezing up. Complex machines often have operating constraints, such as costly enclosures and careful placement to keep dirt or dampness from critical parts, and those constraints take time and money to fulfill and maintain. For much of history complex machines have not simplified life for entrepreneurs; rather, they have added pressure to the process of managing an enterprise. They therefore tended to be embraced only by entrepreneurs who felt a drive to expand production. The challenge of complex machines changed into an opportunity as entrepreneurs figured out how to make machines think for themselves.

It was a dilettante entrepreneur who created the modern road-map for using machines to simplify complex tasks. Joseph Marie Charles, called Jacquard, was born in Lyon, France, a region long associated with the finest silk textiles. (Louis XIV insisted that Versailles be decorated exclusively with Lyonnais silk.) Jacquard's father was a master silk weaver. Jacquard grew up dreaming of a gentleman's life, free of the pressure of having to work for a living. When his father died in 1772, he sold off his inheritance, moved to a prestigious section of town, and tried speculating in real estate. Unfortunately, the good life eluded him. He racked up major losses and escaped bankruptcy only because his new wife used her dowry to save him. Financial disaster averted, they moved to more modest accommodations, and Jacquard started calling himself a silk merchant. Again, he doesn't appear to have been successful. His name never appeared on any of the official or unofficial lists of the hundreds of silk merchants who lived around Lyon at the time.

Next, Jacquard began tinkering with looms. He may have been an indifferent silk merchant, but he had a deep understanding of the mechanics of silk weaving, likely from having watched his father at work growing up. In 1800, Jacquard took out a patent for a foot-powered loom, but he abandoned it a few years later because it didn't work reliably. He kept tinkering, however. In 1803, a loom he designed to automate the making of fishnets received a bronze medal at a Paris industrial exposition. Although this loom never worked reliably either, it caught the attention of both Parisian industrialists and the silk merchants of Lyon. For decades, the French silk industry had sought to automate the complex process required to weave textiles with intricate designs using different-colored threads. Several high-profile prototypes had been made over prior decades, but none had been reliable or practical.

Weaving dates to before the neolithic era. What began with simple baskets and matting led to the development of techniques and tools for weaving finer and finer materials. Cloth suitable for wearing was developed in many neolithic cultures. Fine-textile-weaving processes involve interlacing two types of yarn at perpendicular angles. One set of threads are stronger and finer that the other, as they serve to steady and align the more prevalent threads that give the textile its appearance and feel. The stronger, finer threads are called the "warp." The resulting matrix of threads is durable and can feel soft to the touch. The value of a textile has historically been associated with the yarn materials, how many threads per inch are interlaced with the warp, and the artistry demonstrated in using creative interlaced patterns with threads of different colors or textures. The finer, more colorful, and more beautiful the pattern, the more expensive the textile but also the greater the time and planning involved.

Around Lyon, textiles were produced by a master weaver and an assistant responsible for raising and lowering warp threads in a planned sequence as yarn with color and texture forms the intricate pattern. A single bolt of textile might require thousands of passes, with each pass requiring the assistant to raise and lower a different set of warp threads. Those were the most complex manufacturing processes of their day.

Jacquard's automated fishnet loom sparked renewed interest in the possibility of automated weaving. The city of Lyon gave him a stipend to go to Paris and make a study of an automated loom designed by the legendary Parisian inventor Jacques de Vaucanson. Vaucanson had been famous for his automata, self-operating machines that mimicked living animals and people to the amazement and amusement of his noble patrons. Vaucanson's automata had toured France, attracting large crowds. Some of his more notable creations included a life-sized metal duck capable of quacking, eating, and defecating and a flute player with a repertoire of twelve songs. Sixty years earlier, Vaucanson had built an automated loom, itself an enhancement of two previous attempts by French weaver-inventors, but his didn't work reliably either, and its output was too crude for commercial use.

Once he became intimate with Vaucanson's machine, Jacquard returned to Lyon to work on his own design. He first designed a robust mechanism for storing a complete sequence for raising and lowering warp threads using punch cards. Holes in the cards indicated which threads should be raised and when. Spring-loaded needles would slide along these cards, and when a hole was present, the needles engaged a wire attached to a specific warp thread to raise it. Jacquard then perfected a roller mechanism that could advance one punch card at a time synchronized with the weaver or the assistant "shuttling" an appropriately colored yarn through the warp.

When using Jacquard's loom, neither the master weaver nor the assistant would have to read or remember the warp thread sequences. The yarn could be shuttled through without thinking. This represented a major breakthrough in simplifying the process. Using punch cards to indicate which needles would pick up which warp threads was an idea Jacquard borrowed from an earlier failed attempt, but he developed the reliable spring-activated mechanism for reading them. His roller mechanism for moving the punch cards along in a desired sequence was also novel. Thanks to these two innovations, his automated loom worked well enough to produce large bolts of finely patterned silk cloth on demand (figure 8.1).

8.1 Jacquard loom, ca. 1845.

Source: Alamy, https://www.alamy.com/stock-photo-industry-textile-industry-mechanical-loom-by-joseph-marie-28887196.html.

Jacquard's loom was immediately hailed as a breakthrough. Napoleon visited Jacquard to see his machine. Determined to maintain the superiority of French silk textile production, Napoleon dictated that Lyon would own the patent to the device and that Jacquard would receive a royalty on every loom produced, along with a generous pension for life. Having never aspired to build and operate a factory himself, Jacquard was more than happy to receive a generous pension and licensing income and live the life of a gentleman, which he'd always wanted. Proving reliable for industrial use, especially after a further refinement quickly introduced by Jean Breton, Jacquard's looms quickly won adoption throughout France. English entrepreneurs copied and took Jacquard's invention one step further with a steam-powered version that eventually ruined many of Lyon's master weavers.

Jacquard looms represented a major investment of time and effort. They were more complex to set up and required specialized training. But in return for that effort, they eliminated errors and enabled weavers to change quickly from one pattern to another. They were a major simplification for those master weavers who could intellectually translate their patterns into sets of holes on punch cards, which could be kept on file and reused as needed.

Using punch cards to store and implement detailed process steps was subsequently adopted in the design of other machines, most notably tabulators for counting and accounting as well as in early computers. Jacquard looms produced most patterned textiles for the next two hundred years, until silicon memory chips replaced punch cards and electric motors replaced steam. Jacquard's innovations helped weavers program the looms and increase profitability by making more valuable products more simply than ever before.

Specialize to Simplify

Ancient entrepreneurs developed products and services to simplify the tasks of other entrepreneurs. Our stressed-out friend Heqanakht the ancient Egyptian entrepreneur and the woman named Sitnebsekhtu whom he employed to spin and weave his flax are a prime four-thousand-year-old example of a specialist offering services to simplify the life of another entrepreneur. Although Heqanakht's household comprised twenty-three people, none of them could weave flax into linen well enough that it would be accepted for currency. Egyptian rulers and high officials had scores of weavers working in royal workshops to turn the flax harvested from their own fields into high-quality linen, but someone like Heqanakht couldn't afford to keep specialists full-time in his household, so he contracted out the work. Shalim, the long-distance trader we met in chapter 6, didn't raise the donkeys he used in his caravans. Nor do we believe that he or someone who worked directly for him made all the harnesses he needed—he needed lots of harnesses for all the goods he transported to Kanesh. Even the Stone Age Trobriand chiefs from chapter 1 contracted out the building and outfitting of the oceangoing canoes they needed to lead their *kula* enterprises—they didn't want to drown with the rest of the men in their village in a flimsy canoe.

Roman entrepreneurs established many specialized businesses to simplify the tasks of other entrepreneurs. In Ostia, the town built by entrepreneurs who were scaling supply, there was a large and thriving courier service. It operated out of its own building and appears to have been very successful. The building's floor was laid with expensive mosaics depicting men driving horse-drawn chariots and watched over by mythical creatures. Roman entrepreneurs who expected valuable shipments needed to know when they would arrive at Ostia to arrange for their transport to Rome and subsequent distribution. Entrepreneurs didn't necessarily want to pay a slave to live in Ostia to watch for shipments, so an entrepreneur created a courier service to relieve the pressure of worrying whether or not shipments arrived.

Builders of all types thrived throughout the Roman Empire by supporting traders and merchants. They built efficient and robust barges, freighters, apartment buildings, and warehouses. Special tradesmen designed and made signs and mosaics to advertise the whereabouts or offerings of artisans and merchants. Others made specialized tools for hauling freight. Producing the large ceramic vessels, called *dolia*, that stored vast quantities of grain, oil, and other foodstuffs required highly specialized skill and experience. Rome's supply chain couldn't have worked as efficiently as it did had every entrepreneur made all their own specialized tools and machines. Entrepreneurs thrived in Rome by serving the needs of other entrepreneurs.

Near the midpoint of the Qingming scroll we see a bridge spanning a river with over a dozen freight and passenger barges nearby, each an entrepreneurial business in its own right. These barges were built at shipyards founded by entrepreneurial shipwrights. At the foot of the bridge we see a vendor selling a wide assortment of specialized tools, including iron hand tools resembling pliers and trawls. To the left of the bridge there's a street with a wheelwright. Artisans and merchants could not have operated efficiently if they had had to make their own carts; wheelwrights simplified their lives. The wheelwright shown in the scroll has laid the parts of a wheel on the ground in front of his shop (figure 8.2). We see him and his assistant using specialized tools and fixtures to make perfectly round and rugged cartwheels. Business appears vibrant. The streets are full of carts being used by artisans and merchants to haul products they plan to sell. Entrepreneurs thrived serving other entrepreneurs in Song dynasty China.

8.2 Wheelwright detail from the Qingming scroll.

Source: http://afe.easia.columbia.edu/song-scroll/song.html.

Simplifying with Trust

Entrepreneurs have always fretted about what to do with the valuable assets they accumulate, like silver and gold, to trade in distant places. Keeping track of valuable assets—and keeping them safe—has always been a critical complicating factor for entrepreneurs. Some rulers and governments allowed entrepreneurs to store merchandise and silver in temple vaults or other safe spaces, thereby ensuring that the ruler was paid the taxes on commerce he or she was owed. State-run banks continue to play an important role in supporting commerce in many countries today.

Private banks, founded by entrepreneurs, show up in the historical record a century after Greek city-states started minting coins and sixty years after Athenians adopted democracy. And while entrepreneurs had been offering loans since at least 2400 BC, private banks that took deposits and also made loans didn't appear until around 450 BC. The milestones of minted coins and democracy made it practical to profit from taking deposits. To profit by keeping other people's money safe required a level of trade spurred by standardized coinage. It also benefited from the lightly regulated, trade-focused culture enabled by Athenian democracy.

Pasion (c. 430–370 BC) is perhaps the best known of the Athenian private bankers. Pasion was a slave of Antisthenes and Archestratos, partners in one of Athens's earliest private banks, located on the docks at Piraeus, the ancient city-state's port. Private banks were known as *trapeza*, from the Greek word for table. Bankers sat under awnings at tables on the docks offering services to both foreign and local traders as they arrived and departed. These specialized tables were scored to hold pieces the bankers used to do abacus-like calculations in front of their clients.

By 394 BC, Pasion had been given his freedom. He quickly became one of the richest people in town. To maintain the goodwill of the Athenian citizenry, he supported the city's efforts to defend itself, buying a shield manufacturer and donating at least a thousand of them, as well as building and equipping a trireme and paying for its crew. Acknowledging this generosity, Athenians granted Pasion full citizenship despite his being a freed slave. To ensure that his bank remained effective and profitable after his death, Pasion left the bank, his widow, and a large dowry payment to Phormio, a slave he himself had freed.

No More Sacks of Coins

While banking continued in various forms during Roman times, it went into hibernation in the West with Rome's decline. The absence of regional rulers who could protect property rights beyond the walls of their castles made coins a liability. By the twelfth century, some local rulers whose domains produced a surplus of food began to feel secure enough to build more comfortable, less defense-oriented palaces. They encouraged merchants of their towns to sell their surplus production more broadly to get higher prices. As their local merchants started to travel more broadly, some also started returning with objects of astonishment, which they then sold to their nobles to display, further encouraging royal patronage.

Count Henry of Champagne (1127–81), nicknamed "The Liberal," and his wife, Mary, the daughter of Eleanor of Aquitaine, were able to indulge their refined tastes for objects of astonishment of all types because Champagne enjoyed sizable grain surpluses (wine was not yet grown there). They and their subnobles, children, relatives, and other court retainers attracted fine craftspeople to the towns around their courts, who made the finest objects to wear and display. The craftspeople, needing to find more and more luxurious material to use in the production of a steady stream of fine products, succeeded in luring Flemish cloth merchants to make the week-long trip to Champagne. Word spread, and by the last decades of the twelfth century, cloth merchants from northern Italian city-states were also making a month-long trek to show their wares in Champagne. The merchants started trading their luxury goods among themselves, and then, with the support of the count, they all started showing up in town at the same time each year. Soon cloth traders from around Europe swarmed to attend the cloth fair. Count Henry, happy with the resulting boost to tax revenues, encouraged more fairs to be held regularly in other towns in Champagne. To help these fairs thrive, he minted his own coins, created a system of standardized weights, deployed judges and armed guards to police the gatherings, and arranged for safe passage for traders through the surrounding counties and principalities.

Trading cloth intensively over several weeks, far from inventory, was a particularly complex operation for the Italian merchants, who not only had farther to travel but also needed months to prepare by importing luxurious cloth from Venice and other exotic locations that they could then resell. To attend the Champagne fair, merchants would be away from their homes for three and a half months. The logistics involved in planning these trips and financing the inventory were extensive. These challenges were exacerbated by shortages of coin, the inconvenience of carrying large sacks of coins, and the dangers of being robbed along the way. Merchants therefore were often short of coin to pay for the services they needed or the products they wanted to buy. To simplify the business of long-distance trade, a few of the most successful Italian cloth merchants offered banking services in Champagne. Merchants could both borrow and deposit money at the fair and then access those funds or pay back the debts on their return home. The most reputable wealthy Italian merchants soon generalized the process of intercity banking by creating transferable bills of exchange, which served as a written guarantee of a smaller merchant's debts. Credit was no longer a private two-party transaction; it had become mobile, transferable, and guaranteed wherever and whenever it was needed.

Merchants charged a premium for issuing bills of exchange, and as a result, they accumulated a measurable fraction of the trading wealth created in these urban centers. Banking became the most profitable part of the business for many of these already successful merchants, transforming the most ambitious into merchant bankers. They scaled up their banking operations further by forming partnerships with wealthy relatives and friends as well as by seeking deposits from nobles and wealthy local merchants.

Simple as Doubling Up

Many entrepreneurs swarmed to become bankers—there were hundreds in thirteenth-century Florence alone. Some innovated or adopted technologies developed by others to offer more money management services to more clients. Arabic numerals were introduced to Europe by Fibonacci of Pisa around 1202, and some Italian merchants began to use the new system for their accounting. (Using Roman numerals didn't die out in accounting until the early eighteenth century.) Merchants in several towns funded schools to teach mathematics using Arabic numerals to guarantee a supply of bookkeepers.

With expansion to other cities, ambitious bankers needed to understand the status of their business in even greater detail, including the profits earned on individual transactions. Keeping simple lists of receipts was too primitive for the complex analyses they demanded. Concurrent with the expansion of merchant banking, a more sophisticated system of control evolved through the efforts of multiple banking partners, what we now call double-entry accounting. Fragments of an accounting ledger of an unknown bank from 1211 shows a page with credits on one side and debits on the other. Other fragments from the thirteenth century provide evidence of Italian merchants using other aspects of double-entry bookkeeping. A surviving ledger from the end of the century shows a double-entry system consistent with modern practices.

Giovanni Farolfi & Co.'s was an entrepreneurial merchant bank focused on the import, export, and financing of goods in and around modern-day Provence, France. Almost half of the accounting ledger for the company's office in Salon for the year 1299–1300, maintained by partner Amatino Manucci, survives. It shows a completely evolved double-entry system. The branch's business was varied and complex enough that Manucci kept five simultaneous sets of ledgers. A general ledger held summaries of all the accounts that reconciled the changes in assets and liabilities from subsidiary ledgers required to determine the profitability of specific transactions managed by the office. The general ledger also kept track of loans—including a loan to the regional archbishop at an interest rate of 15 percent, this in spite of the Church's prohibition on charging interest. Credits and debits associated with the Farolfi business of buying and selling commodities like olive oil and wheat were recorded in one of these subledgers. Yet another contained the same for their cloth business. Two other ledgers recorded expenses for the office and its cash receipts. Assets and liabilities were balanced regularly to identify profits and sum up outstanding bills and loans. Transfers of cash or inventory to other Farolfi offices were also recorded so that the financial status and performance of every office was always clear. Manucci would have made a great accounting software entrepreneur if he were alive today.

The implementation of double-entry accounting enabled the further expansion of banking offices and the scale of financing. Merchant bankers have simplified the management of money transfers and credit for merchants and long-distance traders ever since.

Machines You Can Trust

We saw in the last chapter how entrepreneurs since the Song dynasty created businesses offering food and drink in interesting and comfortable environments. Food and drinking establishments that serve dozens of customers from morning till late at night are complex and stressful to own and operate.

After America's Civil War, veterans swarmed to open saloons to make money. Captain James Ritty's popular saloon in Dayton, Ohio, was one such place. In 1878, Ritty decided he needed a break from the stress of running the place and went on a trip to Europe, leaving his saloon in the care of people he trusted. Not knowing how his trusted surrogates would control his other employees caused him to constantly worry that the staff might steal from him. While on a tour of the engine room of a steamship he traveled on, Ritty was captivated by a device that counted the revolutions of the boat's propellers. The counting device led to an idea about how to solve his problem. On the trip home he sketched a design for a machine that would count the value of every transaction as it took place. On his return, he asked his twin brother, John, a mechanic, to help him create a prototype. The machine worked as expected, and they immediately filed for a patent. They called their machine "Ritty's Incorruptible Cashier."

The Cashier consisted of a round dial marked with the numbers 1 to 100, with a pointer that worked like the second hand of a watch (figure 8.3). The hand would move in increments around the dial by

8.3 A replica of Ritty's Incorruptible Cashier.

Source: Wikimedia Commons, https://commons.wikimedia.org/wiki/File:Reproduction_of _Ritty_Dial,_the_first_practical_cash_register.JPG.

the necessary amount as buttons were pushed denoting the amount of a sale. By looking at the position of the pointer and a counter indicating how many revolutions had already been made, an owner could quickly see how much had been sold. When Ritty put his machine to use, it reduced employee pilfering. Not content with merely improving his own saloon's profits, Ritty and his brother started producing their Incorruptible Cashiers for others. Over the next few years, they made key improvements, including an adding mechanism that eliminated the dial and pointer and a crude printer that created a mark on a roll of paper denoting the value of each transaction. In the end, however, they sold few machines, and Ritty sold the business and patents in 1882 for $1,000. He used his share of the money to build a bigger saloon.

Two of the machines they did sell went to an entrepreneur in the coal business who also had a pilfering problem. John Patterson installed the machines at his struggling miners' supply store, and the store immediately became profitable. Recognizing the potential of the Ritty machine to simplify accounting and cash drawer supervision, Patterson sold his coal business and tracked down the company that now owned the Ritty business and patents, buying them for $6,500. Then he started the National Cash Register Company.

Patterson was sure that other entrepreneurs needed help running their businesses, even if they didn't know it. He pushed his machines aggressively as the solution to pilfering, but there were few takers. Why spend $50 for a cash register if you trust your employees and the desk drawer works just fine for storing money? Patterson tried mail campaigns, advertising, testimonials, and sales agents, but the machines didn't move. Noting that one of his sales agents was markedly more successful than all the others, Patterson asked the man, Joseph Crane, to explain his technique.

Crane was the opposite of the typical traveling salesman of the time. He dressed conservatively, looking more like a prosperous accountant. He also used the same pitch with every prospective client. Talking to Crane, Patterson realized the importance of using a system to sell based on best practices rather than letting every salesperson make up their own pitch on the fly. Memorized speeches and a standard Q&A led to an immediate boost in sales. Creating the perfect sales system became Patterson's passion. To Crane's techniques he added his own innovations, which are copied to this day: sales meetings, sales territories, quotas, and big bonuses for his salesmen (it was only men at the time) that exceeded their quotas. By 1892, NCR was selling fifteen thousand cash registers a year and by 1900, one hundred thousand. By World War I, cash registers had become a standard for all businesses dealing in cash. They simplified sales records, kept cashiers honest, and lent an air of importance and professionalism to the operation of the business.

Patterson's success with NCR led other entrepreneurs to see the potential in designing equipment to help entrepreneurs manage their businesses. In 1888, Alexander Dey invented a clock that recorded time and created a company with his brother to produce clocks that noted when employees started and finished work. Their time clock enabled entrepreneurs and all businesses to pay their workers by the hour, which simplified the monitoring of large numbers of employees. The practice caught on, and other entrepreneurs started to manufacture time clocks. Meanwhile, some entrepreneurs combined automatic scales with calculating mechanisms to simplify the operation of butcher shops and businesses that sold goods by weight.

Simplified Counting

In 1890, the U.S. Census Office hired a brilliant inventor to use a machine he invented that simplified the counting of large numbers of people. The machine was so productive and sophisticated that census managers felt they needed Herman Hollerith, the inventor, to train and supervise the people who were assigned to use it. Hollerith's invention combined concepts employed in the design of the telegraph with his awareness of the operation of punch cards used in Jacquard looms. His machine counted and sorted punch cards with holes in specific locations that indicated multiple attributes of each person counted in the census. His machine enabled the census of 1890 to be more detailed than any before it. In 1896, he left to create his own company, the Tabulating Machine Company, to sell his machines to other countries where censuses were conducted, as well as to very ambitious entrepreneurs like Marshall Fields and Thomas Edison, who utilized Hollerith's machine to simplify and speed the analysis of sales data.

Entrepreneurs offering business equipment generally struggle to convince entrepreneurs and professional managers to invest in their products. The idea of accounting for this kind of capital equipment as an investment and not an expense developed in the late nineteenth century. At the time, however, most entrepreneurs had no bookkeeping or financial training. They considered any money spent on equipment as nothing more than an immediate reduction in their bank balance. Selling equipment that simplified business processes to skeptical entrepreneurs required a highly trained and regimented sales force, of which NCR was the only example for several years. Fortunately for the world, the brilliant, autocratic, and megalomaniacal John Patterson recruited and trained hundreds of salespeople and executives and fired most of them if they did anything he didn't like, even top performers. Many of these fired NCR salesmen and executives became entrepreneurs who understood the potential of technology to simplify business challenges. They bought or took over struggling business equipment manufacturers and turned them into profitable companies.

One of the people Patterson fired was Thomas Watson. Watson had already failed as an entrepreneur and been fired as a salesman before he was hired as an assistant to an NCR salesman in Buffalo, New York. This time around, he was determined not to fail and became an exemplary student of Patterson's sales system. After becoming head of the Rochester office and creating a virtual monopoly in the area, Watson was called to NCR headquarters in Dayton to head sales and work on special projects. One such project required Watson to move to New York City to set up a seemingly independent company to buy up all the used cash registers on the market. Secondhand cash registers were starting to flood the market, and NCR protected its prices by buying them.

Unfortunately, Patterson's scheme was brought to the attention of federal prosecutors, who charged Patterson, Watson, and eleven other NCR executives with anticompetitive practices under the Sherman Antitrust Act. They were all convicted and sentenced to a year in jail. All their convictions were eventually set aside on appeal, but Patterson no longer wanted to work with these tainted executives and fired them all, including Watson.

By the time of his firing in 1912, Watson had earned a stellar reputation in the industry as NCR's head of sales. At the time, NCR executives were in high demand at the large, new corporations forming through mergers. Watson's colleagues and family were nonetheless shocked when he chose to take a position at a relatively small company put together by an entrepreneurial financier nicknamed "The Father of Trusts." Copying the business models of John D. Rockefeller and J. P. Morgan, Charles Flint formed a series of monopolies by acquiring the most successful entrepreneurial firms in a market. He created his first when he bought several rubber companies to form U.S. Rubber in the early 1890s, which went on to dominate its market. He then did the same thing for chewing gum with American Chicle and for wool with American Woolen.

In 1911, looking to control the nascent market for business machines, Flint bought six small, struggling business equipment companies to create The Computing-Tabulating-Recording Company (CTR). Among the six were Dey's time clock company and Hollerith's Tabulating Machine Company. But Flint didn't have a vision for how to consolidate the companies, so he offered Watson the job. Watson's experience made him a great fit to lead the firm. To entice him to accept the offer, Flint offered him near total autonomy, and a deal was struck. Watson ran the company with the same structures and philosophies he'd learned at NCR, immediately prioritizing the creation of a professional sales force. Sales increased, and in 1924, Watson renamed the company International Business Machines.

For the next forty years, Watson and then his son, Thomas Watson, Jr., eschewed designing business machines for entrepreneurs. Instead, they focused on the large professionally managed corporations that began to dominate markets all over the world in the early twentieth century at the expense of entrepreneurs (as described in chapter 5). The Watsons felt it would be more profitable to design equipment to simplify the very complex processes associated with government agencies (including in Nazi Germany), large banks, insurance companies, and big industrial and consumer companies rather than deal with the varying needs of different small- and medium-sized businesses. Their focus did not change with their success and dominance with mainframe computers after World War II. The first commercial computers produced by business equipment companies, the UNIVAC by Remington Rand in 1951 and then the IBM 702 in 1953, were extremely expensive, costing more than the total invested capital of any startup and over 95 percent of the corporations of the age. Entrepreneurs were initially on the outside in their ability to tap this new technology and put it to use in simplifying their lives and adding to their profits. They swarmed to break IBM's grip.

Taking Control Over Computers

Georges Doriot (figure 8.4), a professor at Harvard Business School, had written extensively about the need to support entrepreneurs in starting technology-enabled companies. Already in the late 1930s, he was worried about large corporations dominating technologies and slowing innovation. The then president of the Massachusetts Institute of Technology, Karl Compton, had similar feelings. After the war ended, the two of them lobbied prominent New England financial and business leaders to invest in the American Research

8.4 Georges Doriot, ca. 1955.

Business Week, photo by Dick Wolters. Courtesy of the Baker Library Historical Collections.

and Development Corporation (ARDC), which would serve as "matchmaker" between investors and engineers wishing to commercialize their inventions. The company made many small investments in engineers, mostly those involved with new electronics technologies. ARDC was mildly successful, but many of the inventors in whom it invested were unable to scale their companies. Indeed, investors were lukewarm, at best, about ARDC's record for making them money.

In 1957, after months of meetings, Ken Olsen (figure 8.5) and Harlan Andersen finally convinced Doriot to invest $70,000 for 70 percent of their startup, which they named Digital Equipment Corporation (DEC). At the time, Olsen and Andersen were working together at MIT on government contracts to apply the recently invented transistor to computers. They had developed a working

8.5 Ken Olsen, founder of DEC, in 1996, posing with a PDP-8 minicomputer.

Chitose Suzuki/Associated Press.

model of a transistorized computer they felt could be commercialized and sold for much less than IBM or UNIVAC mainframe computers. They were so excited by the prospects of their more affordable computer that they didn't care they had to sell 70 percent of their company to get their chance.

DEC introduced their first computer, the PDP-1, in 1960. The machine sold for the equivalent of $1 million today and was too expensive for anyone except the government. It took another five years to introduce the PDP-8, which sold at the time for just $18,500, less than a tenth the price of the least expensive mainframe computer. (When DEC went public in 1968, ARDC's shares were worth five hundred times more than they paid. DEC was ARDC's one major success.)

The PDP-8's low price opened computers to being exploited by entrepreneurs in startups. The prospects for profits from making computers more affordable set off three different entrepreneurial swarms. One group developed semiconductors that would make computers even more powerful and less costly. Another swarm set off the design of software to simplify using computers to run businesses. And a third set off copying DEC and making better and cheaper computers. IBM, despite employing thousands of engineers and investing tens of millions of dollars a year in research and development to maintain its computer monopoly, could not keep up with the entrepreneurial innovation cycles set in motion by these three swarms.

Simplifying with Silicon

Semiconductor swarms had already emerged before Olsen and Andersen designed their first transistorized computer prototypes. Although transistors were smaller and more reliable than the electronic tubes they replaced, they were still complicated and tricky to use, particularly in computers (transistor radios were the first transistorized products to appear). An emerging cohort of semiconductor engineers raced to produce devices that could mimic some or all of the electronics found in the computers being designed by DEC and their copycats.

Leading this race was one of the founders of Fairchild Semiconductor, Robert Noyce (figure 8.6). He invented the practical integrated circuit in 1959, which enabled several connected microscopic transistors to be produced in large batches ready for use in a computer. Fairchild introduced the first commercial integrated circuit in 1961, giving semiconductor-savvy entrepreneurs and their financiers a template for developing integrated circuits that could mimic and replace much larger, heavier, and more expensive electronic circuits already in use.

In 1968, Noyce and one of his Fairchild cofounders, Gordon Moore, left to found Intel. (Moore had gained fame for Moore's Law, published in 1965, which predicted that technological advancements would enable integrated circuits to double in power and

8.6 Robert Noyce in 1959, holding a design element of the first integrated circuit.

Source: https://en.wikipedia.org/wiki/Robert_Noyce.

complexity every two years for the foreseeable future—which petered out only fifty years later.) Their goal was to make integrated circuit computer memory chips to further decrease the cost and complexity of computers. Noyce and Moore, already legends in what would soon be called Silicon Valley, quickly succeeded in producing the first silicon chips that could store and retrieve bits of information. Three years after Intel's founding, in response to a customer requesting a custom chip for a complex calculator, an engineering team working directly for Noyce developed the Intel 4004 four-bit microprocessor, the first postage-stamp-sized integrated circuit to mimic the performance of the electronic circuits the size of a shoebox at the center of every computer—an actual computer on a chip.

Simplify the Work

A second swarm formed around designing and selling software to simplify running businesses. Inventory management programs called MRP, for manufacturing resource planning, became popular by the mid-1970s when packaged with ever more affordable minicomputers. MRP programs modeled the flow of goods into a company and their flow inside factories as they were transformed and combined with other parts through every step of manufacturing, until they were shipped to customers as finished products. These very complex programs were first developed by IBM for its major industrial customers to run on mainframe computers but then copied by entrepreneurs to run on less expensive machines. When properly implemented, MRP programs would print out instructions that managers could follow regarding how much product to order or which partially completed product to work on next. No thinking required; just like what Jacquard looms did for weavers.

Once again, a swarm of entrepreneurs set out to deliver the power of these programs to entrepreneurs. When programs were not implemented properly, which happened often with managers who had not implemented or used software before, chaos ensued and profits vanished. So MRP and business software entrepreneurs specifically wrote their programs so other entrepreneurs could bundle them along with a minicomputer, consulting services, and training that they would provide. New swarms of computer consultants were unleashed.

As MRP systems demonstrated their success in reducing inventory, new swarms of entrepreneurs set out to create programs that would dictate how their clients ran other parts of their businesses, not just materials and manufacturing. Software began to appear in the 1980s for emulating "best-practice management" in virtually all other business processes, such as human resources, facilities, customer relations, sales, and marketing. New cohorts of consultants, including entrepreneurs founding specialized consulting companies, helped big companies and entrepreneurs implement these programs to ensure the expected results. By the late 1990s, with the ubiquitous availability of high-speed internet in business centers throughout the world, yet another swarm of entrepreneurs offered business optimization software delivered through the internet, dubbed "software as a service," or SaaS.

Simple Enough for the Entrepreneur in All of Us

Six years after the Intel 4004 was introduced, Steve Wozniak used a competing microprocessor chip to design the first practical, affordable, and friendly (for its time) personal computer, the Apple II. Other entrepreneurs, along with established companies like DEC, Siemens, and IBM, raced to produce competing personal computers, further incentivizing semiconductor-savvy executives and engineers to found even more companies aspiring to produce novel integrated circuits that could boost computer performance and lower cost.

Another cohort of entrepreneurs started writing computer programs to make personal computers easier to use for writing, calculating, and specific business applications like accounting. One such entrepreneur was Dan Bricklin. His father was an entrepreneur with a successful printing business. Dan always expected to be an entrepreneur someday because entrepreneurship seemed like a good way to lead a life doing just what he wanted. In high school in the late 1960s, Bricklin was fortunate to have access to a computer and learned to program. While a freshman at MIT, his prior experience enabled him to land a job working for a professor focused on making it easier for humans to control high-performance computers. Dan graduated in 1973 and went to work for DEC, where he was assigned to a team writing the company's first word-processing software. That year, a startup named Vydec had introduced the first word-processing console: a desk built around a minicomputer, keyboard, printer, and early disc drive, with a monitor that displayed what you were typing (figure 8.7). DEC wanted to offer a software package for its general-purpose minicomputers to mimic that capability. Dan was familiar with the requirements of quality typesetting from his father, which propelled him to become project lead.

Still aspiring to start his own company, Dan left DEC to attend Harvard Business School. As he worked through case studies associated with how to optimize a factory or optimize warehousing costs, he was taken with the similarity of describing a business with tables of numbers and formulas that connected those numbers, to the structure of the word processor software he had designed at DEC. Dan realized all the numbers actually were associated with words, or abbreviations, that described them, so manipulating numbers in a table worked in a fashion similar to how words were manipulated by computers.

8.7 Vydec's word-processing computer, ca. 1975.

Source: Internet Archive, https://archive.org/details/Vydec1400-TextEditor-ReferenceManual.

Over a long weekend Bricklin created a program in which when a user changed any number in a table, every other number was automatically recalculated based on formulas that the user had input. Over his final nine months at business school, Dan and Bob Frankston, a friend from his time at MIT, created the interfaces that would make it easy for people to use his software on the newly available Apple II. VisiCalc was introduced to the world in 1979, simultaneously with Dan's graduation from Harvard Business School (figure 8.8).

It took slightly over a year for VisiCalc to start driving sales of Apple computers as both entrepreneurs and professional managers realized how much the program simplified the number crunching inherent in running a business. Scenarios and analyses that used to take hours now took minutes. Entrepreneurs could perform even more detailed analyses of their businesses and began quantifying how they could increase business rather than relying on gut feel. Entrepreneurs were soon expected to create detailed quantitative models of their startup ideas to receive VC funding.

8.8 Dan Bricklin (left) and Bob Frankston (right).

Source: https://upload.wikimedia.org/wikipedia/commons/0/0f/Daniel_Bricklin
_v%C3%A0_Bob_Frankston.jpg.

With computing power, memory storage, and the speed of digital communication doubling every two years, entrepreneurs launched into a game of leapfrog in designing new generations of computers, controllers, and networks of all types, as well as software-based applications to simplify management. Dan Bricklin and Bob Frankston became early entrepreneurial casualties of this phenomenon as an entrepreneur who created programs that added graphing features to VisiCalc soon chose to create a more powerful and easier-to-use version, called Lotus 1-2-3.

Systems Simpler Than People

It has never been difficult to get an entrepreneur to admit that the ideal is to get their business to run on its own so they can spend time doing things they enjoy more, like expanding their business, engaging in a favorite pastime, or spending time with loved ones. They have developed and used tools, machines, and, recently, complex computer-enabled systems run by sophisticated software to get closer to this idealized state.

The latest entrepreneurial swarms seek to use machine learning (ML), the efficient accessing and organizing of all relevant information, and artificial intelligence (AI), software that creates its own algorithms to better identify trends and predict outcomes. AI and ML have the potential to deliver software customized to entice customers to buy, cost-reduce designs, couple with robots to perform difficult or exhausting tasks more effectively, and even motivate remaining staff to work more productively.

Societies have occasionally grappled with the consequences when entrepreneurs try to simplify their enterprises. At the beginning of the nineteenth century, many feared the ramifications of entrepreneurial innovations that forced workers from their homes and into more tightly controlled, machine-driven, simpler-to-manage factories filled with complex labor-saving machines. Luddites destroyed machines that spun cotton and burned the factories. Within a few decades, unions formed not just to fight for higher wages but also to protect jobs from automation. Today, many worry how entrepreneurs will use ML, AI, and robots to eliminate entire classes of workers, including even what the influential business philosopher Peter Drucker called "knowledge workers." The future of work is a new field of entrepreneurial consultation that is spawning a new swarm as I write this.

As we have seen, the most ambitious entrepreneurs seek unprecedented scale and drive many other members of their swarms to copy their successes. The scale of entrepreneurial impact only increases with time. And the impact of entrepreneurial innovation accumulates, for better and for worse. The next two chapters look at the consequences of these accumulating impacts.

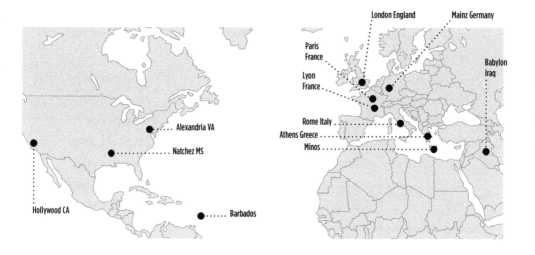

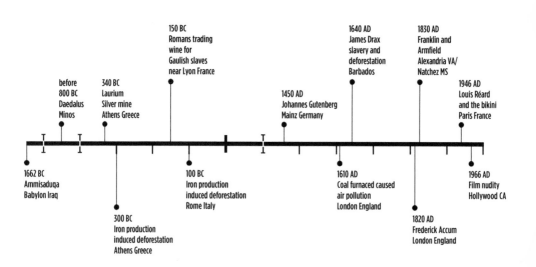

CHAPTER 9

Scaling Consequences

Mechanical arts have an ambiguous or double use, and serve as well as to produce as to prevent mischief and destruction; so that their virtue almost destroys and unwinds itself.

—Francis Bacon, *The Wisdom of the Ancients*, chapter XIX, "Daedalus, or Mechanical Skill," 1609

Francis Bacon's quote uses the myth of Daedalus to warn readers of the double nature of entrepreneurship to "produce" but also "unwind itself." At the beginning of the seventeenth century, Bacon, the father of scientific inquiry, implicitly feared the consequences unleashed by innovative entrepreneurs of his day. This was a time when timber was in short supply in many parts of England, new coal furnaces were belching black smoke into the air around cities, and real estate developers were figuring out how to pack more people into city housing. He felt the need to explain his worry to the learned elite of his day using the example of Daedalus to illustrate his points, but to no avail. Who can resist the allure of innovation and profit?

Entrepreneurs continuously confront impediments to scaling. Many find ways to mitigate or alleviate these impediments while persisting in delivering their products and services. The large number of these impediment-breaking actions cumulatively determine the direction and scale of every entrepreneurial swarm and lead to massive social, economic, and environmental change. These changes, when multiplied many times by scores of other members of a swarm, are often not what any individual entrepreneur expected or what many people in the local culture wanted. Entrepreneurial actions therefore often lead to unexpected consequences. The nature of entrepreneurial swarming, with entrepreneurs copying the best ideas of one another, results in the scaling of many unintended consequences in tandem with the supply of an innovative product or service.

Slavery Scaled

We've already seen some prime examples. James Drax was one of the most effective innovators of supply scaling in history. Aspiring to be the wealthiest sugar baron in the wealthiest sugar colony on the planet, he increased throughput by a factor of five by using wind to power his sugar mills. This innovation set off a series of new challenges that required an unprecedented scaling of his operations, workforce, and controls. His need for hundreds of additional slaves to staff his operations provided the impetus and rationale for a significant increase in transatlantic slave trading. Furthermore, the synchronization of the actions of as many as five hundred slaves working across hundreds of acres on multiple simultaneous processes, each requiring tight controls, inspired Drax to implement a brutal regimentation with no compassion for his slaves. Death and brutality were among the by-products of scaling up the production of sugar to meet the insatiable desire for sweetness.

Death and brutality were not specific goals of Drax or most other sugar barons, but neither were they constraints. While many religious communities of the time considered slavery to be an undesirable consequence of sugar production, for would-be slaves and their families, slavery was a tragic consequence.

Drax did not invent slavery, but he innovated its scale and inspired others to understand how to benefit from it on an unprecedented scale. Slavery was already well documented with Mesopotamian entrepreneurs before 2000 BC—certainly by the time the word for "profit" first came into existence. Slavery was codified in Mesopotamian proverbs, such as, "The strong man lives off what is paid for his strength, and the weak man off of what is paid for his children." Because slaves were central to so much commercial activity, many of the laws listed in Hammurabi's code describe what was permitted in buying, renting, controlling, or punishing slaves.

Many civilizations of the past allowed or encouraged the use of slaves for strenuous or dangerous tasks that enriched their elites and entrepreneurs. Ancient Athenians relied on slaves to produce their agricultural wealth and perform dangerous mining tasks. The mining and metallurgy industry in Athens attracted swarms of entrepreneurs as it generated immense wealth. Entrepreneurs could purchase leases from the Council of 500 to work the nearby rich Laurium silver mine. By 340 BC, about one hundred fifty new three- to seven-year mining leases were being issued a year. Only around 20 percent of the leases were bought by members of the Athenian elite, as swarms of nascent entrepreneurs tried to benefit from finding and working a new vein of silver. Holders of large numbers of leases required up to a thousand slaves to extract all the silver from their mines. An Athenian named Nicias ran a business that acquired slaves from around the region for the purpose of renting them to entrepreneurs holding mining leases. Other entrepreneurs ran businesses that smelted and purified silver or transported materials to and from the mines, using thousands of additional slaves to work the hot furnaces or load and unload tons of material as it moved from mines through various processing steps. Socrates, as described by Xenophon in his *Oeconomicus*, encouraged entrepreneurs to not treat their slaves as expendable assets but to motivate them with recognition and rewards. Some did, but the treatise makes clear that many did not.

In the time of Imperial Rome, wealthy Romans used large numbers of slaves to provide the physical labor required to run their vast estates. Some wealthy Romans explicitly coveted smart, ambitious slaves who could run ancillary agricultural and commercial businesses tied to the estates. Ambitious and shrewd slaves who proved highly valuable were often freed and given funds to enable them to expand a business they had previously run for their owners, enabling their former owners to then participate as an investing partner in the freeman's profit stream.

Entrepreneurs nevertheless scaled up the subjugation of others in innovative ways. For example, in 150 BC, Roman wine merchants suggested that powerful Gauls pay, in the form of slaves, for the expensive Italian wines they coveted. Gauls didn't produce much that Romans wanted, so wine merchants could expand their business only by pointing powerful Gauls toward accumulating commodities they wanted; together they agreed on slaves. Wine sales expanded quickly because what one entrepreneur found successful, others copied. Gaulish slaves became a Roman commodity.

In the first half of the nineteenth century, at the peak of the slave trade, traders counted among the wealthiest people in England and France, alongside their major sugar baron customers. Although today slavery has been outlawed in most all countries, entrepreneurs still perpetuate it in several forms, forcing men, women, and children to work under unwanted and unwarranted conditions with no freedoms and no chance of leaving. We still tolerate the millions of slaves who enrich entrepreneurs in the sex trade and cotton and shrimp industries.

Slavery per se is not an entrepreneurial construct, but the scale of slavery is. Entrepreneurial initiative scaled slavery to new and unprecedented levels. Slavery improved the profits for specific entrepreneurs, and entrepreneurial swarming made slavery into big business. Some of the most single-minded entrepreneurs set aside human values to scale up the supply of slaves, using brutality to overcome the logistical and motivational constraints of human nature. The massive scale of slavery is *all* entrepreneurial.

Throughout time, cheap, plentiful labor has enabled entrepreneurs to scale supply in many types of businesses. In many industries today profitability is directly related to how inexpensively labor can be procured with minimal costs associated with worker safety. Scaling clothing, refuse, mass production, hauling, or toy businesses have always required entrepreneurs to "innovate" the reduction of labor costs. Ambitious, innovative entrepreneurs search the world for low-cost labor in unregulated or poorly regulated regions to offer low-cost labor as a service to other entrepreneurs who do not want to be directly associated with labor exploitation. The fallout from unintended and undesirable consequences of exploited labor remains to this day.

Amplifying the Worst in Some

New entrepreneurial swarms form to facilitate the scaling of other entrepreneurs, which further amplifies undesirable or unintended consequences. Because there are no rules or conditions on who becomes an entrepreneur, society feels the impact of "innovations" instigated by the full spectrum of human motivations. Throughout time, for some entrepreneurs the lure of wealth, power, and sex has transcended social bonds and human decency. Entrepreneurs who are highly ambitious and aggressive and lack empathy ignore societal norms—if not laws—in pursuit of their goals. The social transgressions of some members of lucrative swarms can be particularly dangerous.

Isaac Franklin and John Armfield were two of the richest people in America by the time they retired in 1836 to become socially prominent Southern gentlemen. Their firm, Franklin & Armfield, was so efficient at slave trading that it created a virtual monopoly.

Franklin was born in 1789 on a Tennessee farm that used slaves. As a teenager he started making money buying and selling slaves. After fighting in the War of 1812, Franklin aspired to build a business beyond small-scale local trading. It was an opportune time. Shortly before the war, the U.S. government passed a law banning the importation of slaves while still permitting the sale of slaves already in the country. New farmland opened up west of the Appalachian mountains and north of New Orleans along the Mississippi River, fueling the demand for slaves. At the same time, farmland on the East Coast that had been intensively farmed was being depleted, inducing farmers to sell some of their slaves. Great money could be made by transporting slaves from the east to the major slave-trading market in Natchez, Mississippi.

Franklin traveled extensively throughout the east looking for slaves, but the scale of business he aspired to required a trusted partner with equally good skills at transport and slave buying. He found his ideal partner around 1824 when he met and hired John Armfield. Armfield had run away from his Quaker family in his teens and had lived by his wits until the two met; legend has it that they met when Franklin was a passenger on a stagecoach Armfield was driving. Armfield proved very astute at leading the transport of

9.1 Contemporary photo of Franklin and Armfield's office in Alexandria, Virginia.

Source: Wikimedia Commons, https://commons.wikimedia.org/wiki /File:Franklin_%26_Armfield_Office_front.jpg.

up to two hundred shackled slaves in overland marches to Natchez. By 1828, when the two established their firm in Alexandria, Virginia (figure 9.1), they had become formal partners. In 1834, John Armfield married Isaac's high-strung niece, cementing his close relationship with Franklin and his family.

Franklin and Armfield were shrewd and efficient traders. To transport slaves from the East Coast to where they could be sold for large sums, the partners packed slaves into boats with less space than even in transatlantic ships. But the two were always highly sensitive to how they were perceived socially. To appear "humane" they advertised that they kept families together and did not separate husbands and wives or mothers and their children. Records show they often did not do what they promised, as family groups sold for much less, but none of the people on the East Coast who sold them slaves seemed to have checked. They were diligent in maintaining an outward appearance of being honorable and men of their words. In a profession that had a reputation for being unsavory and dishonest, Franklin and Armfield were trusted by the people they did business with. They were even described by contemporary abolitionists who were able to tour their holding pen in Alexandria as "charming." Nothing could be further from the truth.

Franklin and Armfield were not only driven by the profits, wealth creation, or even by being the biggest; they both relished raping their young women captives. They wrote to one another about their conquests, using euphemisms like being pirates or one-eyed men to refer to what they called their "games." Their activity would not have been condoned by the society from which they wanted respect, and their games remained secret until their correspondence was uncovered decades after they had passed away.

Franklin and Armfield were not the only slave traders who raped their female captives. Swarms amplify behaviors that yield perceived benefits in general, not just profits. Since swarms are made up of all types of self-directed people, including those who seek more than just socially proscribed profit, they bring out the worst in some, and we would be naive to think otherwise.

Want Some Money?

The Liberty Bell, one of the most important artifacts of American independence and freedom, bears an inscription from the Bible, Leviticus 25:10: "Proclaim liberty throughout all the land, and to all the inhabitants thereof." The beauty of the exhortation stands on its own, but the phrase is taken out of context, and its greater meaning has long been overlooked. Leviticus 25 describes the Lord admonishing his followers to forgive all debts every fifty years in order to restore economic equality. This chapter of the Bible is a description of the divinely granted right to economic freedom—specifically freedom from the oppressive mortgages that enslaved many Babylonians, not just Jews, for millennia.

Mesopotamian entrepreneurs invented the secured commercial loan around 2300 BC. Administrators of the temples of powerful cults at the center of Mesopotamian city-states developed loans and written contracts to secure their economic control over the common people. By 3000 BC, large numbers of people had begun to move to urban centers, where they felt safer and where skilled priests could mediate on their behalf with the powerful spirits and gods that controlled lives. Temples expected defined amounts of tribute from citizens. (This was how taxes were invented.) They supported citizens through difficult times by offering loans, with interest, in amounts equal to the tribute they could not pay.

Temple administrators in some city-states wanted to dissociate themselves from the collection of these loans, selling them at a discount to merchants with surplus wealth. These entrepreneurs collected the loans and were allowed to demand that a citizen work off the debt if they could not repay it on time. It did not take long for some entrepreneurially innovative merchants to realize the profit potential of offering loans directly to their fellow citizens. To reduce risk, they explicitly required that their loans be secured by assets such as land. These pioneering entrepreneurs created written contracts that required debtors who did not pay back their loans on time to forfeit their lands and to work as debt-slaves.

Entrepreneurs swarmed to offer profitable loans. The unintended consequences of excess debt and the accumulation of productive lands by wealthy merchant moneylenders became a serious problem for kings in the Near East. It undermined their rule because it reduced the rolls of tribute-paying citizens and the number of citizens who could be expected to serve in the army. It also created powerful and wealthy merchants with large landholdings, who controlled the supply of both essential and desirable commodities, potentially wielding more power than rulers.

To improve their popularity and legitimacy, Mesopotamian rulers issued edicts, called *amargi* (in Sumerian) or *misharum* (in Babylonian), forgiving loans owed to temples for unpaid tribute and taxes irrespective of who had paid for the right to collect the loan. As private debt became more prevalent, these edicts were expanded to include private debt forgiveness, with various degrees of success. Local entrepreneurs obviously did not want to comply with these edicts, giving back forfeited lands and losing their debt slaves, so innovative entrepreneurs added provisions to their loans to get around the edicts. For example, they tried requiring debtors to adopt them as legal heirs. Mortgage holders also started physically seizing assets from debtors who were not late on their payments when they suspected edicts would be issued.

In 1662 BC, the Babylonian king Ammisaduqa issued his misharum as a long legal document with six distinct sections clarifying how it applied to different types of contract clauses that he deemed were attempts to circumvent the edict. It stated that these contract clauses would be considered fraudulent. It also stated that forced collections would not be tolerated. To send the message that entrepreneurs were expected to fully comply with the intent of the edict, the misharum explicitly stated that any attempts to circumvent it would warrant the death penalty.

For over four thousand years too much debt has caused families to lose their "liberty," forcing many into debt-slavery. Societies up to the present continue to struggle with the unintended consequences of too much debt. For millennia entrepreneurs have packaged debt in various forms to circumvent existing regulations and entice borrowers to borrow more money than they can pay back. The unintended consequences are as much a problem today as they were in the time of Ammisaduqa. The use of the word "liberty" in Leviticus directly relates to the idea that "freedom" means being debt-free. The unintended consequences of entrepreneurs offering to lend portions of their wealth to others remain of biblical proportions.

Environmental Impacts

The increase in the scale of misery and brutality of slavery wasn't the only undesired or unintended consequence of the operational and organizational innovations of James Drax and his sugar plantation contemporaries. When Drax was put ashore as one of the original settlers of Barbados, the island was covered with tall trees, forming an impenetrable forest. As stipulated in the contract providing his free passage from England, Drax was given tools and seeds to clear a portion of the forest, where he could cultivate cash crops like tobacco that the Courteen Company could sell in Europe. Drax was one of only a handful of original settlers who succeeded in growing enough poor-quality tobacco to buy staples and build a house to protect him from the elements.

It took fifteen years for Drax to figure out how to produce sugar in large enough quantities with high enough quality to demonstrate the value creation potential of the island. His success triggered a swarm of entrepreneurs, most coming from England, to invest their life savings to enter the sugar business. The swarm members had heard descriptions of the wealth Drax and others were accumulating, and they wanted it too. On arriving, their priority was to secure land, which necessitated clearing a plot of land not already cleared. As Barbados was a tiny island, it took only a few years for it to be almost completely denuded of trees.

The cultivation of every plot of available land unleashed a series of unintended and undesirable consequences that affected everyone on the island. Prices skyrocketed for food and shelter. The cost of living rose, making it more expensive to live on Barbados than in London. In essence, anyone on the island who didn't own a successful sugar plantation or provide essential services to plantation owners became so impoverished that they couldn't even escape the island. The only way off the island was to agree to become indentured and work without pay for five to seven years for another entrepreneur living in another English colony.

Deforestation is a classic unintended consequence of entrepreneurial swarming. Entrepreneurial farmers pioneering new lands almost always start by cutting down the trees. Until coal replaced wood as the primary source of heat, industries like pottery and metals caused the deforestation of large areas. Xenophon complained about the smoke that wafted over Athens from the nearby workshops that were processing lead and silver, warning that it was harmful to human health. The poet Horace (65 BC–8 AD) similarly lamented "the smoke, wealth, the noise of Rome." In 100 AD, iron production in ancient Rome is estimated to have exceeded 80,000 tons a year. This level of iron production would have required a minimum of 10,000 square miles of forest to support. The production of lead, glass, bricks, pottery, and bronze added to demand for wood. By the time of Imperial Rome, virtually all of the forests of Italy had been consumed, requiring timber to be imported from Spain. Today entrepreneurs are responsible for the elimination of half of the Amazonian rainforest (and likely the extinction of countless species).

Deforestation and smoke were not the only unwanted consequences of entrepreneurs working on their own behalf. Entrepreneurially initiated noise pollution was also a big enough problem that the Talmud included the admonition, "one must not open a shop in a courtyard if the noise pollution of customers will disturb the neighbors' sleep."

New Innovations, New Consequences

Spurred by the shortage of labor caused by the Black Death in the fourteenth and fifteenth centuries, entrepreneurs focused on agricultural innovations, introducing new plows, crops, and land management techniques useful to both noble estates and family farms. The resulting food surpluses and favorable climate conditions caused England's population to grow particularly rapidly in the sixteenth and seventeenth centuries, more than doubling between the mid-1500s to the mid-1600s. The increase of three and a half million people spurred many to leave their siblings on the family farm to move to the city and learn a trade, with many opening shops for themselves. Others cleared new land to farm. In many locations in England wood for fuel became scarce and expensive.

By 1540, inflation had started to set in, particularly near urban centers, led by sharply rising timber and charcoal prices. Aspiring entrepreneurs began experimenting with alternative sources of heat. We do not know where and when the "reverberatory" furnace for efficiently converting coal into heat was developed, but the technology was described in the Italian book *De la pirotechnia* in 1540. As with most new technologies, it took a while for entrepreneurs to figure out how to leverage an expensive furnace into an innovation that produced an enticing profit.

Glass-manufacturing entrepreneurs were the first to figure out all the steps required to turn coal into proverbial gold. By 1610, several glassmaking entrepreneurs had figured out where and how to procure and transport the inexpensive coal that was available in parts of England to nearby urban centers, where they set up large reverberatory furnaces. These coal-fired furnaces produced large amounts of heat, which enabled vastly expanded production of glass objects that both urban and rural consumers had begun to covet. Setting up furnaces near urban centers greatly reduced breakage during transport and enabled glass objects to be sold for prices that further increased demand.

Other entrepreneurs swarmed to copy the glass manufacturers' profit models. Within fifty years entrepreneurs were utilizing coal to expand the production and lower the cost of beer, bricks, tile, pottery, soap, paper, lime burning (for construction and agriculture), salt, gunpowder, and brass objects. Urban skies, however, became darkened with soot as the updraft produced by the heat carried with it millions of small coal dust particles. The problem of coal soot, more dangerous to health than soot generated by burning wood, was being widely discussed as an urban blight in the late 1600s. By the mid-1700s, travelers could spot London by its plume of sooty smoke from a hundred miles away.

Because no one found mitigating coal soot to be profitable, the problem continued to grow for another hundred years as entrepreneurs instead focused on reducing the cost of coal through innovations in mining and transport. New swarms of entrepreneurs developed steam-powered machines and railroads, which then stimulated the Industrial Revolution. The problems caused by the by-products of burning coal, including CO, CO_2, and sulphur, still plague the world.

Societies rarely hold entrepreneurs accountable for the unintended consequences of their actions. If it is not profitable to mitigate an unintended consequence, its impact can accumulate for centuries.

Competition Made Me Do It

Some adverse entrepreneurial consequences are intended. Frederick Accum (1769–1838) was a distinguished scientist and successful entrepreneur (figure 9.2). He was also the first person to alert the public to the subterfuges by fellow entrepreneurs who were adulterating the food they sold to the public. His book, *A Treatise on Adulterations of Food, and Culinary Poisons*, published in 1820, was a bestseller, available in multiple editions, and quickly translated into German. Food processing had recently become a new line of business, made possible by technologies like canning and large-scale production of inexpensive mass-produced packaging through

9.2 Photo of an oil painting of Frederick Accum.

Source: Wikipedia, https://en.wikipedia.org/wiki/Friedrich_Accum#/media
/File:Friedrich_Christian_Accum_(Portrait,_sw).jpg.

steam-driven mechanization. At the end of the first quarter of the nineteenth century, local farmers no longer supplied the food to many cities—new swarms of entrepreneurs did. Motivated as both a scientist and an entrepreneur, Accum was driven to understand how food was actually being produced, and he had both the expertise and resources to find out.

The son of a German soap maker and merchant, Accum apprenticed as an apothecary with a prominent German firm that had a branch in London. He moved to London to take classes in the newly emerging field of chemistry, and at the age of twenty-nine published his first scholarly article in England's first chemical journal. To financially support his continued passion for chemical research, Accum launched three successful businesses: a school where students could learn laboratory practices, chemical analysis, and minerology (prime minister Lord Palmerston was a student); a mercantile for chemicals; and a manufacturer and seller of laboratory equipment (some of which can still be found in the archives of places like Yale University). One of Accum's most popular products was a portable laboratory for farmers to use in analyzing soils and rocks.

Accum was appalled by the results of his personal investigations into the composition of food being sold to Londoners. He wrote articles and then a book describing in direct and simple terms what he found and why it was dangerous to consumers' health. He also described what his readers could do to detect adulterations and poisons in their foods. He specifically warned of candies colored with copper salts and vermillion, wines sweetened with lead or fishberries (a naturally occurring addictive intoxicant), and beers "aged" with vitriol or made to be addictive with opium. Accum chose for the cover of his book a design with twelve intertwined serpents forming the frame of a spider web bearing a large, ominous spider. The cover shows a skull and crossbones with a quote from scriptures: "There is death in the pot" (2 Kings, IV:40).

In each chapter of his book Accum describes a different adulteration. He also discharges his "painful duty" to expose the names of entrepreneurs he knew engaged in selling each type of dangerous food product. Accum makes clear his feelings about these entrepreneurial attempts to improve profits by deceiving customers with adulterated products: "The man who robs a fellow subject of a few shillings on the high-way, is sentenced to death; while he who distributes slow poison to a whole community, escapes punishment."

By the time his shocking and popular exposé was published, Accum had become a highly respected member of the scientific elite and a member of the prestigious Royal Institution. His investigations on the production of natural gas for odorless and smokeless lighting led to the creation of the world's first gas-fueled street lighting system. The first entrepreneurial gas company made Accum a director, appointing him to oversee the construction of the world's first gas production facility to assure Parliament that it was reasonable to give permission to operate it. Accum became widely known and respected when the gaslight system proved popular and profitable.

Accum's standing among the London elite did not protect him from being reviled by some in the entrepreneurial community for his exposé, which fabricated a subsequent scandal. Shortly after publication of *A Treatise on Adulterations of Food, and Culinary Poisons*, Accum was accused of ripping pages out of books in the Royal Institution's library. A high-profile investigation ensued, with dignitaries weighing in on both sides. Initially acquitted of the offense because it reflected a trivial amount of paper, a retrial was requested, and Accum, his publisher, and a friend were subsequently convicted of theft in the amount of 14 pence. His publisher and friend paid fines totaling 400 pounds, but Accum, dishonored, fled England and spent the rest of his life writing and teaching in Germany. His books nonetheless remained very popular in England and ultimately led other scientists to investigate food safety, which spurred Parliament to pass the the Adulteration of Food and Drink Act in 1860—forty years after his exposé.

United States lagged England in its concern for food adulteration. In the 1850s, death of children from drinking adulterated milk had become a chronic problem around New York and other cities. Milk in the United States was considered a healthy and energizing drink for both children and adults, which made it a large but competitive market for dairy entrepreneurs. The journalist John Mullaly wrote a popular book, *The Milk Trade in New York City and Vicinity*, which described the practices of milk producers wanting to deliver less and less expensive milk to rapidly growing urban centers. As always, entrepreneurs watched one another carefully and copied techniques that improved profits. Mullaly described how dairymen (and women) started by skimming off the cream and then diluting their milk by a third with lukewarm water. They then added plaster or chalk to make it whiter and a tiny measure of molasses to give the milk a golden quality. To mimic the cream that had been skimmed, liquified calf brain was often included. Finally, formaldehyde was added to keep the milk from spoiling.

The least expensive milk was produced in partnership with brewers or still owners. Cows were lined up to stand immobile in their own waste outside the brewery or distillery and fed the leftovers of the fermentation process, known as "swill." Swill was the lowest-cost source of feed that entrepreneurs could find. Swill produced a drink commonly marketed as "Pure Country Milk," but the milk had none of the expected nutritional value. Doctors openly complained that swill produced sickly children. In summer, when the quantity of formaldehyde was increased to keep milk from spoiling in the heat, children died in the hundreds and even thousands. Customers knew of the hazards, but tainted, adulterated, dangerous milk was the only product available to many low- and middle-income urban families, and many were fatalistic about consuming the product.

After a four-year battle in the city council, with fierce opposition from entrepreneurially oriented aldermen, New York City passed an ordinance in 1862 outlawing swill milk (but not the adulterations). Dairy entrepreneurs simply moved across the river to New Jersey. The first U.S. legislation regulating the purity and safety of food, the Pure Food and Drug Act, was not passed until 1906, after the publication of Upton Sinclair's *The Jungle* created a public outcry that finally forced politicians to ignore the opposition of the food and drink business lobbies.

Even when entrepreneurs knowingly cause harm to some, societies are reluctant to hold them accountable. Only when populations make rulers or officials fear for their right to rule are laws implemented regulating entrepreneurial behavior.

Not My Fault

It's impossible for entrepreneurs to control the evolution of the fruits of their success. The unintended social consequences of some entrepreneurial innovations can change the social fabric in ways that can never be mitigated.

Johannes Gutenberg was fired by his investor and forced out of the pioneering printing business he had created and founded. He never got to sell the bibles he is so famous for having printed; his investor did. Gutenberg was born around 1400. His father was a successful goldsmith who helped design and mint imperial currency. ("Goldsmith" was a generic term for artisans skilled in creating metal molds and forms in all different types of metals.) The family lived in Mainz in present-day central Germany, a town at the center of regional politics that nevertheless suffered bouts of the Black Death (bubonic plague). We know that Gutenberg had gained an understanding of metalworking by the time he decided to leave Mainz around the age of twenty-nine to strike out on his own. With a modest inheritance, he bought a house, hired a couple of servants, and started to tinker with projects of his own choosing.

In 1438, a business idea of Gutenberg's created enough excitement with three local entrepreneurs that they spent considerable time and effort convincing him to let them invest. Gutenberg had an idea about how to make tens of thousands of specialty souvenirs for pilgrims who were expected to show up the following year to see the fabulous holy relics collected by Charlemagne, which were kept in Aachen Cathedral. More than a hundred thousand pilgrims flocked to Aachen every seven years. The souvenir that pilgrims most coveted was a pendant with a convex mirror around three inches in diameter, which they believed would help capture the holy powers exuded by the relics. Pilgrims were willing to pay what would have then been a week's wages for one mirror. Gutenberg claimed he had a process for producing thousands of these convex mirrors, and his entrepreneurial buddies wanted to be part of what they believed would be a very profitable business.

A recurrence of the plague delayed the pilgrimage. Apparently, as part of their discussions on how to deal with the delay, the three investors learned that Gutenberg had been working on a "secret art" that they felt was an even more exciting investment. They convinced him to let them double their investment and shift all the money toward perfecting his secret art. One of the investors died, likely from the plague, shortly after increasing his investment, and his two brothers sued Gutenberg to let them in on the secret and to take over their brother's share of the business. The detailed court testimony is how we know so much about Gutenberg's secret art, which somehow involved "presses," "forms" that could be melted, and "screws" that kept forms in place. Whatever the nature of the secret art, it never materialized into a business that benefited the investors from Strasbourg.

Over the next dozen years Gutenberg meticulously perfected half a dozen technological innovations, each of which was a prerequisite for a new business: mass printing using reusable movable type. He developed new methods for making metal molds, new metal alloys, constant-pressure presses, no-bleed paper, no-bleed inks, and interlocking frames—all under a cloak of secrecy. Gutenberg started his new business in Mainz, having moved back into his parents' old home in 1448 after borrowing 150 gulden from a cousin for his startup. Excited at the prospects of his business, he then turned to a successful Mainz merchant and moneylender for an investment of 800 gulden, about a year's profit of a successful merchant of the day, in the form of a loan at 6 percent interest. With the investment he purchased a new press and other equipment, which he used as collateral for the loan. His investor, Johann Fust, was savvy and understood Gutenberg's business particularly well, since he himself sold block-printed books and his son-in-law, Peter Schöffer, was a professional manuscript copyist. Around the time of the investment Schöffer became Gutenberg's assistant.

The first complete book of twenty-eight pages utilizing Gutenberg's innovations was printed in 1450. The choice of the Latin schoolbook *Ars grammatica*, by Aelius Donatus, appears strategic, as the book was the standard for teaching people how to read the learned books of the day. Nonetheless, what appears to have turned into a mainstay of his business was printing papal indulgences, single sheets of paper printed in the thousands.

Gutenberg's printing business was initially successful enough that he sought and received another 800 gulden from Fust in 1452 to expand the business. Gutenberg thought big and used the new investment to build a bigger press, move into new facilities, and start a monumental project of designing and printing a glorious version of the Bible. All his remaining funds were spent making and casting hundreds of new pieces of type in a brand new typeface and buying supplies for the project. He purchased 250,000 sheets of paper (his Bible was 1,275 pages thick). He also bought 5,000 calfskins, which he planned to use to print a premium version on vellum that could be embellished in colors applied by hand to make it feel like the fabulous illuminated manuscripts many nobles and church officials coveted.

Gutenberg ran out of money before he sold any bibles. The other books that were being printed in his workshop were not profitable enough to finance the difference. Fust demanded his money back and took Gutenberg to court in 1455 to take over the business (made easier because his son-in-law knew the business intimately by then). Fust renamed the business Fust & Schöffer, which became renowned in Germany and France for its ecclesiastical books, profiting from what we now call Gutenberg's Bible.

The church, the most powerful force in people's lives in much of Europe at the time, embraced printing at first. Its wealth increased significantly because Gutenberg printed church indulgences in larger numbers than ever before. The archbishop of Mainz referred to printing as a "divine art." Other church officials, including initially the pope, embraced printing for disseminating church rules and proclamations without mistakes, faster, and more widely.

Printing, like all the other developments in history that turned into very profitable businesses, immediately attracted a swarm of entrepreneurs. The swarming effect was accelerated in the early 1460s by a battle over who would become the next archbishop of Mainz, which forced many of the city's citizens to flee. Dozens of people who had learned the business of printing from either Furst, Schöffer, or Gutenberg or any of their apprentices left Mainz to set up printing shops elsewhere in Germany and as far away as Italy. By 1495, printing had become established in every country in Europe and even Africa, with printers selling more than two million books a year. Knowledge had become rampant.

On All Hollows' Eve in October 1517, the monk Martin Luther, upset by all the indulgences being sold near his monastery in Wittenberg (around two hundred miles from Mainz), nailed a document containing his ninety-five theses to the door of the town's major church. Wittenberg was the site of an important university, which meant that several entrepreneurs had already established print shops there to supply books to professors and their students; one printer had even set up shop in the monastery where Luther lived. Martin Luther wrote his ninety-five theses in Latin by hand, but within sixty days (Luther later claimed fifteen) they had been put to press in both Latin and German and were available throughout Germany. They immediately became a best-seller, and printers throughout Europe started printing the theses in their own languages. A movement had started that the church could no longer control.

Gutenberg never envisioned the potential of his commercial innovation to disrupt the social fabric of Europe. He died in 1468, just as the concerns about the religious and social impact of printing were starting to be discussed. By 1470, Italian censors had taken control of the publication of books by Jews. In 1475, the pope, who had worried about the broad dissemination of knowledge fifty years before Luther, instructed the University of Cologne, near Mainz, to censor all German books and control their distribution. By 1500, many books had already been written about the problems caused by the availability of books—ironically enough, one printed book denounced printing for its adverse impact on book scribes. In 1515, the Ottoman Emperor Sultan Selim I made publishing books punishable by death. That same year Pope Leo X forbade printing any book without the church's approval—with little effect.

No entrepreneur in history has been able to accurately foretell the impact of their innovation. All the most impactful entrepreneurs in history have found success with their innovations through trial and error, almost never by theorizing or scholarship, which means that consequences are rarely considered. Drax did not consider the impact of his vastly expanded sugar production on obesity . . . or slavery and deforestation. Steve Jobs did not think about carpel tunnel syndrome or malware.

The headless, thoughtless entrepreneurial swarm determines which impediments to its overall profit and well-being—and not the public's—are eventually overcome, each thwarted impediment causing its own set of consequences, and those not always positive. Edward Bernays, whom we met in chapter 7, was rewarded handsomely for strategically breaking down the barriers to enabling women to smoke, and only decades later did he take responsibility for his actions after smoking had caused millions of additional cancer deaths. Bernays was very strategic, but even he could not foresee how his innovations, which he openly acknowledged as manipulative, would later be combined with television to persuade people to want cars that were bigger and therefore more polluting, or eventually to create addictive video games. Francis

Bacon already was worried about all these entrepreneurial consequences in 1609. Some entrepreneurs, however, are motivated to explicitly provoke societal condemnation to feel that they've become successful.

Entrepreneurial Shock Waves

Louis Réard was born in 1897, and even though he was trained as a mechanical engineer, he wound up managing his mother's lingerie shop near the Folies Bergères in Paris. Taking control of the shop in 1940, he aspired to a more exciting life and began designing women's swimsuits. On a vacation in the south of France, he noticed how women rolled up and rolled down their bathing suits to expose more of their skin to the sun. Provoked—or inspired—by that observation, Réard sought publicity for his first postwar line of swimwear by staging a "Most Beautiful Swimmer" contest at a popular public Parisian swimming pool in July 1946. To capture the attention of the public, including the newspapers he had invited to cover the event, he designed a two-piece bathing suit that was sure to shock. He called the suit the "bikini" to link it with Bikini Atoll, the site where the United States had conducted the first open-air test of an atomic bomb just five days before.

No professional fashion model would wear the swimsuit that today would be labeled as the scantier "string bikini." Réard had to hire a nineteen-year-old nude dancer from the Casino de Paris to model the design. His design crossed the line of modesty by exposing the navel in public. He proudly advertised that it was the skimpiest bathing suit ever created. The audience of mostly men went crazy, and of course his model won the contest.

9.3 Micheline Bernardini wearing Louis Réard's original bikini, July 1946.

Source: Getty Images.

Two newspapers showed photos (figure 9.3) of the winning model and outfit—but then silence. The fashion world and social elite were scandalized and would not publicly discuss the design. By 1948, the bikini had been officially banned on beaches in Italy and Spain. The following year French officials banned it from beaches on the Atlantic coast (but not on the Mediterranean!). The Vatican magazine wrote of its inappropriate design in 1949. Communist publications condemned it as "capitalist decadence." *Vogue*, the elitist fashion magazine, did not mention the word "bikini" until 1951, stating, "Novelty on the beach and in the sunshine! Beachwear goes decent! We are quite sure that our readers will have had nothing to do with the infamous bikini, which turned some of the coastal shorelines into vaudeville sideshows and music-hall scenarios."

To the horror of social elites, Louis Réard's swimsuit business appeared to have taken off. Nonetheless most, but not all, customers bought his more conservative designs. By the early 1950s, movie stars and aspiring actresses began donning bikinis in public and in their publicity photos. In 1956, Brigitte Bardot wore one in her movie *And God Created Woman*, giving women permission thereafter to expose their navels if they wanted.

Many entertainment entrepreneurs past and present have aspired to shock and poke at the fabric of society, particularly elitist society. In 1960, Alfred Hitchcock pushed his partially nude shower murder scene in *Psycho* to new limits of social acceptability to create a "sensational" movie. By 1966, entertainment entrepreneurs were generating publicity for their movies by experimenting with exposing even pubic hair to their mainstream moviegoing customers. Nudity in film and on TV no longer generates much controversy in the West, and the sight of scanty underwear in public no longer shocks—the morals of many having been changed by entrepreneurs.

But not all. Bikinis are still banned on the beaches of many majority Muslim countries. They continue to serve as a source of international debate on women's rights. Louis Réard, an entrepreneurial provocateur, was proud of having opened this Pandora's Box of discord. Society is almost powerless to stop entrepreneurial provocateurs, as scandal and sex have always drawn the interest of large crowds of potential customers. There likely have been entrepreneurs throughout time who tried to cultivate reputations as social provocateurs, but most have slid into obscurity; their provocations no longer shock.

Who Can You Trust?

An entrepreneur might aspire to tempt people with her crispy croissants to gladly make an extra stop in the parking lot in back of her bakery. Multiply that inducement over all the entrepreneurs with shops in a mall built by an entrepreneur and local traffic can be brought to a standstill. Nobody wants a traffic jam, but we get them because so many entrepreneurs have enticed us into our cars. We tend to accept adverse entrepreneurial consequences even when they affect our health, well-being, and social mores. They are more than we can keep track of, so we don't. We hardly notice any of them at all, at least not until they wind up killing children or cause our blue skies to darken.

All successful entrepreneurs intend to change society. And unless required to do so, they never ask permission. Nobody can sell a product or service without modifying the desires and actions of customers. Entrepreneurs offer products that make customers feel happy—at least momentarily—which entices them to change something about how they live their lives. The changes are usually small to ensure acceptance and avoid triggering annoyance, but hundreds or thousands of small changes induced by swarming entrepreneurs add up. If the allure of a product induces many people to change their lives, the accumulated changes can be monumental.

The consequences are often impossible to fix; only mitigation is possible and only in some cases. Because entrepreneurs are motivated by individual desires, they rarely think about the impact of their innovations beyond what attracts customers to their product or service. And even if they do realize the adverse consequences, they try to hide them. Franklin and Armfield tried to keep their cruelty a secret to be accepted in society. Réard at least was up front about wanting to push past social boundaries. But consequences of entrepreneurial actions are usually left to be dealt with by society as a whole, if or when the problem becomes acute enough. Rulers and governments then step in with rules and regulations for entrepreneurs and often even for the general public. The consequences of these government interventions are also not always what was intended or forecast. We'll next look at some of these interventions, dating from at least forty-five hundred years ago.

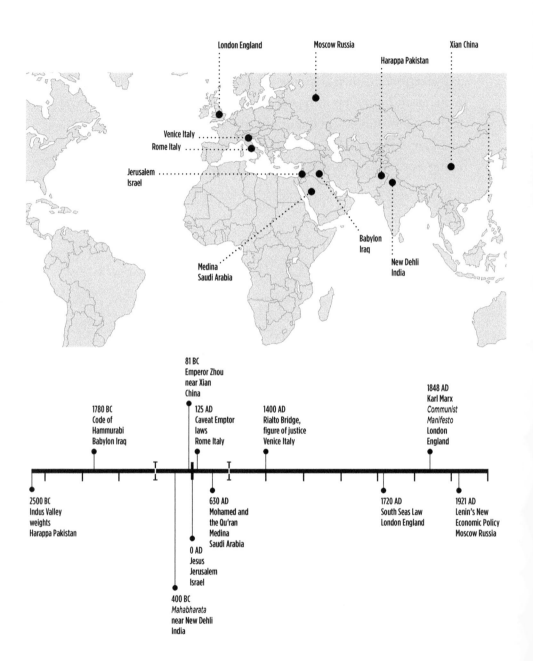

London England

Moscow Russia

Xian China

Harappa Pakistan

Venice Italy
Rome Italy

Jerusalem
Israel

Babylon
Iraq

New Dehli
India

Medina
Saudi Arabia

81 BC
Emperor Zhou
near Xian
China

1848 AD
Karl Marx
*Communist
Manifesto*
London
England

1780 BC
Code of
Hammurabi
Babylon Iraq

125 AD
Caveat Emptor
laws
Rome Italy

1400 AD
Rialto Bridge,
figure of justice
Venice Italy

2500 BC
Indus Valley
weights
Harappa Pakistan

630 AD
Mohamed and
the Qu'ran
Medina
Saudi Arabia

1720 AD
South Seas Law
London England

1921 AD
Lenin's New
Economic Policy
Moscow Russia

0 AD
Jesus
Jerusalem
Israel

400 BC
Mahabharata
near New Dehli
India

CHAPTER 10

Attempts at Control

To found a great empire for the sole purpose of raising up a people of customers, may at first sight appear a project fit only for a nation of shopkeepers. It is, however, a project altogether unfit for a nation of shopkeepers; but extremely fit for a nation whose government is influenced by shopkeepers.

—Adam Smith, *The Wealth of Nations*, 1776, IV:VII:III

The stock exchange is a poor substitute for the Holy Grail.

—Schumpeter, *Capitalism, Socialism, and Democracy*, 1942, 137

S overeigns fantasize that entrepreneurs should behave according to their wishes and expectations, rules, and laws. As we've seen, this is often not the case. The self-directed nature of entrepreneurs, the diversity of their motivations, and the skill sets they offer to others result in frequent misalignment of entrepreneurial actions with the desires and dictates of rulers and social leaders. But rulers and social leaders establish their own roles in how well or poorly entrepreneurs align with their wishes. A lack of understanding of entrepreneurship on the part of almost all rulers results in most government action being reactive and ineffective.

A Teenager's Understanding

In 81 BC, the thirteen-year-old Chinese Emperor Zhao (94–74 BC, ruled 87–74 BC), spurred on by an ambitious regent, invited sixty renowned learned and wise people to the royal palace to debate his famous imperial counselor on the role that entrepreneurs should play in Chinese society. In 87 BC, Zhao succeeded his famous and powerful father, Emperor Wu, when he was just eight. Wu passed over two of his older sons to declare his youngest to be his heir (the palace intrigue is fascinating but not pertinent to our story). Wu appointed his three most savvy political and military advisers as his young son's regents. For several years the regents fought all attempts to usurp the throne, and after one of the regents passed away, the other two jockeyed for position. Engulfed by intrigue, Emperor Zhao started asking his own questions and developed a reputation for being smart and shrewd; he had to develop quickly to survive. He also realized that he needed to chart a different course for his empire if he wanted to be perceived as a great emperor, which required addressing the economic concerns of the people and resolving debates among his counselors. Most puzzling and troubling to the teenager was that he was hearing two contradictory strains of advice from his advisers about how to rule the entrepreneurs in his empire. He had to decide for himself.

The genesis of the debate lies in the words and actions of some of the most important people in Chinese history. On the one side we have Confucius, long dead at that time but fervently studied and quoted by the Chinese elite. He described the rationale, relationships, and fundamental ordering by which all societies could thrive. Confucius, as we learned in chapter 1, knew and respected some but not all entrepreneurs. He entreated entrepreneurs to be respectful of the natural order of things, something he prescribed as "rightness":

"The gentleman understands rightness, whereas the petty person understands profit" (Analects 4, 16).

On the other side was Zhao's father, Emperor Wu (157–87 BC, ruled 141–87 BC), the emperor warrior who doubled the size of his empire and established underlying political structures for ruling vast territories, which included meritocratic selection of government officials. (He also ordered the castration of Sima Qian because the man dared to disagree with him.) He issued an empire-wide standard currency and brought large segments of the economy under the control of the government. Wu's most economically potent programs were instituted by his assistant agriculture minister, Shang Hongyang (152–80 BC), who was known for quantitative brilliance. Shang led the nationalization of the salt, iron, and liquor industries by shrewdly inviting a successful salt and iron merchant to lead new agencies that would control their respective monopolies. Shang's agencies reaped enormous profits (recall from chapter 2 all the fabulously wealthy Chinese iron entrepreneurs listed in the *Chronicles of the Grand Historian*). The profits Shang captured for the emperor provided over half of the state's revenue and enabled Wu to maintain his large armies. Wu promoted Shang to the high position of imperial counselor.

Shang's economic policies were not popular except with Emperor Wu. The populace complained of the high price of salt and the inferiority of the iron tools they bought. Many lower- and mid-level government administrators also did not like Shang's policies. Wu required that civil servants be chosen based on their intellect, as demonstrated through their analysis of ancient Chinese texts, many based on Confucian ideas and ideals. Confucians revered the ideals of harmony and ritual and believed that government should not directly interfere in the daily lives of citizens. A state that monopolized important industries and commercially profited at the expense of the citizenry was anathema to their philosophies. Emperor Wu, confident in his control of the country, generally ignored all complaints. The thirteen-year-old Emperor Zhao wanted the issue resolved and called for Shang Hongyang to debate sixty scholars on whether his economic policies would benefit the populace going forward.

The debate focused on how idealistic or pragmatic a state should be in governing its citizens, specifically its entrepreneurs, who generated a large proportion of the value created in the empire. Both sides agreed on the need for a central government and taxes. Both sides also espoused disdain for merchants who amassed great wealth by profiting off of the meager earnings of commoners. But they disagreed on how value should be extracted from the wealthy artisans and merchants.

Shang and his assistants argued that the state must be pragmatic and utilize all its resources as necessary. This included usurping the profits of its merchants and artisans as needed to defend itself and to redistribute wealth to ensure that citizens receive a form of economic justice. Shang described how citizens often suffered excessively from economic shocks created by natural disasters that were amplified by price swings caused by hoarding merchants. Government should aggressively intervene to stabilize prices by maintaining inventories of grain to be sold when supply was tight. Shang also related how the salt and iron profits enabled individual taxes to remain low.

Two of the wise and learned men took turns refuting Shang and his assistants. They believed that the emperor should act only to institute the balance and harmony of nature. It was natural for farmers to provide sustenance, artisans to make useful objects, and merchants to balance supply with demand. They described farmers, artisans, and merchants as idealized citizens who, if left alone, naturally created balance by focusing on self-sufficiency.

They invoked the model of the fabled Duke of Zhou as immortalized by Confucius, who claimed that his right to rule came directly from Heaven. According to Confucius, the duke had focused his efforts on maintaining harmony on Earth consistent with Heaven, becoming a model of ritual and respect. His heavenly inspired behaviors motivated his subjects to be respectful and work together as families to be self-sufficient.

The Confucian fundamentalists felt that reducing government consumption would establish a model for the general decrease in consumption that would naturally reduce the wealth of merchants. The ministerial pragmatists did not place much faith in the empire's becoming an idealized state. They felt they should not be impeded in accumulating wealth for the state, even if that required controlling the largest sources of wealth creation as well as the interregional movement of goods.

The debate, as recorded in *Discourse on Salt and Iron*, appears to be a fair representation of the discussion, which remained dignified throughout. After deliberating, the young emperor and his regent made a few changes to Shang Hongsang's policies. The liquor monopoly was abolished (nobody seemed to feel it was working effectively anyway), but the salt and iron monopolies were maintained. Ultimately, the young emperor and his regent felt the revenues generated by the monopolies were too important to the economic might of the state. The validity of the state should not be jeopardized by letting the populace be freely self-directed in their creation of value.

Within a year Shang was executed for supporting a plot to overthrow the emperor. After all, he was not popular. Nonetheless, his salt and iron monopolies, and many of his pragmatist ideals, remained in place for another two centuries, waning only when rulers were too weak to enforce them. The monopolies reemerged in the successful Tang and Song dynasties and again during Mao Zedong's leadership, as those rulers were willing to challenge the power of their self-directed entrepreneurs.

The positions in the debate on whether governments should control entrepreneurs have remained unchanged in the intervening two millennia. They are independent of time and place. They revolve around how much power and wealth rulers should let entrepreneurs create and keep for themselves. Should entrepreneurs be taxed like everyone else or under special circumstances, and should the most successful entrepreneurs be taxed even more or even have their enterprises taken away, to be used by the state for its own best interest and the best interests of the populace? Although the idealized behaviors associated with Chinese heavenly balance, or the Western equivalent of Adam Smith's "invisible hand," exist only in theory and not in practice, they remain part of the debate as justification for minimal regulation and taxation. Ultimately, the revenue-generating potential of successful entrepreneurs is too tempting a source for governments to ignore. In most countries today the debate narrows down to incremental changes in tax rates.

Nineteenth- and twentieth-century debates and experiments around communism focused on the control of capital, which has to do with investors—that is, capitalists—rather than with control of all entrepreneurs. We'll shortly explore how Marx's theories manifested themselves in experiments on state control of entrepreneurs. Emperor Zhao's desire to understand the purpose of state control over entrepreneurial endeavors was perhaps the last time the debate has been so carefully considered by the leadership of a nation.

Setting Expectations

From the fabled city of Babylon, Hammurabi (ruled 1795–50 BC) controlled an extensive territory with a significant population. Around 1780 BC, he issued a set of legal directives to help the kingdom's widely dispersed judges and administrators rule in a more consistent fashion. He had the directives carved on stone monu-ments that he situated around the major population centers of his kingdom. About a quarter of the 283 explicit legal directives that are still legible today on the monument in the Louvre (figure 10.1) specify how to properly exchange property or services for the equivalent of money in those days, or how to award recompense

10.1 The stele of the Code of Hammurabi.

Source: Wikipedia, https://en.wikipedia.org/wiki/Code_of_Hammurabi#/media
/File:P1050763_Louvre_code_Hammurabi_face_rwk.JPG.

and dispense justice for faulty products and services. Improperly constructed buildings seem to have been an important enough issue that five directives stipulate punishments and fines when a portion of a building collapses and destroys goods or injures people. The penalties were tough: if part of the building collapsed and killed a citizen, the builder should be put to death. Fourteen directives regulated loans and the repayment of debts. Shipbuilding, tavern-owning (which we've already learned is described using feminine pronouns), and the contracting out of land to tenant farmers are all covered by multiple rules.

We know from documents from the same period that specific courts were set up to rule on disputes between entrepreneurs and between partners in ventures. The city-state ruler or local temple administrator often appointed an experienced merchant to act on their behalf on more mundane and common disputes as well as to ensure that merchants treated one another and their customers fairly.

Hammurabi's laws were not the first; they are just the most complete set that have been discovered. (Carving them in stone as opposed to on clay tablets helped their preservation.) Evidence points to rulers having designated officials to watch over markets and entrepreneurs even before writing was standardized. As we saw in chapter 1, entrepreneurs from the ancient Indus Valley civilization (2500–1900 BC) were technically sophisticated, with particular expertise in producing colorful and beautiful jewelry. The civilization used similar technology and methods to produce the most elegant, beautiful, and finely crafted weights and measures (figure 10.2).

Standard weights throughout the Indus Valley were made from chert, a hard rock formed from microscopic quartz crystals. Chert modules were chipped and polished into cubes whose weights were based on the repeated halving or doubling of the civilization's

10.2 Standardized weights from the Indus Valley city of Harappa, ca. 2500 BC.

(*Source*: Copyright J. M. Kenoyer/Harappa.com/Courtesy Dept. of Archaeology
and Museums, Govt. of Pakistan, https://www.harappa.com/slide/weights-harappa.

fundamental unit of weight, around 13.7 grams, or about half an ounce. The thousands of weights that have been recovered and measured to date were produced, over centuries and in different distant cities, with an impressive reproducible accuracy of +/– 2 percent. This level of repeatability and accuracy leads archeologists and anthropologists to believe that the weights were produced not by self-directed entrepreneurs but by some self-perpetuating standard-setting group.

The wealth and well-being of the Indus Valley civilization relied heavily on commodities that needed to be weighed to be valued, from basic foodstuffs to exotic and valuable minerals like lapis lazuli. Entrepreneurs were not to be trusted to measure on their own. Traders, merchants, and artisans all utilized these standard weights, almost certainly used with a simple balance scale, to settle their exchanges. In some markets the quality of the product and produce also were likely monitored.

In ancient China, urban markets were surrounded by walls and had few entrances. A civil servant monitored the hustle and bustle of the market from a watchtower. All transactions outside the confined space of the market had to be in writing, which created widespread literacy in contractual language even among commoners who could not read or write contracts themselves. Scribes could be found in all towns and cities to draft contracts that were dictated by illiterate sellers, buyers, and witnesses.

Even with standardized weights and measures, customer and entrepreneur disagreements remained common, and almost all successful governments and rulers have felt forced into playing the role of adjudicator. But all try to minimize their involvement and adjudicate at a distance and only under prescribed conditions.

Caveat Emptor

Ancient Rome evolved laws to govern the responsibilities of entrepreneurs in being forthright in selling goods and services. Rome's rules have formed a basis of Western jurisprudence that fall under the broad heading of *caveat emptor*, buyer beware. In the early Republic period, the government intervened on behalf of a buyer only if they had a written contract the seller did not comply with. This was also the basis for many of Hammurabi's rules and was similar to what was practiced in China. But a larger fraction of Roman commerce was controlled by self-directed entrepreneurs than was the case in China, where the contemporaneous Emperor Wu controlled critical industries and infrastructure. Furthermore, with time more and more Roman entrepreneur-to-entrepreneur transactions were made at a distance with intermediaries, resulting in buyers not being able to know the condition of the goods they would receive when they entered into written agreements.

By the time of Hadrian (ruled 117–138 AD), the *curule aediles*, appointed for a year's time to supervise specific markets or supply chains and rectify any problems, had begun to accept arguments that sellers were obliged to tell buyers of defects in their products (the most important of which were slaves) and that customers could return a product for up to a year when a defect appeared that had been present before the transaction but unnoticed by the buyer. By the time of Justinian's Digest, which listed in writing all the laws of the empire (533 AD), even defects unknown to the seller were grounds for returning goods, whether or not that provision was noted in the written contract. This was the genesis of the implied warranty that is implicit in the "good faith" that is assumed in most commercial law today.

Most visitors crossing the famous Rialto Bridge in Venice today do not notice the statue that overlooks the bridge and its entrance plaza (figure 10.3). Five hundred years ago, the case was very different. The statue, depicting the figure of Justice with scales, was erected to serve as a warning to sixteenth-century Venetian entrepreneurs that their honesty and fairness were being constantly

10.3 Figure of Justice overlooking the Rialto Bridge, Venice, Italy.

Source: Evelyn S. Welch, *Shopping in the Renaissance: Consumer Cultures in Italy 1400–1600* (New Haven, CT: Yale University Press, 2005), fig. 77; photo by the author.

monitored and tested. In the Middle Ages statues and plaques depicting the scales of justice were common in European markets, signifying that market transactions were being monitored under conditions that were similar to those in Imperial Rome.

Governments only reluctantly feel compelled to intervene to ensure that entrepreneurs do not take advantage of their customers. In the discussion of the previous chapter on how entrepreneurs adulterated mass-produced food and milk, we saw that governments did not intervene until the populace threatened to throw them out of power. I speculate that virtually all the rules and laws concerning commerce were the result of common entrepreneurial malfeasances that caused sufficient outrage that the ruler or government of the time had to intervene.

Rulers appear to want to ignore the transgressions of their entrepreneurs, at least until they cause unrest from making large numbers of customers feel they've been treated unfairly. But entrepreneurial injustices accumulate with time, leaving thousands of rules and laws in effect. All the legal systems of the world—independent of the political "ism" to which they are associated—invest significant resources in adjudicating actions by or initially inspired by entrepreneurs. Entrepreneurs play a disproportionate role in inspiring laws that regulate exchange, faulty workmanship, or the consequences of their innovations. And once a rule or regulation is enacted, subsequent rulers rarely get rid of it—so regulations grow with time.

Caveat Shareholder

As already discussed, financing startups by selling shares to strangers was commonplace in England after 1690. In the first months of 1720, more than one hundred new companies per month advertised their shares for sale. By spring, startups were attempting to raise over 1.5 million pounds, an astronomical amount for the age.

This frenzy alarmed businessmen who ran an established English company known as the South Seas Company, which had a royal charter and a not very profitable monopoly on delivering slaves to Spain's American colonies. The company was about to receive a contract that would allow new investors to buy shares in the company using discounted government debt at face value, full price—a major inducement partly inspired by John Law's actions selling Mississippi Company shares in France. For Parliament, the interest on England's debt was a big concern, and although the South Seas Company's offer to consolidate the government's debt under more favorable terms and a lower interest rate was enticing, many members still baulked at the potential risks. When the company gave its "friends" (their term, not mine) in Parliament and government generous grants of discounted shares, the deal became too good to pass up.

South Seas management became concerned that the hundred startup "bubbles" trying to sell shares in Exchange Alley would siphon investment away from the company's shares, lessening the stock's price momentum, which had developed when its deal with Parliament had been announced. The strategy was to compel the company's "friends" in Parliament to outlaw all new joint-stock startups to protect investors. A committee in Parliament had recently concluded an investigation into recent egregious bubble scams. With the committee composed of many South Seas shareholders, it explicitly did not look into the validity of South Seas' recent stock offerings. The committee's findings were used to justify a bill with the title *An Act for better securing certain Powers and Privileges, intended to be granted by His Majesty by Two Charters, for Assurance of Ships and Merchandize at Sea, and for lending Money upon Bottomry; and for restraining several extravagant and unwarrantable Practices therein mentioned.* (The nickname "The Bubble Act" did not take hold for another hundred years.) The bill outlawed all joint-stock companies not authorized by Parliament while granting last-moment incorporations to two marine insurance companies started by friends of the king. The bill passed within days. The seriousness of the bill could be found in the penalties for issuing shares in unauthorized joint-stock companies; they were expressly unlimited in either fines or imprisonment.

The legislation worked . . . for a few weeks. Exchange Alley emptied except for the few jobbers that specialized in trading South Seas Company shares, which continued its climb. It also used provisions of the bill to prevent established companies from selling any new shares. The shares of all established companies—including even the East Indies Company and the Bank of England—dropped precipitously. These stock drops induced some South Seas shareholders to want to sell and take the profit on their shares. Soon most shareholders were selling their shares for any price that was offered; within weeks South Sea shares dropped from 700 to 120. An ensuing investigation uncovered the complicity and corruptness of the Parliamentary deliberations and of many high-ranking government officials, including the Prince of Wales and the king's favorite mistress.

The Bubble Act and the South Seas bubble are broadly misconstrued today. First, the word "bubble" means two different things in these two monikers. The Bubble Act forbade further bubbles, meaning startups that raise money by selling stock. The term "South Seas Bubble" describes the 1720 stock market collapse; it came into use much later, after the public came to employ the word "bubble" to mean the rapid rise and fall in asset prices, which is how we use it today. Second, many people think that what we now call the Bubble Act was passed as a reaction to the collapse in South Seas stock when it actually was passed to help maintain momentum in the rise of the stock price. Third, the South Seas Company was not a startup, and its stock bust was not specifically the result of entrepreneurial exuberance or fraud. Rather, it was the result of managers ignoring their company's rules for governing. South Seas managers had tried to use their established company to increase their personal status and wealth using bribery and fraud, using entrepreneurs as their diversion (some of whom were independently using fraudulent tactics to sell shares).

This episode bears on the story of entrepreneurship because it demonstrates how entrepreneurs and their startups are often viewed as fodder to support the personal desires of rulers, civil servants, and elected officials. Even with rapidly increasing investor and consumer interest, in 1720, there was still little Parliamentary interest in understanding the emerging phenomenon of raising money for new companies by selling shares to the public. No joint-stock companies were authorized in Britain for the next 105 years, and they remained in disfavor and difficult to form for 42 years after that. Consequently, the successful enterprises of the Industrial Revolution, such as created by Matthew Bolton (chapter 6) or Josiah Wedgwood (chapter 7), were based on traditional forms of partnership.

Entrepreneurs' offerings of stock in their companies did not come under scrutiny until the late 1800s. In the United States individual states hold the jurisdiction for registering incorporations and deciding on what information is required to legitimize the creation of a company. Pressed by voters who had been misled into investing in new stock offerings, states began to pass "blue sky" laws in the early 1900s to prevent unscrupulous entrepreneurs from raising money for "fly-by-night concerns, visionary oil wells, distant gold mines and other like fraudulent exploitations." These laws also required stockbrokers and brokerage firms to register. These laws were largely ignored. The then newly conceived Investment Bankers Association even instructed its members in 1915 to get around the laws by selling any new issue of shares in more than two states. The U.S. government did not institute national legislation to protect shareholders until 1933, after the 1929 Wall Street crash and the Hoover administration had been voted out of office. Again, only popular outrage stimulated legislation to regulate the sale of shares in startups.

Edicts and legislation aimed at entrepreneurs are rarely deliberated with the care exercised by the thirteen-year-old Emperor Zhao. Short of making sure they're not being personally cheated, self-interested rulers and legislators have rarely enacted effective rules, laws, regulations, or even guidelines for helping entrepreneurs innovate in the best interests of the state.

Heaven's Say

Religions are an independent cultural force in society's attempts to control entrepreneurs. Religions use connection with otherworldly forces to deliver definitions and examples of good and evil. Almost all religions explicitly or implicitly attempt to both encourage and constrain the actions of their entrepreneurially motivated followers. In many cases religions use stories with good and evil entrepreneurial role models to motivate the thoughts and actions of their followers in their finite and constrained worldly existence. Of course, the general influence of any religion on the behavior of entrepreneurs depends on the specific religious interpretations of a region's ruler as well as the interpretations of the religious leaders he or she relies on, if any.

Hinduism is the world's third-largest religion and perhaps has the most ancient roots. Over the millennia it has fragmented into many forms. Entrepreneurs seeking profit, wealth, and status nonetheless have played critical roles in formulating Hindu ethics since the formation of fundamental epic stories such as the *Mahabharata*. An important thread in the story involves the creation and destruction of both individual and societal value through self-directed action, some of which is entrepreneurial in nature.

Hindu epics together teach how four aspects of human behavior proscribe the future. *Dharma* has no direct translation into any Western language and has different meanings in the various religions of present-day India. Most people in the West associate the word with its Buddhist, not its Hindu meaning. In classic Hindu texts it roughly translates into "the ways of moral living," which include devotion to ritual, adherence to societal laws and expectations, individual righteousness, and duties to others. Dharma tends to be interpreted in one of these more specific senses depending on where and how it is used in a sentence. *Artha* also does not directly translate but is generally associated with actions to create value, wealth, or profit. Hindu entrepreneurs follow artha. *Kama* is the pursuit of pleasure and happiness, explicitly including sexual pleasure. *Moshka* is the bliss attained by renouncing earthly constraints.

Hinduism pays great attention to how an individual's actions affect their future and the future of the universe. The religion stresses the importance of creating balance between dharma, artha, kama, and moksha. In the *Mahabharata*, Balarama, the god of strength and one of the avatars for the omnipotent god Vishnu, describes why a greedy king has been allowed by the gods to die, admonishing the survivors of a vengeful battle: "Dharma is properly practiced by the virtuous, but two things cause it to fail: the pursuit of wealth [artha] by those who desire it too strongly and the pursuit of pleasure [kama] by those that are addicted to it. The person who pursues dharma, wealth, and pleasure, all three, without suppressing two of them, whether dharma and wealth, or dharma and pleasure, or pleasure and wealth, he is the one that finds greatest happiness" (book 9.60).

This balance is achieved differently depending on one's role in the pursuit of worldly prosperity. *Vaishya* is the Hindu term for those who pursue wealth for the community and is close in meaning to entrepreneurship in both its social and commercial contexts. Following the words of Balarama, entrepreneurs should pursue wealth and profit but do so morally and without creating an imbalance of pleasure.

We've already encountered Confucius in this chapter. He is not technically a religious leader but an interpreter of Heavenly affect and effect nonetheless. His teachings focus on rightness and leading a life on Earth that mirrors life in Heaven. His descriptions of rightness have distinct similarities with descriptions of dharma. Confucius agreed that morals and ritual should take priority over profits.

A similar path to entrepreneurial enlightenment is prescribed by Mohamed in the Qu'ran. Unique among the founders of major religions, Mohamed was a first-generation trader himself and married a very successful caravan owner, who helped him learn to trade. By the time God dictated the Qu'ran to Mohamed, he was astute and experienced in the pursuit of profit. But profit never was his primary motivation, and the Qu'ran asks that devotion always precede entrepreneurial endeavors: "When the prayers are ended, disperse and go in quest of Allah's bounty and remember Allah much so that you may prosper" (62:10). Islam and the Qu'ran are explicit in forbidding usury, which is usually interpreted as forbidding the charging of interest on loans: "O believers, fear you God; and give up the usury that is outstanding, if you are believers" (2:275). This admonition appears in various forms in twelve different verses.

Judeo-Christian religions vary in their interpretation of the relevance of biblical stories on the virtues of entrepreneurship. In Genesis, God appears to encourage innovation by allowing humans to name plants and animals. God nonetheless also destroys most of humanity twice—once with a flood and later with the destruction of Sodom and Gomorrah—because of the selfish and hedonistic nature of emergent culture, two characteristics closely associated with entrepreneurial action. Even God's wrath does not eliminate problematic entrepreneurial behavior, as we saw in previous chapters.

The Old Testament goes on to admonish entrepreneurs for their loans and credit collection techniques and for making too much noise, among other transgressions. The New Testament goes further in proscribing some entrepreneurial actions. This oft-quoted verse can be interpreted as describing the incompatibility of religious virtue with commerce and entrepreneurship: "And they come to Jerusalem: and Jesus went into the temple, and began to cast out them that sold and bought in the temple" (Matthew 21:12, and a similar verse appears is Mark 11:15).

In practice, religious teachings and edicts control the behavior of relatively few entrepreneurs. The implicit nature of the proscriptions of certain entrepreneurial behaviors, in stories or parables, enables entrepreneurs to innovate and work according to their personal interpretations.

In countries such as Iran and Saudi Arabia, where rulers explicitly rely on sharia law derived directly from Qu'ranic teaching, religious teachings have effectively influenced the behavior of their entrepreneurs. (The reliance of the leadership of Laos on a radical sect of Buddhism is another rare example.) How Islamic laws have affected entrepreneurial behavior is beyond the scope of this book (I give a good reference for further investigation in the bibliographic notes), but they helped shape the dominating role that Muslim entrepreneurs played in creating trading empires that spanned from West Africa to what is now Indonesia and China from the ninth through fifteenth centuries. Sharia law has appeared in different varieties and with different interpretations over the past thirteen centuries. At several times and in several places it has created uncertainty as to whether entrepreneurial innovation was legally acceptable. This was particularly true with sharia interpretations of *bid'a*, harmful innovations that are incompatible with Islam. Some Islamic religious leaders and jurists have labeled any activities, products, and services that were not established when Mohamed was alive as forbidden. Innovative entrepreneurial activity is minimal in areas where these extreme religious views are held and supported by local and regional leaders.

Eliminate Them All

Karl Marx (1818–83) developed a socioeconomic theory in which entrepreneurs were no longer needed. He developed this theory in spite of being an entrepreneur in its truest sense. He founded one newspaper, *The New Rhineland News*, and failed at finding investors for two others. He received varying amounts of money for the dozens of articles he wrote as a freelancer. Hoping to make money on a book rejected by publishers, he self-published *The Poverty of Philosophy*. It did not make him any money.

Marx was completely self-directed in his actions; he supported himself and his family based on his skill as a writer and his unique knowledge and scholarship about the history and dynamics related to socioeconomic classes within different economic systems. What value he received for his work was always a product of double opt-in exchange. Entrepreneurship was frustrating for Marx, but, like many other entrepreneurs throughout time, he didn't feel comfortable working for others.

Marx didn't covet the money; he coveted influencing thousands of people by what he wrote—that was the entrepreneurial value he wanted in return for investigating and writing about how the proletariat was subjugated by the bourgeoisie. Marx was no different from most entrepreneurs in history, in that he prioritized other forms of value that he wanted to receive from customers over money. The money he received barely kept his family housed and fed.

Marx would rather have been an academic. He grew up with a comfortable middle-class upbringing in a small Prussian town. He studied law to please his father but spent more time drinking and hanging out with philosophy professors and students. Although his friends found him jovial, he had stubbornness and confrontational streaks that made him difficult to work with. Sarcasm pervaded much of what he wrote about people and the description of things he did not like. He sabotaged his own academic career when he wrote, against the advice of his professor, about his atheistic beliefs in the thesis that he needed to apply for an open professorship of Protestant theology.

Without academic prospects, Marx turned to journalism, but he aspired to run his own show and be able to write and commission articles that changed the way people thought. He leveraged his knowledge of law and philosophy with his experience in academic argumentation to write very controversial articles and essays. His interest in the economics of social structures was partly sparked by articles he wrote as the editor of a small political newspaper, the *Rhineland News*, about struggling entrepreneurs. Poverty was growing among the winegrowers in the Moselle Valley, and Marx was drawn to the story because his father, a liberal lawyer, had had a small vineyard there as a side business when he was alive. Marx investigated the situation.

In 1842, always the confrontationist, Marx wrote two articles in what he expected to be a series of five. The all-German tariff union of 1834 eliminated the duties that protected Moselle winegrowers from less expensive wines of southern Germany, which caused their prices and profits to fall precipitously. Marx noted that the locals were impoverished, yet the Prussian government lauded its creation of a less expensive and more competitive wine industry. He assailed the government for assuming it always represented the common good and for assuming that its critics were wrong and it was always right. In the second article of the series, he self-righteously offered a solution to the problem of governmental self-righteousness: a free press populated with people like himself, who could act as honest brokers between bureaucracy and special interests. Prussian censors did not allow the series to continue, and soon the newspaper was forced to stop publishing. Marx then made it his mission to bring down regimes and the social classes that impoverished their own people.

At the time, communism and socialism were synonyms and a well-established concept. Marx began to embrace the tenets of shared property after leaving Prussia to write without censorship in Paris. His academic training drove him to figure out how communism could prevail over capitalism. The narrative he described, a revolutionary form of socialism that would inevitably destroy capitalistic systems, proved both exciting and believable to the growing numbers of communists and socialists in mid-nineteenth-century Europe. The fact that Marx claimed his theories were developed based on scientific analysis of history made them all the more palatable. Marx competed with many other socialists to be the philosophical leader of European communists; his particular theories had visceral appeal that other formulations did not. Who isn't excited to learn that they will be on the winning side of history?

Even in his three-volume *Das Capital*, finished after he died and published by Fredrich Engels, Marx's analysis of history is very broad-brush. It is his 1848 *Communist Manifesto* that people actually read, believe, and quote. In the *Manifesto* Marx ties all entrepreneurs to the bourgeoisie, the social class of people who own property and businesses. In turn, he ties the bourgeoisie to both the triumphs and pitfalls of industrial capitalism.

> Society as a whole is more and more splitting up into two great hostile camps, into two great classes, directly facing one another: Bourgeoisie and Proletariat. . . .
>
> Modern industry has established the world-market. . . . This market has given an immense development to commerce, to navigation, to communication by land. This development has, in its time, reacted on the extension of industry; and in proportion as industry, commerce, navigation, railways extended, in the same proportion the bourgeoisie developed, increased its capital, and pushed into the background every class handed down from the Middle Ages. . . .
>
> The executive of the modern state is but a committee for managing the common affairs of the whole bourgeoisie. . . .
>
> What the bourgeoisie, therefore, produces, above all, is its own grave-diggers. Its fall and the victory of the proletariat are equally inevitable.

Marx's work was important in identifying communism as the natural endpoint to capitalist systems. He asserted that capitalist systems continually descend into crisis because of the greed and competitiveness of the bourgeoisie. He described how competition among business owners drives down prices to the point that profits disappear, with commensurate drops in salary and wages, to the point that the proletariat—the social class that works for wages— become impoverished. The lack of profit coupled with widespread poverty creates repeating crises in capitalistic systems that eventually result in worker rebellion and the assumption of communistic economic systems.

Even though Marx was himself an entrepreneur, he never mentions them in his *Manifesto* and only uses the word in *Das Capital* when quoting and belittling bourgeoise economists. Entrepreneurs are nothing special to Marx. He lumps them with elites living off inherited wealth, multigenerational self-supporting traditionalist farmers and artisans, as well as the professional managers who had started appearing and were running large railroads and trading companies.

What is important to how governments have attempted to control entrepreneurs is that Marx's broad formulation of revolutionary socialism appealed to Lenin. Besides historic inevitability, the fact that Marx never exactly described how communism would work postcapitalism was also a benefit to Lenin, who wanted to decide how communism would work. He initially followed the teaching of Marx in lumping all entrepreneurs in with the bourgeoisie; at first Lenin agreed they would need to be eliminated. Then he decided it was a mistake.

We Need Them After All

As with almost all rulers who preceded him, Lenin found he could not control the Russian economy without entrepreneurs, what he called "the new bourgeoisie." Soviet entrepreneurs were also referred to as "Nepmen" after Lenin renewed the legality of personal property and profit-seeking as part of the New Economic Policy (NEP) of 1921. Since all private property had been banned after Lenin led the formation of the Soviet Union in 1918, it meant any new private business that began operating legitimately would have to be led by an entrepreneur. The other forms of profit-making relying on legacy assets and wealth or from running large corporations owned by stranger-shareholders still could not exist.

Between 1918 and 1921, Lenin focused on consolidating power and defeating anticommunist insurgents and competing social revolutionaries. As he refocused on the devastated Russian economy he found that much of what still worked hinged on entrepreneurs. He realized that local worker committees did not have the experience or skills to manage commerce. He concluded that he could not revive growth in the Soviet Union without new bourgeoisie. He told a meeting of Moscow party officials, "Wherever there is small-scale production and free exchange, capitalism will appear. But need we fear this capitalism if we control the factories, transportation systems, and foreign trade? . . . I think it is incontrovertible that we need have no fear of this capitalism."

Lenin's NEP was controversial among party members who feared the return of capitalism by allowing entrepreneurs to operate freely in many segments of the economy, including small- and medium-scale manufacturing. NEP rules and regulations were therefore inconsistently applied. The insistence of most farmers to sell their grain to independent merchants and buy their goods from independent stores prevented petty officials from eliminating entrepreneurship from their jurisdictions (as had been demonstrated consistently dating back at least four thousand years).

With entrepreneurs allowed to operate freely—at least in agricultural, commercial, and smaller-scale industrial businesses—the economy quickly rebounded. NEP continued as state policy until Stalin consolidated power five years after Lenin's death. In 1929, Stalin refocused the Soviet economy on central planning and large-scale agriculture collectives and industrial production; there would be no need for Nepmen. Entrepreneurship was again outlawed. As always, it didn't disappear, with estimates that upward of a quarter of the Soviet economy resided in unofficial black-market transactions until the Soviet Union collapsed in 1991.

In 1978, under the leadership of Deng Xiaoping, China abandoned Stalinist central planning and adopted policies that invited entrepreneurs to help grow its service and retail sectors, while inviting successful established foreign companies to form joint ventures to help its industries grow. Deng acknowledged that "perhaps the most correct model of socialism was the New Economic Policy of the USSR." Of course, from a historical perspective, Deng was also following in the footsteps of the thirteen-year-old Emperor Zhao in deciding which industries would serve the interest of the state and which would remain to be developed by entrepreneurs.

Improving the Imperfect

Rulers have an almost perfect record of not being able to control their entrepreneurial swarms, even when they belatedly implement rules and regulations to prevent behaviors that their publics find unfair or distasteful. Entrepreneurial swarms are chaotic, unpredictable forms that contain scores of individuals, each with their own set of motivations, values, and social attachments, each self-directed in their response to demand that they find for their product or service. Some entrepreneurs in a swarm, particularly larger and more frenzied ones, will therefore act in ways many would consider unscrupulous, if not strictly illegal. Rulers and governments, for their own self-interested reasons, ignore these behaviors until the frustration of customers causes them to fear for their legitimacy, then only begrudgingly implementing rules that some still do not follow.

The ineffectiveness of rules aimed at entrepreneurs has three components. First, rarely do rulers or responsible government officials take the time to understand the motivations that drive individuals leading entrepreneurial swarms. Only by understanding the span of self-serving motivations within swarms can regulators accurately understand where and how entrepreneurial actions are misaligned with civic objectives. Second, rulers and government officials are unable to act completely dispassionately, in the best interest of their subjects, because they can directly benefit by inserting themselves or the institutions they control into the swarm. Third, rarely do the powers that be invite entrepreneurs to suggest how best to control their fellow entrepreneurs. As we saw in chapter 5, entrepreneurs are often extremely effective in controlling their competitors.

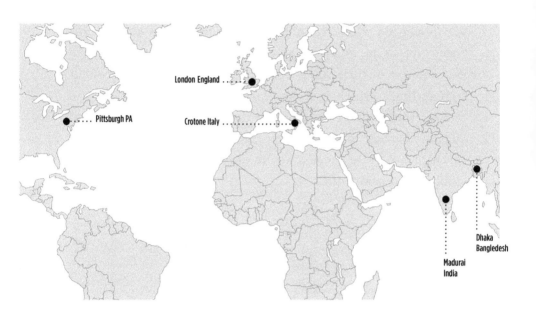

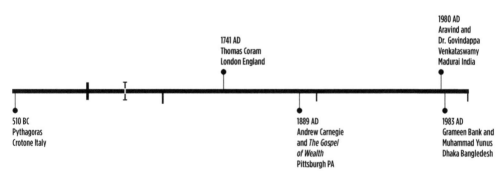

1980 AD
Aravind and
Dr. Govindappa
Venkataswamy
Madurai India

1741 AD
Thomas Coram
London England

510 BC
Pythagoras
Crotone Italy

1889 AD
Andrew Carnegie
and *The Gospel
of Wealth*
Pittsburgh PA

1983 AD
Grameen Bank and
Muhammad Yunus
Dhaka Bangledesh

CHAPTER 11

Value Beyond Money

I believe every one ought, in duty to do any good they can.

—Thomas Coram, 1738

The amassing of wealth is one of the worse species of idolatry. No idol more debasing than the worship of money.

—Andrew Carnegie's note to himself, 1868, at the age of 33

For at least seven thousand years before money was invented, entrepreneurs understood their potential to create value that their neighbors coveted. The bead factory entrepreneurs described in chapter 1 traded the beads they manufactured for sheep or goats. The livestock they received supplied these innovative hunter-gatherers with a new source of food and clothing and, without a doubt, an increased feeling of security and well-being on top of the additional calories. Many entrepreneurs trade the goods they deliver for more than money: control, security, status, knowledge, pleasure, and so on.

The concept of money as an objective unit of value was codified long before governments started minting standardized coins
around 600 BC. As we saw in our discussion of ancient Mesopotamia, entrepreneurs easily computed the value of their textiles in
equivalent weights of silver, tin, and barley. They also codified a
word for profit as the objective measure of the value gained from
an exchange. From that point forward, sometime before 2000 BC,
many entrepreneurs and their customers stopped trying to measure
value in anything other than money.

Some entrepreneurs wanted more than merely silver in return
for their work, but to get it, they had to innovate new forms
of exchange. There is much to learn from these supramonetary
entrepreneurs.

Divine Value

Pythagoras (ca. 570–495 BC) knew things nobody else had ever
dreamed of (figure 11.1). He was an idealist as well as an entrepreneur. His followers—his customers—believed he could deliver
wisdom and, perhaps, the secret of immortality. In return, Pythagoras wanted control of both them and their worldly possessions.
This was the form of exchange that Pythagoras the entrepreneur
innovated. Many of his customers were referred to as mathemati-
cians (meaning "deriving from science" in ancient Greek). Some
historians claim that Pythagoras created the first sect, but it would
be more accurate to say he created a business.

Pythagoras moved from the Greek island of Samos, where he
was already famous, to the southern Italian coastal town of Croton
in order to establish a community for his customers, who would
be taught how to live harmoniously with the universe and therefore become immortal. Chief among the Pythagorean teachings

11.1 Roman copy of a Greek original from the 2nd century BC, depicting Pythagoras.

Source: Wikipedia, https://en.wikipedia.org/wiki/Pythagoras.

was a proscription against beans. It isn't clear why beans disrupted universal harmony—flatulence?—but they were forbidden. Vegetarianism, a new concept at the time, was also essential in the community. Followers (customers) of Pythagoras could listen to him and others lecture about the universe, music, science, and what we now call mathematics, but they could not talk, let alone ask questions, for their first five years in the community.

An interesting feature of Pythagoras's business model was that if someone left or was forced to leave because they could no longer comply or keep up with their studies and practices, they were given twice the value of their investment. This might be the first instance of a "double your money back" guarantee. The policy shows that Pythagoras created his teaching and living infrastructure not for the profit but for the desire to receive something more than money

326 Value Beyond Money

from his customers. We cannot know his true motivations, but I speculate that Pythagoras wanted to feel like the smartest and most idolized person in the room and designed a business model to feed that desire.

Hundreds of customers came from around the Greek world to live with Pythagoras. We know that he and his followers interacted with the neighboring town and that, at first, they were sought after as administrators and advisers to the local ruler. The Pythagoreans were credited with helping Croton conquer Sybaris in 510 BC. The coalition's victory, however, triggered a violent disagreement over whether Croton should adopt democratic principles, following a trend among other Greek city-states. Pythagoras opposed democracy, which led to his community's being attacked by the democracy-supporting citizens of Croton, and the community was burned to the ground. Many died, but Pythagoras appears to have escaped, along with the few surviving customers.

Some of the survivors dispersed throughout Greece, forming their own Pythagorean communities. Though these franchises appear to have been financially self-supporting, locals were suspicious of their teachings and nonconformist attitudes. Some appear to have been burned to the ground as well. Pythagoras learned what many entrepreneurs before and since have figured out: openly challenging the elite usually leads to your destruction. In the end, this entrepreneur was oblivious to the disharmony he created in the world.

Plato, Aristotle, and other educational entrepreneurs copied portions of Pythagoras's business model. They invited customers to learn from them, though not necessarily to live together. Since then countless educational and spiritual entrepreneurs have dispensed knowledge while crediting the adoration of students as a value received—and sometimes the only one sought.

An Ancient Double Bottom Line

Entrepreneurs are often thankful for help they receive from external forces in achieving their success. There was a widespread belief in classical Athens that a democratic structure granted every citizen personal advantage for which they should be grateful. Successful individuals were expected to show that gratitude to their fellow citizens. Socrates, as quoted in Xenophon's *Oeconomicus*, lists a half-dozen expectations that citizens had of their rich brethren, particularly wealthy entrepreneurs: paying for religious festivals, maintaining choirs, entertaining visitors, paying for city improvements as well as the maintenance of its defenses. These costly social responsibilities were called "liturgies." Some were assigned like a tax on the wealthy, while others were voluntary, with the magnitude of the social expectation dependent on the public perception of one's wealth. Most successful Athenian entrepreneurs were honored to use a significant fraction of their profits to improve the city and benefit their fellow citizens. In any case, if they did not meet these formal and informal expectations, they were socially shunned and could even be ostracized.

The city prospered during this entrepreneurial golden age, but liturgical expectations waned in Hellenistic times. Rome had similar expectations of its wealthiest citizens, but not necessarily of its newly wealthy freed slave entrepreneurs. No major culture since Rome has set expectations on the contribution—other than taxes—of their entrepreneurs to social well-being.

For the next seventeen hundred years, entrepreneurs generally did not feel compelled to contribute to the overall well-being of their communities. Entrepreneurs in most cultures felt that well-being was the responsibility of the government and sometimes also organized religion. They concentrated on adding value by creating profit and paying taxes.

Three-Sided Exchanges

The feeling among entrepreneurs that they could create value beyond monetary wealth ultimately did change—at least for a few. Dead children were the trigger. William Hogarth was the most expensive portraitist in England in the first half of the eighteenth century. The portrait considered his masterpiece was not a noble commission but the painting of a man he admired. Thomas Coram created the first private philanthropy (figure 11.2).

11.2 Thomas Coram, portrait by William Hogarth.

Source: Wikipedia, https://en.wikipedia.org/wiki/Portrait_of_Captain_Thomas_Coram.

In Hogarth's painting, a proud but not quite comfortable Coram sits by a desk dressed as the prosperous sea captain merchant he was. On the desk is a document titled "Royal Charter." In the distance beyond Coram's desk, merchant ships at sea indicate how he spent much of his life. Off his right shoulder a curtain is drawn back to reveal, barely visible in the shadows of another room, a young mother with a child at her breast posed like the Madonna and child. At Coram's feet sits a globe, positioned to highlight the Atlantic. Coram's right hand leans on the desk and clutches the official seal of the Foundling Hospital, the first privately funded joint-stock corporation dedicated to creating a public good rather than a profit. The Foundling Hospital was a place where orphaned or abandoned children could be looked after and educated. (In Coram's time, the word "hospital" meant a place where people were treated hospitably.)

Coram's mother died when he was young. He was sent to sea at the age of eleven by his newly remarried father. On his return, Thomas was apprenticed to a shipwright. He became adept at ship design and construction. In fact, Coram became so skilled during his apprenticeship that he was soon hired as a naval surveyor. That job brought him to the attention of a London merchant, who hired him to oversee the construction of his ships, with the goal of building them less expensively in the American colonies. In 1693, at the age of twenty-five, Coram went to Boston and soon after set up his own shipbuilding firm.

With little formal education, and having spent most of his youth around seamen, Coram was gruff and coarse in his manner. He was not liked by his New England neighbors or his competitors. This animosity was compounded by the fact that he was a devout Anglican in a land of Puritans. Having achieved considerable entrepreneurial success in America over a decade despite frequent threats of physical harm, Coram returned to England with his American wife. Back home, he captained merchant boats that traded widely (never in the slave trade and mostly in naval provisions) while promoting ideas to fellow merchants and trade administrators on leveraging the resources and energies of the colonies. Frequent trips to London for both trade and his lobbying efforts took Coram through some of the country's poorest areas. There he saw many abandoned children, both starving and dead. These scenes must have been particularly traumatic for someone who had lost his mother at a young age and been ostracized by his father.

In 1722, Coram petitioned the king to create a government body to look after foundlings. His proposition was met with skepticism, if not derision. Nobles and royals felt that if the government looked after foundlings, it would encourage illegitimacy and prostitution. Rebuffed, Coram turned his attention to proposals to colonize present-day Maine and Nova Scotia, which also did not receive support. He actively promoted programs to aid debtors by sending them to a new colony that would become Georgia, which ultimately did go forward, but only after he was excluded from the effort. These efforts brought him into contact with more powerful and influential people in the British government, but he remained unable to generate interest in helping foundlings.

During a trip to Paris, Coram learned that wealthy French widows often provided shelter and meals for foundlings. This changed his thinking—he had been asking the wrong people to become involved. In 1729, he solicited support from English noblewomen to petition the queen to support his efforts. He also sought their financial support for a privately funded, fully chartered corporation whose only mission would be caring for foundlings. Coram collected signatures from twenty-one of the most prominent and wealthy ladies of the day. At that point, his proposal began to be taken seriously—at least by the husbands and relatives of those prominent women. Still, it took another eight years of petitions, proposals, and lobbying to receive a royal charter from the king's privy council. The corporation would be funded by private individuals, not the government, and it would be exclusively dedicated to supporting foundlings.

In 1737, after twenty years of effort, the charter was granted, and Coram recruited 375 wealthy and influential individuals to serve as "governors"—what we would consider a very large board of directors—and help him secure funding on an ongoing basis. In a sense, these individuals would be both his customers and his salesforce. The Foundling Hospital opened and, in 1741, moved into larger buildings with separate wings for boys and girls. Once it was well established, the governors agitated for Coram to be removed from oversight of the hospital and the corporation for having been "indiscrete with his criticisms"—he still hadn't mastered his manners. Nonetheless, Coram remained credited with having created this new type of institution.

A different customer/entrepreneur relationship

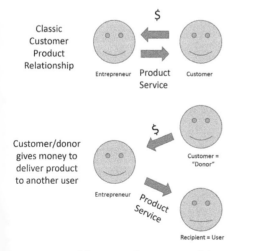

Classic Customer Product Relationship

Entrepreneur Product Service Customer

The most basic entrepreneurial interaction involves an entrepreneur delivering a product or service directly to a customer and receiving money or something more valuable in return

Customer/donor gives money to deliver product to another user

Customer = "Donor"

Entrepreneur Product Service

Recipient = User

The most basic model of a charitable enterprise involves the entrepreneur seeking funds from "donors" and delivering a product or service to a recipient that is made "better off." The donor is technically "the customer" because they are handing over the money. The recipient is often thought of as a "customer" too, but technically they are the "user."

11.3 Three-way business model common to charities.

Coram's enterprise used a new business model (figure 11.3). The users of the product or service (i.e., the foundlings) weren't its customers; wealthy donors were. In return for their donations, the hospital's customers received positive feelings and a sense of well-being for their altruism. Coram's model remains the primary one used for charities and philanthropies today.

As would be predicted, Coram's success inspired swarms of entrepreneurs motivated to deliver products and services to groups who did not have the ability to pay for them. This three-pronged funding model has been used by millions of entrepreneurs to create charities and philanthropies. (Charity tends to imply an organization that provides short-term help, whereas philanthropies are associated with organizations making longer-term efforts. Many, however, consider the words synonymous.) Today charities and philanthropies exist to provide services for humans in practically any form of distress: physical, mental, or social. They also fund activities with a net social benefit including scientific progress, education, artistic endeavors, and the protection of natural resources.

Profitable Nonprofit Models

Dr. Govindappa Venkataswamy was known to everyone as Dr. V. Born in a poor southern Indian village without electricity or running water, he learned to read by drawing words in the sand with his fingers. As a child, deeply affected by the death of a cousin in childbirth, Govindappa decided to become a medical doctor. An uncle used his savings to send his precocious nephew to school, making Govindappa the first in his village to go to college and obtain a medical degree.

Dr. V's career as a doctor in the Indian Army Medical Corps at the end of World War II was cut short by an attack of rheumatoid arthritis so severe that he remained bedridden for a year.

His disability made it impossible for him to practice obstetrics any longer, so he returned to medical school to pursue an additional specialization in ophthalmology. Starting in 1951 and continuing for the next quarter century, Dr. V practiced ophthalmology at various Indian government hospitals and agencies, ultimately winning global recognition for regional and national programs that he created to stem and mitigate blindness. In 1976, at the age of fifty-eight, he reached the government's mandatory retirement age.

Spiritually driven to help people, the newly retired Dr. V (figure 11.4) borrowed money from relatives and mortgaged his house to fund the creation of an eleven-bed eye surgery hospital

11.4 Dr. Govindappa Venkataswamy at his desk.

Source: Wikimedia Commons, https://commons.wikimedia.org/wiki/File:Chief_in_desk.jpg.

(figure 11.5), Aravind, named after a revered spiritual leader. His funding model was one that entrepreneurs had shunned for millennia: "pay what you can." He staffed the hospital with altruistic siblings and in-laws, some of whom he'd helped become ophthalmologists. To make a profit—or "surplus," as many nonprofits call it—the team streamlined its surgical processes, eventually performing more than ten times as many eye surgeries as a normal hospital of equivalent size. Aravind became so effective that its customers had fewer complications. Ultimately, costs had been reduced through increased efficiency to such an extent that wealthier patients paying the standard cost of eye surgery generated enough surplus to cover the treatment of two patients who could pay nothing, with money left over to fund rapid expansion. Today, Aravind has fourteen hospitals throughout India, a division to manufacture low-cost implantable lenses and ophthalmological equipment, a training institute, and a research institute. Dr. V died in 2006, but the company continues to thrive. As of 2020, Aravind has conducted more than 7.8 million eye surgeries.

11.5 Aravind's first eleven-bed eye hospital.

Source: Aravind Eye Care Center, "Our Story," https://aravind.org/our-story/.

The organization also shares its processes with others, inspiring copycat entrepreneurs to provide similar eye-care facilities in India and other developing countries.

Virtuous Loans

Seven years after Dr. V opened his revolutionary hospital, a professor in Bangladesh opened a bank many considered equally audacious. In 1983, Muhammad Yunus (figure 11.6), head of the Economics Department at Chittagong University, had successfully turned some early experiments aimed at mitigating poverty in small villages into an authorized bank designed to bring services to the rural poor.

11.6 Muhammad Yunus.

Source: https://en.wikipedia.org/wiki/Muhammad_Yunus.

Yunus had begun by making microloans funded out of his own pocket. The loans were often just a dollar and went to women aspiring to create small businesses to provide supplemental income for their families. Most of the women who received his loans were successful in creating small craft, retail, or service businesses. Their profits increased their families' disposable income, and Yunus was able to train other villagers to make and keep track of these small loans, minimizing his overhead costs. With this low-cost structure, the 99 percent repayment rate yielded a tiny profit despite interest rates similar to those big banks offered to creditworthy customers. Based on these encouraging results, Yunus incorporated a for-profit bank dedicated to making microloans, calling it Grameen (Bengali for "rural") Bank. The subsequent success of Grameen set off a swarm of thousands of entrepreneurs offering similar services in most poor regions of the world, even in the United States.

As would be expected in any large swarm, some entrepreneurs used questionable practices to sustain their business and make a profit. With so many microloan entrepreneurs administering their businesses expediently rather than deliberately, not all loans have resulted in successful businesses, leading to indebtedness and family discord rather than value creation. Even the actions of the best-intentioned entrepreneurs create unintended consequences. That said, most have improved a family's well-being. In 2006, Grameen Bank became the first entrepreneurial enterprise to receive the Nobel Peace Prize, along with founder Muhammad Yunus.

Thomas Coram, Dr. V, and Muhammad Yunus created a spectrum of models that entrepreneurs now use to help others: not-for-profit businesses, for-profit businesses that use their profits to subsidize not-for-profit components, and businesses that profit by helping those in need. There is heated debate among entrepreneurs, academics, government officials, and leaders of nongovernment organizations about which of these models is more effective and what role entrepreneurs can or should play in mitigating poverty and improving overall health and well-being. Some have coined the term "social entrepreneurship" to describe for-profit models that improve the well-being of the disadvantaged, but nobody claims to know exactly which parts of this spectrum of models fall under this loosely defined term and which do not.

Settling Up

Andrew Carnegie (figure 11.7) felt that his good fortune was not simply related to hard work, let alone divine intervention, contrary to the declarations of his successful contemporaries. Carnegie was

11.7 Andrew Carnegie.

Source: https://en.wikipedia.org/wiki/Andrew_Carnegie.

an ardent follower of the British philosopher Herbert Spencer, considered the father of social Darwinism. Spencer coined the phrase "survival of the fittest." He viewed society as a constantly evolving—and improving—organism driven by fundamental forces of nature, particularly human nature. Carnegie considered Spencer's views a direct description of the forces that had shaped his own success, which he attributed to his constant search for improvements in how work was performed.

Carnegie extrapolated Spencer's ideas into a personalized description of how entrepreneurs, in making improvements, created inequality. According to Carnegie's *Gospel of Wealth*, "The contrast between the palace of the millionaire and the cottage of the laborer with us to-day measures the change which has come with civilization." Specifically, social inequality was a necessary by-product of entrepreneurs improving products and making them more affordable. He admitted that some paid a great price for this progress: "We assemble thousands of operatives in the factory, in the mine, and in the counting-house, of whom the employer can know little or nothing, and to whom the employer is little better than a myth." He argued that it was not hard work but "talent for organization and management . . . rare among men" that distinguished successful entrepreneurs in their ability to "accumulate wealth." There was "no middle ground"; you had the talent or you didn't. This was not good luck or hard work. It was evolutionary selection.

Carnegie felt that his inherited talents came with a responsibility. He argued that "not evil, but good has to come from the accumulation of wealth by those who have the ability and energy to produce it." Rather than leave their fortunes to their families, he believed that successful entrepreneurs had a duty to use all their earnings in their own lifetimes to benefit others less fortunate.

Carnegie wrote extensively on this unprecedented concept. His first exposition of this idea came in an article titled "Wealth," published in 1889 in the *North American Review*. He later amplified it in his famous monograph, *The Gospel of Wealth*. Carnegie was a man of his word, from that time forward spending more and more time donating money to parks, libraries, universities (including Black institutions), and many grant-making institutions that now bear his name. He was famously direct when he wrote, "The man who dies thus rich dies disgraced."

Carnegie's solution to the unintended entrepreneurial consequence of inequality was to use his accumulated profits to mitigate what he had indirectly helped to exacerbate. He felt that inequality was inevitable. Rather than dampen entrepreneurial profit motives and slow progress, hurting what he saw as the rightful competitive superiority of the most talented entrepreneurs, society would best be served by the use of entrepreneurial profits to fight the side-effects. It goes without saying that most entrepreneurs, including the most successful, have not followed Carnegie's lead.

Ignoring the social consequences of your startup with the aspiration to give at least half of your wealth to charity is now a fashionable trend, with hundreds of billionaire entrepreneurs from two dozen countries publicly signing The Giving Pledge, nicknamed the "Billionaire's Pledge." An attempt by Bill Gates and Warren Buffett to goad fellow entrepreneurs into following in Carnegie's footsteps has, as of this writing, resulted in over $600 billion being pledged. Relatively little has yet been spent, with some notable exceptions.

Rediscovering Value

Socially responsible entrepreneurship is something many government officials, academics, and aspiring entrepreneurs seek to understand and foster. The challenge is that all entrepreneurs are self-directed in their actions. It is naive to expect most entrepreneurs to focus their actions on improving overall well-being and to substantially mitigate unintended consequences such as inequality and product-induced suffering and illness. Defining entrepreneurial success with the single metric of profit has eliminated social values and nonmonetary value creation from the discussion of entrepreneurship. In the last chapter, I'll discuss what history suggests we can do about this challenge.

CHAPTER 12

The Possibilities of Our Entrepreneurial Future

The first thing we do, let's kill all the lawyers.

—William Shakespeare, *Henry VI*

I n social and some professional gatherings, this quote always gets a laugh at attorneys' expense. I like to play a game with my students by substituting "entrepreneurs" for "lawyers" and seeing where the prompt takes the class. They usually come up with a vision of a dystopia.

Take away everything entrepreneurs have ever innovated and you would be left with only what governments and religious organizations have provided: government-built buildings, government-issued clothing, government-produced food, and temples and places of worship built by religious groups. We would have only government-developed technology, which tends to be long on weaponry—and short on everything else.

The world would be bleak and undeveloped, indeed: no lights, cars, commercial flights, or even bicycles. There would be no entertainment—only government-sanctioned communications, and none of it electronic because electricity was put to practical use exclusively by entrepreneurs.

We wouldn't have much trade, either. Attempts to control trade by Egyptian pharaohs, Chinese emperors, and even some twentieth-century communist states show that trading without entrepreneurs is cumbersome. Rulers and governments trade critical materials among themselves on a quid pro quo basis, with a great deal of formality and care to ensure neither side feels dishonored.

We would have science, but not much technology. Great scientists like Newton, Galileo, and Pasteur were not entrepreneurs. Their theories were essential for understanding how to build longer bridges and make our food safer, but it was entrepreneurs who actually built the bridges and pasteurized cauldrons of milk.

As rulers have always been interested in their own health, we would have holistic medicine and folk remedies but might have nothing that requires sophisticated chemical or biological processing, because those industries were created by entrepreneurs.

On the positive side, the world would have virtually no obesity (we'd get our sweetness from natural honey, not processed sugar or corn syrup) and far less trouble with addictions. Most types of pollution would not exist, and the massive waves of deforestation that began when entrepreneurs figured out how to produce iron in large quantities would never have occurred.

The point is that the cumulative impact of entrepreneurs has been to deliver to all of us—even the citizens of North Korea—most of what we recognize as modern civilization. Virtually every big business originated with an entrepreneur. Every factory in the world has an entrepreneurial legacy, no matter where it is. Our health, our fun, our very lives are almost totally dependent on entrepreneurial activity. Even most government services could not be delivered without products and services that were created by entrepreneurs.

Beyond Our Power?

Our review of the nature of entrepreneurship shows that its impact is pervasive. Entrepreneurial innovation has ever-increasing impact. These innovations are mostly incremental, but when summed over the large number of simultaneously innovating entrepreneurs, incremental effects become substantial. The scale of entrepreneurial impact dwarfs the impact of any other social force, including that of any government or religion. It operates at the level of the individual, of society, the planet, and even beyond.

Entrepreneurs pervasively shape our daily lives. Our freedom is both increased and restricted because entrepreneurs chose what to create and deliver. The products that are available, how we travel and communicate with one another, where we live, how we are entertained, what we eat, what we wear, and even who we court have all been both enabled and constrained by innovations scaled by entrepreneurs. Granted, some pioneering entrepreneurial enterprises eventually become big, risk-adverse businesses run by professional managers. But virtually all professional managers look to the entrepreneurial firms in their markets to decide what changes to make to their own products. Entrepreneurs take the risks; big businesses copy what pans out. One way or the other, entrepreneurs drive change like no other force. As described throughout the book, the world would be unrecognizable if entrepreneurs had never emerged to act for themselves. We just assume the world is what it is, never considering how many of our choices are made for us by entrepreneurs. Our actions are products, more than anything else, of their efforts.

Entrepreneurs create desire for products and services we would not otherwise want. They must do so to survive. The entrepreneurial innovation cycle drives swarms of entrepreneurs to figure out how to get us to want more of what they can give us. As we have seen, this manipulation is not the result of malevolent intention—at least, not usually. It is the direct consequence of swarms of individuals enticing us to exchange money for what they have to offer.

On a macro level, entrepreneurship provides members of society with objects and services that existing power structures do not want to or cannot provide. As we have seen, based on the number and impact of the products and services that entrepreneurs have pioneered, governments shape only a small fraction of its citizens' activities and behaviors. Political leaders interfere with entrepreneurs only when the unintended adverse consequences of their efforts rile the citizenry. Most of the laws regulating how we act in society are, fundamentally, consequences of past entrepreneurial efforts run amok.

Culturally, entrepreneurs set many of our social norms: what is cool, what is scandalous, what is convenient, what is private. They even change the way we speak: "Google it," "post it," and "blog" are recent examples. "Mathematician" goes back to 530 BC. Much of what we think of as society is shaped, in fact, by entrepreneurial innovation.

The fundamental outputs of entrepreneurial swarms are innovation and scale. Today, some of these swarms have achieved planetary and extraplanetary scale. Social media, smartphone apps, and cybercriminal hacking products are examples of instantly served, global-scale markets. Social media sensations change the behaviors of millions of people around the world almost simultaneously. And today, at least four billionaire entrepreneurs are racing to send customers to space. Others pursue asteroid mining. Entrepreneurial scaling doesn't stop at the stratosphere.

A Hidden Social Tax

Swarms focused on individual customers prioritize delivering short-term pleasure over long-term well-being. This has been the case since early entrepreneurs supplied objects of astonishment that made customers feel powerful and worthy of respect. Today, technologies developed by entrepreneurs make it easier than ever to design products and services that addict customers. An entire branch of digital design now deals with taking advantage of the brain's reward centers to "entice" potential customers and keep existing customers "engaged"—they call it "persuasion technology." Entrepreneurs are quick to use new techniques to capture customers faster and keep them longer. Business models that leverage these new technologies produce the largest and most innovative swarms. The fastest-growing swarms are innovating products with more unintended consequences, not fewer. Businesses focused on delivering long-term well-being grow more slowly, making them less appealing to the venture capitalists who accelerate the pace of the EIC.

Governments eventually jump in when the adverse consequences of a product grow so acute that large numbers of citizens threaten unrest. But that can take decades, and the regulations are always minimal. If those regulations cannot mitigate a problem to the satisfaction of the citizenry, governments feel forced to step in and pay to fix the problem directly. Even when governments step in, it is the consumer who ultimately pays to mitigate entrepreneurial unintended consequences. And these costs accumulate. For example, we are taxed today to pay for the consequences of entrepreneurs who originally figured out how to use coal as a source for power four hundred years ago. Insurance policies are more expensive because they cover treatments for entrepreneurially created medical conditions. Individuals pay directly for products such as air filters or more electricity for air conditioning to mitigate entrepreneurial-induced problems like air pollution and warmer temperatures. A portion of our taxes pays for government programs to regulate, monitor, and enforce pollution standards.

The hidden entrepreneurial innovation tax is substantial. I estimate that a family of four in the American Midwest, with both parents working and earning $80,000, with health care, pays around $2,500 a year. For a small-business owner in the American Southeast, again with a family of four, the tax could be over $7,500, as they pay for health insurance directly and work longer hours.

The tax may be worth it, at least for now. We don't want to live without all the things entrepreneurs have delivered to us, so we should be willing to pay to mitigate the consequences of those innovations. But we should know the cost. It will only grow with time as the scale and magnitude of the EIC increases. Now that we realize this tax exists, we can figure out what we can do to bring the costs down.

To Trust or Not to Trust?

There is scant evidence that entrepreneurs, primarily motivated to stay competitive with others in their swarm, spontaneously mitigate the consequences of their innovations. Nonprofit swarms focused on enhancing overall well-being have not yet developed methods to scale demand for their products and services. Individual entrepreneurs have yet to globally impact climate change, plummeting fish populations, deforestation, addiction, income inequality, or other entrepreneurially induced existential threats. But hundreds of millions of entrepreneurs could.

We should expect even more adverse consequences from future entrepreneurial innovations. As the scale of the EIC increases, the potential magnitude of unintended consequences grows. We're seeing entrepreneurial medical doctors illegally clone children. Entrepreneurs have made machines that almost anyone can learn to use to fabricate new DNA and RNA strands. Will all that new genetic material prove beneficial? Powerful open-source artificial intelligence programs are now widely used to manipulate people into acting against their best interest.

Francis Bacon, in his retelling of the story of Daedalus in 1609, implored society to mitigate the unintended consequences of entrepreneurial action. Our latest generations of technology-driven entrepreneurs surpass the capabilities of Daedalus and can create Minotaurs. Based on how entrepreneurship has worked for the past nine thousand years, we cannot count on entrepreneurs to obey laws and regulations or come to our existential rescue. If anything, they will only create more adverse consequences.

Andrew Carnegie felt that Bacon was an idealist and called entrepreneurship a force "beyond our power to alter." Don't even bother trying. Carnegie felt that encouraging entrepreneurs to give away their wealth before they died was the best that could be done to align entrepreneurial impact with societal well-being. The most common rejoinder to both Carnegie and Bacon, from the rare entrepreneur or politician who gives a second thought to unintended consequences, is that entrepreneurs have always addressed unintended consequences with new products and services once those consequences have created demand for a solution. Perhaps we can't cure lung cancer or Type 2 diabetes—the unintended consequences of Washington Duke, James Drax, and others we met earlier—but, they argue, entrepreneurs *have* helped to develop drugs that partly ease the suffering and extend the lives of those afflicted. Likewise, cars take many lives, but entrepreneurs eventually developed seatbelts (Irving Air Chute Company and others) and airbags (Breed Corporation) that can help people survive accidents. Today, entrepreneurs are hard at work on solutions to keep our data private, now that many of us see this as a major problem. And they are already working on the problem of climate change. "It just takes time," the optimists say. "Trust the system." Considering the scope of the global problems we face, the truth is that no one knows if we have the time to wait for the entrepreneurial innovation cycle to solve them. We must figure out how to deal with swarms.

What Is Within Our Power?

We have developed a far more complete understanding of how entrepreneurship works than Carnegie, Bacon, or even Marx and Schumpeter. Entrepreneurial forces are mightier than even they realized. But we can now find ways to steer these forces. How might we create an environment in which we can trust entrepreneurs to build businesses that not only make money but also improve overall well-being?

Can we control existing swarms to act in certain ways and not others? The evidence presented shows that governments have rarely succeeded in preventing entrepreneurs from innovating once the ability to make a profit has been established. The rules imposed by rulers or governments are seen as optional for the self-directed; entrepreneurs simply choose whether to accept the risks associated with noncompliance. Because swarms contain large numbers of individuals, with each member utilizing similar techniques to create value for themselves, innovation is uncontrolled and unpredictable. The uncontrolled nature of who joins a swarm results in all types of self-directed people deciding which rules or social constraints they will abide by and which to ignore. The story of how entrepreneurs continued to offer mortgages and other loan products that evaded new restrictions demonstrates that, short of the brutal enforcement of laws, some entrepreneurs will find a workaround and many others will follow.

Entrepreneurs innovate around constraints. Brutal enforcement dissuades some entrepreneurs in a swarm from risking certain activities, but others move to black markets. America's Prohibition and entrepreneurial drug cartels are well-known examples of governments failing to stop existing swarms from innovating. Entrepreneurs innovate around social constraints if there is money to be made in doing so.

Can we bias swarms? Instead of trying to prevent certain entrepreneurial behaviors, can we do more to encourage others?

Today, some claim that tax rates bias entrepreneurs to act differently. Although tax breaks may motivate some entrepreneurs to act differently, we have seen those entrepreneurs who are at the leading edges of swarms, where the greatest innovation takes place, focus on scaling up profits, not scaling down taxes. Entrepreneurs around the world flock to Silicon Valley, one of the most heavily taxed metropolitan areas in the country. Big businesses change behaviors to minimize taxes but not the most ambitious entrepreneurs. Politicians must realize that entrepreneurs and professional managers are different. Ambitious entrepreneurs focus on innovation, and the success of these entrepreneurs is what others copy. Taxes are rarely an effective method for biasing the behavior of a swarm.

On the other hand, tangible incentives and subsidies can shift the direction of entrepreneurial swarms and the focus of EICs. Lucrative incentives make some entrepreneurs more successful, and others copy them. Scores of Roman freed slaves focused on delivering grain to Rome after the Senate offered them citizenship for doing so—a major tangible benefit for noncitizen freed slaves and their families.

A recent example is the swarm of solar energy entrepreneurs that created large arrays of solar panels to supply electricity at guaranteed prices. When governments subsidized utilities to offer long-term contracts for solar-generated electricity (called "feed-in tariffs"), they enabled entrepreneurs to lock in profits for large installed solar arrays for a decade or more. These low-risk large profits shifted the focus of solar entrepreneurs from making or installing solar panels to raising large amounts of capital to install acres of panels. The focus of several solar energy entrepreneurial swarms and their EICs shifted quickly toward capturing this new source of revenue. When the feed-in tariffs stopped being offered because taxpayers balked at higher utility bills, solar entrepreneurs went back to doing business the way they had before. Fabricating new sources of profitable revenues or offering tangible perks like citizenship can bias the direction of entrepreneurial swarms. But it is expensive.

Can we create swarms? Around 3000 BC, the rulers of Uruk enticed citizens to take on the risks of trading the city's textiles to secure badly needed supplies to support its growth. They created a swarm of long-distance traders who continued innovating for the next two millennia. Success required that the ruling elite of Uruk made creating this entrepreneurial swarm their top priority. To ensure success, they dealt with only a small group of individuals who they already trusted and were clearly motivated by the profit potential of the proposed ventures.

Recently, the U.S. government created a swarm of entrepreneurs and big businesses to develop COVID-19 medications and vaccines by offering to pay for both research and development as well as quantities of doses to ensure profitability. Most of the first wave of vaccines and medications approved as of this writing were developed by companies led by entrepreneurs who teamed up with a big business to scale as quickly as possible. Guaranteeing a profit and quick return by also funding product development can create new swarms. It is fast, though expensive.

As described in chapter 2, inventions don't trigger swarms, but innovations—best practices newly embraced by groups of people—do. Funding the development of new technologies does not necessarily trigger new entrepreneurial swarms. This is a fallacy held by many. New technologies can—sometimes—be used by entrepreneurs to make entirely new products or products that are radically cheaper or easier to use than established products. Often the innovation enabled by utilizing a new technology to produce a better version of an old product requires little creativity to implement. Bronze weapons substituted for copper weapons wherever bronze technology was available. Bronze technology didn't trigger a new entrepreneurial swarm. That credit goes to the first successful bronze weapon manufacturer, who inspired copycat behavior by nearby copper weapons entrepreneurs.

Of the eleven million patents granted to date in the United States, only a few tens of thousands have ever yielded the owner of the patent, whether an individual or a business, more than the expense of development and patenting. Only certain technologies trigger new swarms. Technologies that make existing products vastly cheaper to produce (e.g., windmills to crush sugar cane, plastics for containers), or vastly easier to use (e.g., pullies for lifting, gyroscopes for navigating), or vastly more reliable (e.g., the boring machine that made steam engines more reliable, or transistors replacing vacuum tubes) are quickly adopted and spur innovations. Occasionally a new technology inspires an entrepreneur to use it to offer a new type of product or service, which then triggers a new swarm to form once an instigator entrepreneur's efforts prove successful. In 4000 BC, it was metallurgy; in 1956, it was the transistor; today it is AI, artificial intelligence. History shows us that entrepreneurs will continue to mix new and mature technologies to innovate products and services, both new and existing.

Inspiring Entrepreneurs to Make a Better World

We are now armed with an understanding that points to specific actions we can take to better align entrepreneurial actions with overall well-being, possibly mitigating the planet's multiple existential crises along the way. I present here five simple, basic, and inexpensive actions to consider.

First, a little entrepreneurial education will go a long way toward motivating subsequent generations to understand the impact of entrepreneurs, support good entrepreneurs, and ostracize those who do harm. Inserting a learning module in elementary school on what "good" entrepreneurs do (I'll define this in a moment) will stimulate interest in being innovative and begin to set a moral compass for future entrepreneurs. This can be done naturally when children learn about professions. Later, in high school, students could specifically study the impact of entrepreneurial innovation, both intended and unintended. This would fit into existing world history modules, pointing to how much of the world we live in today was created by swarms of entrepreneurs relentlessly innovating. All high school graduates will then be in a position to decide by which entrepreneurs they want to be enticed and which to shun, as well as whether to try to be one themselves.

Second, we should expect entrepreneurs to understand and educate the public about the potential unintended consequences of buying and using their products and services. This enables customers to make informed decisions about the impact of their purchases. This can be done simply, by requiring entrepreneurs—and all businesses, for that matter—to post a notice on their websites and physical premises that publicly discloses the potential adverse consequences that could arise from using their products or services. For most entrepreneurs, particularly those not aspiring to scale their businesses, this disclosure would be standard and pro forma. Major benefits would ensue if ambitious entrepreneurs contemplated and shared the potential adverse consequences of their innovations with the public. The public could then decide when and whether to act on any of those potential consequences. We have already moved in this direction with food labeling. A more informed population will both support entrepreneurial innovation and hold entrepreneurs accountable for the consequences of their actions.

Third, we would all benefit if the hidden entrepreneurial innovation tax were made explicit. Understanding the magnitude and composition of the costs associated with mitigating entrepreneurial innovation will lead to discussion, debate, and action. I project that we will decide that these costs should be paid by successful entrepreneurs and not the unsuspecting public. Doing so would hold entrepreneurs, as a swarm, accountable for the unintended consequences of their actions. A small tax—say, 1 percent on the profits of products with market shares greater than 50 percent—would generate billions of dollars a year that could be used to mitigate entrepreneurial unintended consequences and learn how to better project consequences going forward.

Fourth, we would all benefit if entrepreneurs formed a national or international academy of role models. We have national academies of scientists, engineers, artists, and inventors, and their prestige shapes the behavior of their peers. Officially recognizing entrepreneurs for their beneficial accomplishments will shape the behavior of anyone aspiring to large-scale success. Many will adjust their actions to be recognized by their esteemed peers. This would be an effective body for shaping entrepreneurial ethics in a way that inspires entrepreneurs to be more considerate and sensitive to overall well-being.

Finally, perhaps working in conjunction with a national academy of entrepreneurs, governments and philanthropists could offer profitable contracts for anyone to develop and deliver not-yet-available products and services that mitigate undesirable consequences of previous entrepreneurial actions. The government portion of these contracts could be paid for by the monopoly tax. The objective of these contracts would be to create swarms aimed at supplying products and services that mitigate previous or anticipated entrepreneurial adverse consequences. The target of the new swarms and the nature of the contracts offered could be decided by the national academy. Contracts would be constructed to trigger new swarms with the lure of minimal-risk profits, as well as status and recognition. The phasing of these contracts could be like those used for Project Warp Speed and the development of COVID-19 vaccines. They would also be similar to what the rulers of Uruk put into place five thousand years ago to secure enough lumber, metal, and precious stones to keep their city growing and their citizens happy.

What Is a Good Entrepreneur?

We are finally in a position to answer the question that started this deep dive into the origins and impacts of entrepreneurship. The mechanisms of entrepreneurial swarming and its entrepreneurial innovation cycle are embedded in our humanity. We cannot stop them, nor do we want to stop them. We need to encourage them in a way that expects entrepreneurs to act in the best interests of every customer and all of us. We should expect that "a good entrepreneur delivers value to society without harmful consequences." This is a reasonable expectation based on our understanding of how entrepreneurship works and how much it influences what we do and how we act.

Expecting our entrepreneurs to "be good" is a higher standard than most people have of entrepreneurs today. A more typical definition of a good entrepreneur is along the lines of "someone who makes lots of people very wealthy, very quickly." Most people have positive feelings toward products and services created by entrepreneurs and want more individuals like Steve Jobs to fill the world. By encouraging people to aspire to enormous wealth creation through innovation, we turn a blind eye to consequences like the ecological damage of iPhone manufacturing. Producing a six-and-a-half-ounce iPhone contaminates twenty-six gallons of water and creates eighty pounds of rubble. We will eventually care about the unintended consequences of smartphones, but as we've seen in previous chapters, that won't happen until a great deal of harm has already been done. We need to expect all entrepreneurs to care about the consequences of their actions, no matter how ambitious they are. The world will be better and more sustainable if some iPhone profits go toward the reclamation of water contaminated in its production.

Entrepreneurial apologists who argue that we should trust the system to correct itself espouse a utilitarian perspective: we should expect our entrepreneurs to deliver more happiness than pain. If an entrepreneur has created net positive utility during their life, they can feel good about their innovating. The problem is that the people entrepreneurs make happy are usually different from those they hurt. By adopting a definition of good entrepreneur that requires only net positive utility, we make an arrogant judgment that the happiness of people who benefit first from innovations are more important than the pain of those who do not, cannot, or don't want to.

As the history of entrepreneurship shows, many entrepreneurial innovations cause pain to many noncustomers, and these consequences accumulate and accelerate with time. We should not let our entrepreneurs feel so privileged that they do not have to care about the pain they cause. It is in society's best interest to expect entrepreneurs to accept responsibility for the consequences of their actions, intended or otherwise.

Directly benefiting from enticing others to purchase products entrepreneurs create leads them to figure out how to deliver products or services that make people happy enough to gladly offer something more valuable in return. Every entrepreneur delivers some form of happiness to their customers, however fleeting. This happiness needs to last only long enough for the exchange to take place. It is a fundamental construct of entrepreneurship that only the entrepreneur and customer matter. Consequences for everyone else do not. We want good entrepreneurs to care about those consequences. We can and should expect entrepreneurs to create innovations that deliver lasting happiness, not only to their customers but to everyone involved in making and delivering the product and to everyone living nearby. We should express these expectations not only through laws—as we have seen, laws are never entirely successful in directing entrepreneurs—but also through social appreciation of our good entrepreneurs.

A prevalent meme within high-tech entrepreneurship circles is epitomized by a slogan Mark Zuckerberg propagated within Facebook: "Move fast and break things." This is widely interpreted as meaning that entrepreneurs have permission to take large risks and ignore rules because they deliver innovations to the world. As we have seen, entrepreneurs have believed they have special permission to ignore rules from as long ago as we have documentation. Remember Shalim-Assur, the Assurian caravan owner in chapter 6 who instructed his caravan driver to smuggle bolts of textiles into the town of Timelkiya. Being self-directed means that entrepreneurs feel, to one degree or another, that they can decide which rules they will follow. Entrepreneurial innovation is directly linked to this self-direction. But being self-directed does not—and should not—exempt entrepreneurs from the consequences of ignoring those rules.

Likewise, entrepreneurs should never create or enable actions, legal or illegal, that can potentially cause physical or mental harm. If an innovation takes longer to develop because it needs to be done safely, then patience must be expected.

These are fundamental expectations we should have of all entrepreneurs. Beyond being subject to whatever fines or constraints are imposed for violating rules, society should shun entrepreneurs and their products that have caused harm to others—whether customers, employees, suppliers, or anyone in the vicinity.

Creators of Value

We need entrepreneurs. We cannot live without them. But we have been naive in our understanding of how entrepreneurship works and why forces beyond their control lead them to act in ways that are not considerate of others, particularly noncustomers. We need good entrepreneurs to innovate products and services that enhance our lives, and we need them to look after our well-being, not just our momentary pleasures.

Understanding how and what entrepreneurs have accomplished in the past offers a powerful understanding of primal forces that drive some to be self-directed, to accept the risks of loss, and to be different and apart. We are fortunate that archeologists, anthropologists, economists, sociologists, and bystanders have uncovered so much new information about past entrepreneurial actions that we can now place entrepreneurship into a broader and more consequential systems context. Self-directed people who are driven to make and do things differently and are willing to live off what they can entice others to give them in return for their actions have shaped the world and our place in it. Entrepreneurs shape our future. That future may be burdened to an even greater degree by pollutants, inequality, and diminished resources. I believe that a deeper understanding of this force shows that it doesn't have to be.

We must acknowledge the contributions of entrepreneurs even as we hold them accountable for the problems they have caused. Punishment has never worked; enticement is key. We now know what a good entrepreneur is. We can use some of the same methods they use to entice us to steer their own behavior. More informed, respectful, mutual enticement will be immensely rewarding to all.

Entrepreneurship is the most important force shaping our lives, our world, and soon our solar system. It deserves and demands to be understood. I hope I have succeeded in pushing that understanding to a new level.

Notes on the Definition of "Entrepreneur"*

Formulating a history of anything requires that we know exactly what it is we are seeking to understand. This is especially true with entrepreneurs, as the word is now overused and can mean anything. We need a definition that is as valid for 2000 BC as it is for 2000 AD and is precise enough to categorically identify who is an entrepreneur and who is not.

We need to formulate an operational definition of "entrepreneur." That requires the following:

- Its criteria must yield a yes or no answer to the question, "Is this person an entrepreneur?"
- Its criteria must be measurable and replicable; the answer to who is an entrepreneur cannot change or be interpreted differently at different times or under different conditions.
- Whoever applies the criteria should reach the same conclusion.

---

* A more detailed explanation of the derivation of this definition can be found in my 2022 *Journal of Management History* article, "The Pre-Historic Entrepreneur: Rethinking the Definition."

As we are investigating a topic that could predate history and writing, the definition must use criteria discernable in any combination of archeological, anthropological, or historical records.

None of the hundreds of existing definitions, described generally in chapter 2, work as historically consistent operational definitions. State-of-mind definitions, like those associated with risk-taking, don't work because we can't tell what a person in the past was thinking unless they described it in writing or in an interview—assuming we could know how to adjust for a person's natural tendency to glorify and justify their actions. (This does not prevent us from concluding based on assembled evidence that there may be certain relationships between traits and motivations and entrepreneurial success in certain places and during certain periods.)

Definitions based on starting or running a company don't work either. Corporations are relatively new legal constructs, and those constructs have morphed over the past few centuries. Using any definition that relies on a legal structure would tie entrepreneurship to the actions of the people who created the laws. We would be making a hidden assumption that societies create entrepreneurs. We need a definition that stays clear of any structural linkage with legal, political, social, or religious constructs.

Similarly, if we want to be open-minded about what entrepreneurship is and has been, the definition cannot depend on any historic milestones, including the invention of money, the introduction of capitalism, or the emergence of "modern" economies. Our criteria must focus strictly on things people made and how nonhousehold members used those objects. We want to spot when, where, and how people create things that nonfamily members value.

We need to look at outcomes and objects. Fortunately, experienced and esteemed archeologists, anthropologists, and historians have learned to uncover and identify objects that people used and cared about and determine who made them. I cite here two articles with complete bibliographies that identify criteria for detecting objects in the archeological record that were made to be exchanged with others. Christopher Garraty's "Investigating Market Exchange in Ancient Societies: A Theoretical Review"[1] and Sussane Kerner's "Craft Specialisation and Its Relation with Social Organization in the Late 6th to Early 4th Millennium BCE of the Southern Levant"[2] are great summaries of these criteria. The works of Cathy Lynne Costin have proven essential for identifying products in the archeological record that were produced by self-directed individuals rather than individuals or groups directed by an overarching institution or social or political hierarchy.[3]

From these works and those of many others, we are directed to look for items produced with the quality and uniformity indicative of a deliberated set of repetitive actions, perhaps using specialized tools, beyond the abilities of the surrounding population. These products are made in places controlled by the producer and stored in places controlled by the producer or a trader. For our purposes we then look for these entrepreneurial products not just in the producer's home, workshop, store, or factory but in nonfamily members' homes—that is, with customers.

Whereas archeologists teach us how to identify self-directed individuals who make products for others, we need the help of anthropologists to teach us how to identify which types of trades are entrepreneurial and which are not. Who is a customer, as opposed to who is performing a ritual or being dictated by others to exchange? Malinowski's description of the seven types of Stone Age exchange used in the Trobriand Islands identifies *gimwali*, bartered exchange, as distinct from ritual exchange and gifting.[4] Some anthropologists have identified other forms of ritual exchange, but the practice of gimwali has similar characteristics everywhere it is practiced. The essence of what Malinowski observed is the double

362   Notes on the Definition of "Entrepreneur"

opt-in nature of nonritual, nonreciprocal exchange. Both parties independently agree to enter into a negotiation, which *may* result in an exchange of objects of independently assessed value. We are looking for evidence of double opt-in exchange.

How do we spot double opt-in exchange in the archeological record? Garraty notes that double opt-in exchange takes place in markets, but it is not limited to markets. As mentioned in chapter 2, there are many forms of double opt-in exchange; gimwali is just the most primal one we've observed directly. As ritual exchange and gifting are forms of one-to-one exchange tied to ceremony or social obligations, they are not well suited for individuals exchanging large quantities of similar products with strangers. If we find evidence of independently controlled, factory-like production of very large quantities of products beyond the needs of the local community, some of those products would need to have been exchanged without ritual or reciprocal exchange. In chapter 1 we identify two examples of prehistoric large-scale production sites, and a third, Shiqmim, is described in chapter 3. Because we cannot explicitly tie these producers to the exact form of exchange they used, I label them "proto-entrepreneurs."

We can tell with a high degree of certainty

- if an individual was self-directed in how they created value;
- if the individual created value sought by others; and
- if they captured value for themselves through double opt-in exchange.

Fortunately, these three characteristics suffice for creating criteria that allow us to identify individuals throughout time whom we would instantly recognize as entrepreneurs.

In this book we are really identifying and discussing a subset of entrepreneurs: successful ones. We are looking for and at entrepreneurs who have made a discernable difference. We are not finding all of them, but those we have found left traces that have persisted for hundreds or thousands of years. We can adjust these three criteria to define a successful entrepreneur by using an iterative approach. Using the understanding we have developed through the examples discussed in this book, we can identify a minimal set of modifiers that distinguish an entrepreneur whose products were exemplary in the quality and quantity of their production from those of people or persons having little long-term success at being an entrepreneur.

All entrepreneurs throughout time have been self-directed, whether they have been successful or not. There is no need to modify this criterion.

A successful entrepreneur does more than creating value sought by others. As we have seen, to remain part of a swarm for long enough to be discerned in the archeological record, you need to produce products that some group you serve considers to be the best of what is available. A product that some group considers to be the best *is* the definition of an innovation. In the case of entrepreneurs, they must serve some group within the culture they serve. In the definition from chapter 2, I cite "perceived" value. Value is always perceived, but because that is not widely realized, I insert it as a clarification. Wealth is an outcome that is absolutely measurable, but we have seen some entrepreneurs seek other forms of value for their innovations, like fame or acknowledgment.

To keep the book nontechnical, I did not want to use the term "double opt-in" in my definition in chapter 2; I describe it instead. I also add a modifying phrase, "entice others," to signify that the double opt-in exchange is not a random encounter in the case of a successful entrepreneur.

The test of a good definition is whether or not it is compact. Does losing any criteria make it too broad, labeling some people as entrepreneurs whom we would not recognize? Does adding any other criteria narrow its scope and exclude people who are consensus entrepreneurs? I admit that we can lose the word "perceived" whenever the definition of "value" is well understood. Other than that, I think this definition can stand the test of time.

Notes on the Definition of "Entrepreneur"

1. Christopher P. Garraty, "Investigating Market Exchange in Ancient Societies: A Theoretical Review," in *Archaeological Approaches to Market Exchange in Ancient Societies*, ed. Christopher P. Garraty and Barbara L. Stark (Boulder: University Press of Colorado, 2010), 3–32.
2. Susanne Kerner, "Craft Specialisation and Its Relation with Social Organisation in the Late 6th to Early 4th Millennium BCE of the Southern Levant," *Paléorient* 36, no. 1 (2010): 179–98.
3. Cathy Lynne Costin, "The Study of Craft Production," in *Handbook of Archaeological Methods*, vol. 2, ed. H. Maschner 2 (Lanham, MD: Altamira, 2005), 1032–1105; Costin, "Craft Production Systems," in *Archaeology at the Millennium*, ed. G. Feinman and T. Price (New York: Kluwer), 273–327.
4. Bronislaw Malinowski, *Argonauts of the Western Pacific: An Account of Native Enterprise and Adventure in the Archipelagoes of Melanesian New Guinea* (New York: Routledge, 2002); Marcel Mauss, *The Gift: The Form and Reason for Exchange in Archaic Societies* (New York: Routledge, 2002).

Bibliographic Notes

C reating a view of entrepreneurship that spans millennia and the globe requires significant digging through archives and help from many experts and scholars. My objective with these notes is to describe the most accessible references I used in understanding each of the topics discussed. (I describe the help I received from experts and scholars in the acknowledgments.) I have chosen to list the most compact set of references; by studying the references cited by these sources, anyone can start exploring any subject area to the depth that interests them.

One noteworthy reference that I do not cite in its entirety is a compendium of academic papers assembled by three distinguished economists of the late twentieth century. The articles they chose to include in their book describe entrepreneurship at several different periods and in different parts of the globe. It is a very academic work, but if you are deeply interested in the subject, it is worth the effort:

Landes, David S., Joel Mokyr, and William J. Baumol, eds. *The Invention of Enterprise: Entrepreneurship from Ancient Mesopotamia to Modern Times.* Princeton, NJ: Princeton University Press, 2012.

I do not reference Diderot's 1751 encyclopedia of trades and industry specifically, but it is full of fascinating illustrations depicting the machines and processes used in all the industries of his time, before factories and steam power further accelerated the ability to scale supply.

Diderot, Denis. *A Diderot Pictorial Encyclopedia of Trades and Industry*, 2 vols., ed. Charles Coulston Gillispie. New York: Dover, 1959.

Introduction

Qingming Scroll

Valerie Hansen's illustrated description of the Qingming scroll is a fun and charming introduction to this work of art that is not appreciated enough in the West. This paper is also easily accessible on the internet:

Hansen, Valerie. "The Beijing Qingming Scroll and Its Significance for the Study of Chinese History." *Journal of Sung-Yuan Studies* (1996). https://history.yale.edu/sites/default/files/files/Hansen-Beijing%20Qingming%20Scroll.pdf.

There are libraries full of descriptions of China during this entrepreneurial golden age. These two sources are very well written, impeccably researched, and not too academic:

Kuhn, Dieter. *The Age of Confucian Rule: The Song Transformation of China.* Cambridge, MA: Harvard University Press, 2011.
Lewis, Mark Edward. *China's Cosmopolitan Empire: The Tang Dynasty.* Cambridge, MA: Harvard University Press, 2009.

Daedalus

Francis Bacon is a very important contributor to Western philosophy and considered by many to be the father of the scientific method. Although I only quote his version of the story of Daedalus, the rest of his essays are worth reading, too.

Bacon, Francis. *Bacon's Essays and Wisdom of the Ancients.* Little, Brown, 1884.

If you are fascinated with the story of Daedelus, here are three versions from Roman times:

Ovid's *Art of Love*, book 2, lines 1–110; Ovid's *Metamorphoses*, book 8, lines 153–259; and Virgil's *Aeneid*, 6.1–40.

North Korea

I allude to North Korean entrepreneurship several times in the book. This reference is both valuable and accessible:

Kim, Byung-Yeon. *Unveiling the North Korean Economy: Collapse and Transition*. Cambridge: Cambridge University Press, 2017.

Chapter 1

Ötzi

Ötzi is perhaps the world's most interesting mummy. Everything about him is fascinating. These five pieces will give you a good overview; the Wierer and the Artioli references are technical.

Artioli, Gilberto, et al. "Long-Distance Connections in the Copper Age: New Evidence from the Alpine Iceman's Copper Axe." *PLoS One* 12, no. 7 (2017): e0179263.
Gannon, Meegan. "Scientists Reconstruct Ötzi the Iceman's Frantic Final Climb." *National Geographic*, October 30, 2019. https://www.nationalgeo graphic.com/history/article/scientists-reconstruct-otzi-iceman-final-climb.
Krosnar, Katka. "Now You Can Walk in the Footsteps of 5,000-Year-Old Iceman—Wearing His Boots." *The Telegraph*, July 17, 2005. https://www .telegraph.co.uk/news/worldnews/europe/italy/1494238/Now-you-can -walk-in-footsteps-of-5000-year-old-Iceman-wearing-his-boots.html.
Rosenberg, Jennifer, "Otzi the Iceman." ThoughtCo. https://www.thoughtco .com/otzi-the-iceman-1779439, updated January 4, 2020.
Wierer, Ursula, et al. "The Iceman's Lithic Toolkit: Raw Material, Technology, Typology and Use." *Plos One* 13, no. 6 (2018): e0198292.

Trobriands

The *Argonauts of the Western Pacific* is a classic of many disciplines, including economic anthropology. It reads like a travel log.

Malinowski, Bronisław. *Argonauts of the Western Pacific: An Account of Native Enterprise and Adventure in the Archipelagoes of Melanesian New Guinea*. London: Routledge, 2002.

Bead Factory Tribe

The bead factory tribe is a tantalizing example of entrepreneurship from over nine thousand years ago. This article summarizes the exquisitely excavated, researched, and described body of work that uncovered and analyzed these artifacts.

Wright, Katherine, and Andrew Garrard. "Social Identities and the Expansion of Stone Bead-Making in Neolithic Western Asia: New Evidence from Jordan." *Antiquity* 77, no. 296 (2003): 267–84.

Cabezo Juré

Francisco Nocete wrote an engaging summary of his excavations and findings of this almost five-thousand-year-old copper tool factory.

Nocete, Francisco. "The First Specialised Copper Industry in the Iberian Peninsula: Cabezo Juré (2900–2200 BC)." *Antiquity* 80, No. 309 (2006).

Heqanakht

You can't help but feel for Heqanakht. James Allen's review of the Heqanakht papyri is an amazing piece of scholarship. The book can be hard to find, but it is worth the search. If you can't find Allen's book, or you just want to learn more about ancient Egypt, try the classic textbook authored by Barry Kemp.

Allen, James P. *The Heqanakht Papyri*. New York: Metropolitan Museum of Art, 2002.
Kemp, Barry J. *Ancient Egypt: Anatomy of a Civilization*. London: Routledge, 2006.

Uruk and Ancient Mesopotamia

There is no shortage of material on ancient Mesopotamia. The book by Gil Stein is a good source of material of how long-distance trade evolved into an entrepreneurially dominated field.

Stein, Gil. *Rethinking World-Systems: Diasporas, Colonies, and Interaction in Uruk Mesopotamia*. Tucson: University of Arizona Press, 1999.

These four works are my favorite descriptions of the economy of Mesopotamia.

Aubet, Maria Eugenia. *Commerce and Colonization in the Ancient Near East*. Cambridge: Cambridge University Press, 2013.

Garfinkle, Steven J. "Ancient Near Eastern City-States." In *The Oxford Handbook of the State in the Ancient Near East and Mediterranean*, 94–119. New York: Oxford University Press, 2013.

Postgate, Nicholas. *Early Mesopotamia: Society and Economy at the Dawn of History*. London: Routledge, 2017.

Veenhof, Klaas. " 'Modern' Features in Old Assyrian Trade." *Journal of the Economic and Social History of the Orient* 40, no. 4 (1997): 336–66.

This is the reference for the etymology of the word "profit." It is not an easy reference.

Roth, Martha, T. ed. *The Assyrian Dictionary of the Oriental Institute of the University of Chicago* (CAD). https://oi.uchicago.edu/research/publications/assyrian-dictionary-oriental-institute-university-chicago-cad.

Indus Valley

The Indus Valley civilization is fascinating. It is tantalizing because we do not find any evidence of how it was ruled, and the civilization had a written language we cannot read. These three references will give you a good sense of what we know.

Kenoyer, Jonathan M. "Trade and Technology of the Indus Valley: New Insights from Harappa, Pakistan." *World Archaeology* 29, no. 2 (1997): 262–80.

Miller, Heather M.-L. "Associations and Ideologies in the Locations of Urban Craft Production at Harappa, Pakistan (Indus Civilization)." *Archeological Papers of the American Anthropological Association* 17, no. 1 (2007): 37–51.

Wright, Rita P. *The Ancient Indus: Urbanism, Economy, and Society*. Cambridge: Cambridge University Press, 2010.

China

The emergence of Chinese entrepreneurs has not been studied extensively, and Chinese scholars have not been interested in understanding it. The record of the teachings of Confucius as recorded by his followers is where any search starts.

The Analects. London: Penguin, 1979.

A good place to begin an understanding of Chinese archeology and historic evidence of independent artisans and merchants are these two books:

Liu, Li, and Xingcan Chen. *The Archaeology of China: From the Late Paleolithic to the Early Bronze Age*. Cambridge: Cambridge University Press, 2012.

Von Falkenhausen, Lothar. *Chinese Society in the Age of Confucius (1000–250 BC): The Archaeological Evidence*, vol. 2. Los Angeles: Cotsen Institute of Archaeology, University of California, Los Angeles, 2006.

A good general overview of how the Chinese economy coalesced and evolved can be found in

Von Glahn, Richard. *An Economic History of China: From Antiquity to the Nineteenth Century*. Cambridge: Cambridge University Press, 2016.

Discovering the etymology of the Chinese word for profit, "Li" 利, required a great deal of digging and assistance from Joshua Seufert, head of collections at Princeton's East Asian Library, and Charles Aylmer, the head of Chinese Collections at Cambridge University, aided by Yuzhou Bai's expert translations. The key source for the oracle bone evolution of 利 are set out on pp. 1515–20 of 李孝定，甲骨文字集釋，台北　1974. (Li Xiaoding, *Jiagu wenzi jishi*, Volume 4.)

Chavín

The diversity of trade and trading goods in ancient Chavín can be discerned from the meticulous work of Isabelle Druc.

Druc, Isabelle C. "Ceramic Diversity in Chavín de Huántar, Peru." *Latin American Antiquity* 15, no. 3 (2004): 344–63.

Mesoamerica

Susan Evans's book is a good place to start your understanding of the evolution of civilization in Mesoamerica. It is important to remember in reading her book that many ancient forms of trade were not entrepreneurial. Evans points to several examples of very ancient trade, but we need to spot marketplaces to be sure people are behaving entrepreneurially.

Evans, Susan T. *Ancient Mexico and Central America: Archeology and Culture History*, 3rd ed. London: Thames & Hudson, 2008.

This article by Feinman and Nichols explicitly and conclusively traces the emergence of market exchange in Oaxaca.

Feinman, Gary M., and Linda M. Nicholas. "A Multiscalar Perspective on Market Exchange in the Classic Period Valley of Oaxaca." In *Archaeological Approaches to Market Exchange in Ancient Societies*, ed. Christopher P. Garraty and Barbara L. Stark, 85–98. Boulder: University Press of Colorado, 2010.

Demarest's book is a great place to start learning about the Mayan civilization.

Demarest, Arthur. *Ancient Maya: The Rise and Fall of a Rainforest Civilization*, vol. 3. Cambridge: Cambridge University Press, 2004.

These three books paint a comprehensive picture of Aztec merchants and entrepreneurs.

Cowgill, George L. *Ancient Teotihuacan*. Cambridge: Cambridge University Press, 2015.
Hirth, Kenneth G. *The Aztec Economic World: Merchants and Markets in Ancient Mesoamerica*. Cambridge: Cambridge University Press, 2016.
Nichols, Deborah L., et al. "Chiconautla, Mexico: A Crossroads of Aztec Trade and Politics." *Latin American Antiquity* 20, no. 3 (2009): 443–72.

Sub-Saharan Africa

Sub-Saharan Africa is the one spot on the globe where I did not detail the emergence of entrepreneurship. It is there, but the archeology is more complex, and I have not found the single best story to tell. Graham Connah has written a summary of African archeology, which is a vast field due to widely varying and sometimes challenging terrains and access constraints.

Connah, Graham. *African Civilizations: An Archaeological Perspective*. Cambridge: Cambridge University Press, 2015.

Finally, Bruce Trigger has written a brilliant analysis of similarities and differences in the emergence of trade and commerce among characteristic early civilizations, including the Yoruba from Africa.

Trigger, Bruce G. *Understanding Early Civilizations: A Comparative Study*. Cambridge: Cambridge University Press, 2003.

Chapter 2

Sima Qian

This is the classic English translation of the *Shiji*. Its introduction also describes the conditions under which Sima Qian compiled his history.

Sima, Qian. *Records of the Grand Historian: Han Dynasty*, vol. 65. New York: Columbia University Press, 1993.

Socrates and Xenophon

This volume of the collected works of Xenophon includes a good biographical sketch in the preface.

Xenophon. *Oeconomicus*, trans. O. J. Todd Cambridge, MA: Harvard University Press, 2013.

Creative Destruction

Schumpeter even admitted that his writing style and constant references to esoteric economic works meant that "few if any people have read my ponderous volumes really through." So true, but that hasn't stopped people from quoting him. The passage that includes the term "creative destruction" can be found in

Schumpeter, J. A. *Capitalism, Socialism, and Democracy*. Edinburgh: Edinburgh University Press, 2016.

The most accessible way to learn about Schumpeter is from this recent biography:

McCraw, Thomas K. *Prophet of Innovation*. Cambridge, MA: Harvard University Press, 2009.

You can read about the evolution of the concept of entrepreneurship in this monograph:

Hébert, Robert F., and Albert N. Link. *A History of Entrepreneurship*. London: Routledge, 2009.

Entrepreneur Definition

Cantillon, Richard, and Antoin E. Murphy. *Essay on the Nature of Trade in General*. Carmel, IN: Liberty Fund, 2015.

How I Derived the Definition

My derivation of a time- and place-invariant definition of entrepreneur relied on the work and insights contained and cited in these works:

Costin, Cathy Lynne. "Craft Production." In *Handbook of Archaeological Methods*, vol. 2, ed. H. Maschner, 1034–1107. Lanham, MD: Altamira, 2005.
Costin, Cathy Lynne. "Craft Production Systems." In *Archaeology at the Millennium: A Sourcebook*, ed. Gary M. Feinman and T. Douglas Price, 273–327. New York: Springer, 2001.
Garraty, Christopher P. "Investigating Market Exchange in Ancient Societies: A Theoretical Review." In *Archaeological Approaches to Market Exchange in Ancient Societies*, ed. Christopher P. Garraty and Barbara L. Stark, 3–32. Boulder: University Press of Colorado, 2010.
Kerner, Susanne. "Craft Specialisation and Its Relation with Social Organisation in the late 6th to Early 4th Millennium BCE of the Southern Levant." *Paléorient* 36, no. 1 (2010): 179–98.
Mauss, Marcel. *The Gift: The Form and Reason for Exchange in Archaic Societies*. London: Routledge, 2002.

My academic article on the pre-historic definition of entrepreneurship is:

Lidow, Derek. "The Pre-Historic Entrepreneur: Rethinking the Definition," *Journal of Management History*, forthcoming, 2022.

Entrepreneurial Swarm

Here is the quote that describes Schumpeter's concept of entrepreneurial swarming: "The question may now be formulated as follows: why is it that economic development in our sense does not proceed evenly as a tree grows, but as it were jerkily; why does it display those characteristic ups and downs? The answer cannot be short and precise enough: exclusively *because the new combinations are not . . . evenly distributed through time . . .* but *appear, if at all, discontinuously in groups or swarms*" (Joseph Schumpeter, *The Theory of Economic Development*, New York: Oxford University Press, 1961, 223; emphasis in the original).

Two distinct schools of thought have emerged to quantitatively describe entre-preneurial swarming. Epstein and Axtell created a computer model of a society composed of agents who discover valuable objects and trade them. Their model demonstrates why entrepreneurs swarm and trade. You can read their book, or you can get a simpler overview in Beinhocker's book on how and why established economic theories don't effectively describe how the world, including its entrepreneurs, really works.

Beinhocker, Eric D. *The Origin of Wealth: Evolution, Complexity, and the Radical Remaking of Economics*. Cambridge, MA: Harvard Business Press, 2006.
Epstein, Joshua M., and Robert Axtell. *Growing Artificial Societies: Social Science from the Bottom Up*. Washington, DC: Brookings Institution Press, 1996.

A very mathematical formulation of entrepreneurial swarming can be found in this article:

Justman, Moshe. "Swarming Mechanics." *Economics of Innovation and New Technology* 4, no. 3 (1996): 235–44.

Stephen Klepper's book meticulously traces the development of several prominent entrepreneurial swarms.

Klepper, Steven. *Experimental Capitalism: The Nanoeconomics of American High-Tech Industries*. Princeton, NJ: Princeton University Press, 2015.

Shiqmim

If you are interested in the emergence of metallurgy or the copper-producing enclave of Shiqmim, these two references are great places to start.

Golden, Jonathan M. *Dawn of the Metal Age: Technology and Society During the Levantine Chalcolithic.* London: Routledge, 2016.
Golden, Jonathan, Thomas E. Levy, and Andreas Hauptmann. "Recent Discoveries Concerning Chalcolithic Metallurgy at Shiqmim, Israel." *Journal of Archaeological Science* 28, no. 9 (2001): 951–63.

Chapter 3

Sitnebsekhtu and Women Entrepreneurs in Ancient Egypt

These three works get into enough detail to discern female entrepreneurs in ancient Egypt.

Allen, James P. *The Heqanakht Papyri.* New York: Metropolitan Museum of Art, 2002.
Muhs, Brian. *The Ancient Egyptian Economy: 3000–30 BCE.* Cambridge: Cambridge University Press, 2016.
Zingarelli, Andrea. *Trade and Market in New Kingdom Egypt: Internal Socio-Economic Processes and Transformations.* London: BAR Publishing, 2010.

Women Entrepreneurs in Mesopotamia and Kanesh

"Code of Hammurabi, c. 1780 BCE," trans. L. W. King. Ancient History Sourcebook. https://sourcebooks.fordham.edu/ancient/hamcode.asp.

Özgüç, Tahsin. *Kültepe: Kanis/Nesa: The Earliest International Trade Center and the Oldest Capital City of the Hittites*, 184. Tokyo: Middle Eastern Culture Center in Japan, 2003.

Women Entrepreneurs in the Indus Valley

Rita Wright's works are always very accessible and carefully researched.

Wright, Rita. "Women's Labor and Pottery Production in Prehistory." In *Engendering Archaeology: Women and Pre-History*, ed. Joan M. Gero and Margaret W. Conkey, 194–223. Hoboken, NJ: Wiley-Blackwell, 1991.

Women Entrepreneurs in Ancient China

This is a wonderful book, revered by academics but little known to the public:

Barbieri-Low, Anthony Jerome. *Artisans in Early Imperial China.* Seattle: University of Washington Press, 2007.

Women Entrepreneurs in Ancient Greece

These references are important for understanding female entrepreneurship in Greece.

Acton, Peter. *Poiesis: Manufacturing in Classical Athens.* Oxford: Oxford University Press, 2014, particularly 274–78.
Kamen, Deborah. *Status in Classical Athens.* Princeton, NJ: Princeton University Press, 2013.
Xenophon. *Oeconomicus*, 3.15–16.

Yoruba Women

This classic work on understanding the emergence of civilization contains several references to the roles women have played in the emergence of general trade and the crafts.

Trigger, Bruce G. *Understanding Early Civilizations: A Comparative Study.* Cambridge: Cambridge University Press, 2003, particularly 348.

Other Examples of Women Entrepreneurs

These references offer a good sense of the scale of successful women entrepreneurs in different contexts.

Berdowski, Piotr. "Roman Businesswomen. I: The Case of the Producers and Distributors of Garum in Pompeii." *Analecta Archaeologica Ressoviensia* 3 (2008): 251–71.
Kwolek-Folland, Angel. *Incorporating Women: A History of Women and Business in the United States.* New York: Twayne, 1998.
Phillips, Nicola Jane. *Women in Business, 1700–1850.* Woodbridge, England: Boydell, 2006.

Russia before the Soviets was perhaps the least-constrained culture for women entrepreneurs.

Ulianova, Galina. *Female Entrepreneurs in Nineteenth-Century Russia*. London: Routledge, 2015.

Raskolniki

Finding references on this very interesting Russian minority can be challenging. This reference provides background and context.

Gerschenkron, Alexander. *Europe in the Russian Mirror*. London: Cambridge University Press, 1970, particularly 21.

Ummidia Quadratilla

Ummidia was a very interesting individual and worth knowing about.

Sick, David H. "Ummidia Quadratilla: Cagey Businesswoman or Lazy Pantomime Watcher?" *Classical Antiquity* 18, no. 2 (1999): 330–48.

Madame Tussaud

Pamela Pilbeam's book on Tussaud and the history of waxworks is fascinating.

Pilbeam, Pamela. *Madame Tussaud and the History of Waxworks*. London: Hambledon/Continuum, 2006.

Black Entrepreneurs

These four references are essential reading for gaining an understanding of the poorly understood and underappreciated history of Black entrepreneurship in America.

Butler, John Sibley. *Entrepreneurship and Self-Help Among Black Americans: A Reconsideration of Race and Economics*. Albany: State University of New York Press, 2012.
Ruef, Martin. *Between Slavery and Capitalism: The Legacy of Emancipation in the American South*. Princeton, NJ: Princeton University Press, 2016.
Walker, Juliet E. K. *The History of Black Business in America: Capitalism, Race, Entrepreneurship*, vol. 1. Chapel Hill: University of North Carolina Press, 2009.

Wills, Shomari. *Black Fortunes: The Story of the First Six African Americans Who Escaped Slavery and Became Millionaires.* New York: HarperCollins, 2018.

Specific information about William Johnson and Henry Boyd came from these sources:

Davis, Edwin Adams, and William Ransom Hogan. *The Barber of Natchez.* Baton Rouge: Louisiana State University Press, 1973.
Preston, Steve. "Our Rich History: Henry Boyd, Once a Slave, Became a Prominent African-American Furniture Maker," *Northern Kentucky Tribune,* February 11, 2019. https://www.nkytribune.com/2019/02/our-rich-history -henry-boyd-once-a-slave-became-a-prominent-african-american-furniture -maker/.
Van Cleave, Timothy. "The Barber of Natchez." National Park Service. Accessed March 30, 2015.

Other Outsider Entrepreneurs

I found these two insightful sources about Chinese and Mexican American entrepreneurs.

Butler, John Sibley, Alfonso Morales, and David L. Torres, eds. *An American Story: Mexican American Entrepreneurship and Wealth Creation.* West Lafayette, IN: Purdue University Press, 2009.
Zhou, Min. *Chinatown: The Socioeconomic Potential of an Urban Enclave.* Philadelphia: Temple University Press, 2010.

Chapter 4

Amur-Ištar

Larsen's book on Kanesh is the classic and very accessible.

Dercksen, Jan Gerrit. "On the Financing of Old Assyrian Merchants." In *Trade and Finance in Ancient Mesopotamia: Proceedings of the First MOS Symposium (Leiden 1997).* Istanbul: Nederlands Historisch-Archaeologisch Instituut, Istanbul, 1999.
Larsen, Mogens Trolle. *Ancient Kanesh: A Merchant Colony in Bronze Age Anatolia.* Cambridge: Cambridge University Press, 2015.

Larsen, Mogens Trolle. "Partnerships in the Old Assyrian Trade." *Iraq* 39, no. 1 (1977): 119–45.

Monumetum Ephesenum

Malmendier, Ulrike. "Roman Shares." In *Origins of Value: The Financial Innovations that Created Modern Capital Markets*, ed. William N. Goetzmann and K. Geert Rouwenhorst., 31–42. New York: Oxford University Press, 2005.

Ho-Pen

Ho-pen are not widely described in references translated into English. Here are a few references that will enable you to piece together a sense of these early Chinese joint-stock associations.

Chin, Tamara T. *Savage Exchange: Han Imperialism, Chinese Literary Style, and the Economic Imagination*. Cambridge, MA: Harvard University Asia Center/Harvard University Press, 2020.
Ebrey, Patricia Buckley, and Anne Walthall. *East Asia: A Cultural, Social, and Political History*. Belmont, CA Cengage Learning, 2013.
Kuhn, Dieter. *The Age of Confucian Rule: The Song Transformation of China*. Cambridge, MA: Harvard University Press, 2011.
Lewis, Mark Edward. *China's Cosmopolitan Empire: The Tang Dynasty*. Cambridge, MA: Harvard University Press, 2009.
Von Glahn, Richard. *An Economic History of China: From Antiquity to the Nineteenth Century*. Cambridge: Cambridge University Press, 2016.
Yoshinobu, Shiba, and Mark Elvin. "Commerce and Society in Sung China." Trans. Mark Elvin. Ann Arbor: Center for Chinese Studies, University of Michigan, 1970.

Russia Company

The importance of the Russia Company to entrepreneurs has been overlooked.

Sandman, Alison, and Eric H. Ash. "Trading Expertise: Sebastian Cabot Between Spain and England." *Renaissance Quarterly* 57, no. 3 (2004): 813–46.

Walker, C. E. "The History of the Joint Stock Company." *Accounting Review* 6, no. 2 (1931): 97–105.

Willan, Thomas Stuart. *The Early History of the Russia Company, 1553–1603*. Manchester, UK: Manchester University Press, 1956.

Dutch East Indies Company (VOC)

These two references give a good sense of how and why the VOC was created and how its shares became widely traded speculative investments.

Gelderblom, Oscar, and Joost Jonker. "Completing a Financial Revolution: The Finance of the Dutch East India Trade and the Rise of the Amsterdam Capital Market, 1595–1612." *Journal of Economic History* 64, no. 3 (2004): 641–72.

Petram, Lodewijk. *The World's First Stock Exchange*. New York: Columbia University Press, 2014.

South Seas

You'll need all three of these references to get a good sense of what caused this bubble and how the English Parliament made matters worse.

Carswell, John. *The South Sea Bubble*. Dover, NH: Alan Sutton, 1993.

Harris, Ron. "The Bubble Act: Its Passage and Its Effects on Business Organization." *Journal of Economic History* 54, no. 3 (1994): 610–27.

Temin, Peter, and Hans-Joachim Voth. "Riding the South Sea Bubble." *American Economic Review* 94, no. 5 (2004): 1654–68.

Exchange Alley

This hundred-year-old reference is filled with fascinating examples of early joint-stock companies.

Scott, William Robert. *The Constitution and Finance of English, Scottish and Irish Joint-Stock Companies to 1720*, vol. 1. Cambridge: Cambridge University Press, 1912.

John Law

These three biographies emphasize different aspects of John Law's career.

Gleeson, Janet. *Millionaire: The Philanderer, Gambler, and Duelist Who Invented Modern Finance*. New York: Simon & Schuster, 2001.

Hyde, H. Montgomery. *John Law: The History of an Honest Adventurer*. Amsterdam: Home & Van Thai, 1948.

Murphy, Antoin E. *John Law: Economic Theorist and Policy-Maker*. Oxford: Oxford University Press, 1997.

Samuel Slater

The accomplishments of Samuel Slater are not fully appreciated today.

Nicholas, Tom. *VC: An American History*. Cambridge, MA: Harvard University Press, 2019.

Tucker, Barbara M. "The Merchant, the Manufacturer, and the Factory Manager: The Case of Samuel Slater." *Business History Review* 55, no. 3 (1981): 297–313.

Chapter 5

Cornelius Vanderbilt

This is a great biography.

Stiles, T. J. *The First Tycoon: The Epic Life of Cornelius Vanderbilt*. New York: Knopf, 2009.

John D. Rockefeller

Chernow's biography of Rockefeller is the benchmark.

Chernow, Ron. *Titan: The Life of John D. Rockefeller, Sr.* New York: Random House, 1998.

Understanding how Rockefeller justified his actions is a great example of an entrepreneurial memoir and why you cannot trust many of those written today.

Rockefeller, John D. *John D. Rockefeller: The Autobiography of an Oil Titan and Philanthropist*. CreateSpace Publishing, 2016.

J. P. Morgan

Chernow's biography of J. P. Morgan is a bit dry, but Morgan didn't have much of a personality, and this is the best there is.

Chernow, Ron. *The House of Morgan: An American Banking Dynasty and the Rise of Modern Finance*. New York: Grove, 1990.

The source of the *New York Times* quote on the formation of U.S. Steel:

Bayles, James C. "The Merger of Iron and Steel Interests." *New York Times*, March 10, 1901. https://timesmachine.nytimes.com/timesmachine/1901/03/10/118462210.html.

J. Presper Eckert and John Mauchley

Eckert and Mauchley are underappreciated entrepreneurs.

Cortada, James W. *Before the Computer: IBM, NCR, Burroughs, and Remington Rand and the Industry They Created, 1865–1956*. Princeton, NJ: Princeton University Press, 2000.
Fishman, Katherine D. *The Computer Establishment*. New York: Harper & Row, 1981.

William Shockley, Arthur Rock, and Sherman Fairchild

These are the best-researched books about the birth of the semiconductor industry.

Lécuyer, Christophe. *Making Silicon Valley: Innovation and the Growth of High Tech, 1930–1970*. Cambridge, MA: MIT Press, 2006.
Seitz, Frederick, and Norman G. Einspruch. *Electronic Genie: The Tangled History of Silicon*. Urbana: University of Illinois Press, 1998.

This is the only accessible reference on Sherman Fairchild.

"Multifarious Sherman Fairchild," *Fortune*, May 1960, 170.

This article describes business practices among entrepreneurs and professional managers a hundred years ago.

Russell, Malcolm B. "Captive Supplier or Partner? Sears, Whirlpool and Washer Design." *Business and Economic History* 25, no. 1 (1996): 143–53.

Netscape

This interview with several Netscape insiders gives an excellent sense of how entrepreneurial decisions were made at the dawn of the internet.

Lashinsky, Adam. "Remembering Netscape: The Birth of the Web." *Fortune*, July 25, 2005. Accessed via CNN. https://web.archive.org/web/20060427112146/ and http://money.cnn.com/magazines/fortune/fortune_archive/2005/07/25/8266639/index.htm.

Chapter 6

James Drax

The story of sugar is more important to the history of entrepreneurship than the more widely told story of cotton. Sugar was not as important to American slavery, but its more complex processing played a pivotal role in shaping entrepreneurial structures and processes. Reconstructing the role of sugar and the primary role of James Drax in making it a global commodity requires reconstructing this pivotal time and set of events from multiple references.

Craton, Michael. "The Historical Roots of the Plantation Model." *Slavery and Abolition* 5, no. 3 (1984): 189–221.
Deerr, Noël. *The History of Sugar*, vol. II. London: Chapman & Hall, 1950.
Galloway, Jock H. *The Sugar Cane Industry: An Historical Geography from Its Origins to 1914*, vol. 12. Cambridge: Cambridge University Press, 2005.
Higman, Barry W. "The Sugar Revolution." *Economic History Review* 53, no. 2 (2000): 213–36.
Hills, Richard Leslie. *Power from Wind: A History of Windmill Technology*. Cambridge: Cambridge University Press, 1996.
Ligon, Richard. *A True Exact History of the Island of Barbados (1657)*. London: Forgotten Books, 2018.
Mintz, Sidney Wilfred. *Sweetness and Power: The Place of Sugar in Modern History*. New York: Penguin, 1986.
Pares, Richard. *Merchants and Planters*. Cambridge: *Economic History* Review/Cambridge University Press, 1960.
Parker, Matthew. *The Sugar Barons: Family, Corruption, Empire and War*. New York: Random House, 2011.

Sheridan, Richard B. *Sugar and Slavery: An Economic History of the British West Indies, 1623–1775*. Kingston, Jamaica: University of the West Indies Press, 1994.

Thompson, Peter. "Henry Drax's Instructions on the Management of a Seventeenth-Century Barbadian Sugar Plantation." *William and Mary Quarterly* 66, no. 3 (2009): 565–604.

Walvin, James. *Sugar: The World Corrupted, from Obesity to Slavery*. London: Robinson, 2018.

Lombe's Factory

The Joshua Freeman book is an engaging read, and Lombe's factory is featured in the first chapter. The Jones article is a more in-depth analysis of why entrepreneurs adopted the factory organization structure. The link to Drax has not been well understood until now.

Calladine, Anthony. "Lombe's Mill: An Exercise in Reconstruction." *Industrial Archaeology Review* 16, no. 1 (1993): 82–99.

Freeman, Joshua B. *Behemoth: A History of the Factory and the Making of the Modern World*. New York: Norton, 2018.

Jones, Stephen Richard Henry. "Technology, Transaction Costs, and the Transition to Factory Production in the British Silk Industry, 1700–1870." *Journal of Economic History* 47, no. 1 (1987): 71–96.

Grimes Graves

These Grimes Graves references can get technical very quickly. The English Heritage website leads to many of the informative displays you can find at the Grimes Graves visitor center.

Barber, Martyn, David Field, and Peter Topping. *The Neolithic Flint Mines of England*. Swindon, UK: English Heritage, 1999.

Russell, Miles. *Flint Mines in Neolithic Britain*. Stroud, UK: Tempus, 2000.

Sieveking, G. de G., et al. "A New Survey of Grimes Graves, Norfolk—First Report." *Proceedings of the Prehistoric Society* 39 (1973): 182–218. https://www.english-heritage.org.uk/visit/places/grimes-graves-prehistoric-flint-mine/history/.

Shalim-Assur

Larsen, Mogens Trolle. *Ancient Kanesh: A Merchant Colony in Bronze Age Anatolia*. Cambridge: Cambridge University Press, 2015.

Ostia

The Meiggs book contains more than you'll ever need to know about Ostia. The Holleran and Ellis books go into detail on how Rome's entrepreneurs created a retail golden age. The Aldrete and Mattingly article describes the magnitude of Rome's entrepreneurial supply chain accomplishments, while the Oleson book is a compendium of Roman, mostly supply-chain-oriented, innovations.

Aldrete, Greg S., and David J. Mattingly. "Feeding the City: The Organization, Operation, and Scale of the Supply System for Rome." In *Life, Death, and Entertainment in the Roman Empire*, ed. D. S. Potter and D. J. Mattingly. Ann Arbor: University of Michigan Press, 1999.

Ellis, Steven J. R. *The Roman Retail Revolution: The Socio-Economic World of the Taberna*. Oxford: Oxford University Press, 2018.

Holleran, Claire. *Shopping in Ancient Rome: The Retail Trade in the Late Republic and the Principate*. Oxford: Oxford University Press, 2012.

Meiggs, Russell. *Roman Ostia*. Oxford: Clarendon, 1973.

Oleson, John Peter, ed. *The Oxford Handbook of Engineering and Technology in the Classical World*. Oxford: Oxford University Press, 2008.

Eurysaces

Eurysaces created the world's most interesting and compelling entrepreneurial funeral monument.

Petersen, Lauren Hackworth. "The Baker, His Tomb, His Wife, and Her Breadbasket: The Monument of Eurysaces in Rome." *Art Bulletin* 85, no. 2 (2003): 230–57.

Matthew Bolton

Bolton's mint is vastly underappreciated as both an engineering and entrepreneurial milestone.

Tungate, Susan. *Matthew Boulton and the Soho Mint: Copper to Customer.* Worcestershire, UK: Brewin, 2020.

Baltimore and Ohio Railroad

Historians tend to talk about the impact of railroads in a general sense, yet the real story from an entrepreneurial perspective is how the first railroads were too complex for even the most ambitious and capable entrepreneurs of the age. These four references discuss the B&O from different perspectives and enable us to piece together how the railroad almost failed and why it survived to prosper.

Chandler, Alfred D., Jr. *The Visible Hand.* Cambridge, MA: Harvard University Press, 1993.

Dilts, James D. *The Great Road: The Building of the Baltimore and Ohio, the Nation's First Railroad, 1828–1853.* Stanford, CA: Stanford University Press, 1996.

Reizenstein, Milton. *The Economic History of the Baltimore and Ohio Railroad 1827–1853.* Baltimore, MD: Johns Hopkins Press, 1897.

Stover, John F. *History of the Baltimore and Ohio Railroad.* West Lafayette, IN: Purdue University Press, 1995.

Andrew Carnegie

Nasaw's biography of Carnegie is my favorite.

Nasaw, David. *Andrew Carnegie.* New York: Penguin, 2006.

Chapter 7

Josiah Wedgwood

The Dolan biography is a great, well-researched read. The McKendrick article adds intriguing and little-known facts—like Wedgwood selling knock-off products as his own—that make it a worthwhile read.

Dolan, Brian. *Wedgwood: The First Tycoon.* New York: Viking, 2004.

McKendrick, Neil. "Josiah Wedgwood: An Eighteenth-Century Entrepreneur in Salesmanship and Marketing Techniques." *Economic History Review* 12, no. 3 (1960): 408–33.

Objects of Astonishment

The workmanship and innovation represented in dozens of objects of astonishment from this huge hoard of copper objects is astonishing and underappreciated.

Bar Adon, P. *The Cave of the Treasure*. Jerusalem: Israel Exploration Society, 1980.

Golden, Jonathan. "New Light on the Development of Chalcolithic Metal Technology in the Southern Levant." *Journal of World Prehistory* 22, no. 3 (2009): 283–300.

Goren, Yuval. "The Location of Specialized Copper Production by the Lost Wax Technique in the Chalcolithic Southern Levant." *Geoarchaeology: An International Journal* 23, no. 3 (2008): 374–97.

Moorey, P. Roger S. "The Chalcolithic Hoard from Nahal Mishmar, Israel, in Context." *World Archaeology* 20, no. 2 (1988): 171–89.

Shalev, Sariel, and Jeremy P. Northover. "The Metallurgy of the Nahal Mishmar Hoard Reconsidered." *Archaeometry* 35, no. 1 (1993): 35–47.

Hospitality

The hospitality breakthrough is not understood or appreciated by business historians and deserves to be recognized as a major entrepreneurial accomplishment. These references paint a detailed picture of hospitality in China in comparison to medieval Europe and the Middle East.

Braudel, Fernand. *Civilization and Capitalism, 15th–18th Century, vol. I: The Structures of Everyday Life*. London: Collins, 1981, particularly 183.

Braudel, Fernand. *Civilization and Capitalism, 15th–18th Century, vol. II: The Wheels of Commerce*. Berkeley: University of California Press, 1992.

Ebrey, Patricia Buckley. "The Attractions of the Capital." In *Chinese Civilization: A Sourcebook*. New York: Simon and Schuster, 2009.

Hanna, Nelly. *Making Big Money in 1600: The Life and Times of Isma'il Abu Taqiyya, Egyptian Merchant*. Syracuse, NY: Syracuse University Press, 1998.

Kuhn, Dieter. *The Age of Confucian Rule: The Song Transformation of China.* Cambridge, MA: Harvard University Press, 2011.

Lewis, Mark Edward. *China's Cosmopolitan Empire: The Tang Dynasty.* Cambridge, MA: Harvard University Press, 2009.

Spufford, Peter. *Power and Profit: The Merchant in Medieval Europe.* London: Thames & Hudson, 2002.

Welch, Evelyn S. *Shopping in the Renaissance: Consumer Cultures in Italy 1400–1600.* New Haven, CT: Yale University Press, 2005.

West, Stephen H. "Recollections of the Northern Song Capital." In *Hawai'i Reader in Traditional Chinese Culture*, ed. Victor H. Mair, Nancy Shatzman Steinhardt, and Paul Rakita Goldin, 405–22. Honolulu: University of Hawai'i Press, 2005.

Harry Selfridge

Selfridge thought well of himself, but he really did understand the consumer. He was able to get even the most jaded customer to find something they never knew they needed.

Soucek, Gayle. *Marshall Field's: The Store that Helped Build Chicago.* Mt. Pleasant, SC: Arcadia, 2013.

Woodhead, Lindy. *Mr Selfridge.* Madrid: Punto de Lectura, 2014.

William Randolph Hearst and Joseph Pulitzer

Like Selfridge, Hearst and Pulitzer thought well of themselves and really understood their readers. They also understood how to make reading the newspaper every day addictive.

Juergens, George. Joseph Pulitzer and the New York World. Princeton, NJ: Princeton University Press, 2015.

Morris, James McGrath. *Pulitzer: A Life in Politics, Print, and Power.* New York: Harper, 2010.

Nasaw, David. *The Chief: The Life of William Randolph Hearst.* New York: Houghton Mifflin Harcourt, 2013.

Procter, Ben H. *William Randolph Hearst: The Early Years, 1863–1910*, vol. 1. Oxford: Oxford University Press, 1998.

Pulitzer, Joseph. "The College of Journalism." *North American Review* 178, no. 570 (1904): 641–80.
Whyte, Kenneth. *The Uncrowned King: The Sensational Rise of William Randolph Hearst.* Toronto: Vintage Canada, 2009.

Edward Bernays

Like the other entrepreneurs in this chapter, Bernays thought well of himself. His impact on consumerism is vastly underappreciated, as are the potency of his methods.

Bernays, Edward L. *Propaganda.* Brooklyn, NY: Ig Publishing, 2005.
Curtis, Adam. *Century of the Self,* vol. 17 (DVD). London: BBC Four, 2002. https://www.youtube.com/watch?v=eJ3RzGoQC4s.
Cutlip, Scott M. *The Unseen Power: Public Relations: A History.* New York: Routledge, 2013.

Chapter 8

Jacquard

Everything reliable we know about Jacquard comes from the Eymard publication in French by the city of Lyon. The other three references focus on different perspectives of his life and impact on subsequent innovations.

Delve, Janet. "Joseph Marie Jacquard: Inventor of the Jacquard Loom." *IEEE Annals of the History of Computing* 29, no. 4 (October–December 2007): 98–102.
Essinger, James. *Jacquard's Web: How a Hand-Loom Led to the Birth of the Information Age.* Oxford: Oxford University Press, 2004.
Everything2, https://everything2.com/title/Joseph+Marie+Jacquard.
Eymard, Paul. *Historique du Métier Jacquard.* Lyon, France: Imprimerie de Barret, 1863, particularly 9. Reprinted in *Annales des Sciences Physiques et Naturelles d'Agriculture et d'Industrie* 3rd ser., 7 (1863): 34–56.

Passion

Passion is an important entrepreneurial success story in several dimensions, including the Greek banking innovations that reshaped how entrepreneurs would forever expand their businesses.

Shipton, Kirsty M. W. "The Private Banks in Fourth-Century BC Athens: A Reappraisal." *Classical Quarterly* 47, no. 2 (1997): 396–422.

Champagne Faires

The Champagne faires marked the end of the "dark ages" from an entrepreneurial perspective. Both the Spufford and Braudel books are fascinating and important, even if you look only at the illustrations.

Braudel, Fernand. *Civilization and Capitalism, 15th-18th Century, vol. II: The Wheels of Commerce.* Berkeley: University of California Press, 1992.
Spufford, Peter. *Power and Profit: The Merchant in Medieval Europe.* London: Thames & Hudson, 2002.

Italian Banks

The world knows the Medicis, but they were mere copycats. These four references will give you an appreciation for the entrepreneurial accomplishments of Italian bankers centuries earlier.

Del Punta, Ignazio. "Principal Italian Banking Companies of the XIIIth and XIVth Centuries: A Comparison Between the Ricciardi of Lucca and the Bardi, Peruzzi and Acciaiuoli of Florence." *Journal of European Economic History* 33, no. 3 (2004): 647–62.
Hunt, Edwin S. *The Medieval Super-Companies: A Study of the Peruzzi Company of Florence.* Cambridge: Cambridge University Press, 2002.
Kohn, Meir. "Merchant Banking in the Medieval and Early Modern Economy." Working Paper 99–05. Hanover, NH: Dartmouth College, Department of Economics, 1999.
Origo, Iris. *The Merchant of Prato: Daily Life in a Medieval Italian City.* Middlesex, UK: Penguin, 2017.

Double Entry

The origins of double-entry bookkeeping are also not well understood or appreciated.

Lee, Geoffrey A. "The Coming of Age of Double Entry: The Giovanni Farolfi Ledger of 1299–1300." *Accounting Historians Journal* 4, no. 2 (1977): 79–95.

Smith, Fenny. "The Influence of Amatino Manucci and Luca Pacioli." *BSHM Bulletin: Journal of the British Society for the History of Mathematics* 23, no. 3 (2008): 143–56.

James Ritty

I never knew about James Ritty, and his story is a challenge to piece together. He is nonetheless the instigator of the business machine entrepreneurial swarm.

Ohio History Connection, https://ohiohistorycentral.org/w/James_Ritty.

History Computer, https://history-computer.com/james-ritty/.

John Patterson

Somebody needs to write an updated biography of John Patterson. He is the epitome of the "larger-than-life" cliché.

Crowther, Samuel. *John H. Patterson: The Romance of Business*. London: Geoffrey Bles, 1923.

Dayton Innovation Legacy, http://www.daytoninnovationlegacy.org/patterson.html.

Alexander Dey

The importance of time clocks is vastly underappreciated.

National Museum of American History, https://americanhistory.si.edu/collections/search/object/nmah_856741.

Worldclocks, http://www.workclocks.co.uk/dey.html.

Herman Hollerith

Hollerith was an interesting character. This biography only begins to tell his story.

Austrian, Geoffrey D. *Herman Hollerith: Forgotten Giant of Information Processing.* New York: Columbia University Press, 1982.

Charles Flint

Charles Flint is never mentioned in discussions of the major robber barons, but he put together more successful monopolistic trusts than any other person except J. P. Morgan.

IBM, https://www.ibm.com/ibm/history/exhibits/builders/builders_flint.html.

"C. R. Flint Is Dead. 'Father of Trusts'; Former Industrialist Was a Pioneer in Consolidation of Large Corporations. Helped Form U.S. Rubber. Retired at 78, but Returned to Activities Two Years Later. Owner of Speedy Yachts." *New York Times*, February 14, 1934. https://www.nytimes.com/1934/02/14 /archives/c-r-flint-i8-dead-fatr-of_trusts-former-industrialist-was-a -pioneer.html.

Thomas Watson, Sr.

There are several good sources for information about the de facto founder of IBM.

Fishman, Katherine D. *The Computer Establishment.* New York: Harper & Row, 1981.

Maney, Kevin. *The Maverick and His Machine: Thomas Watson, Sr. and the Making of IBM.* Hoboken, NJ: Wiley, 2003.

Watson, Thomas J., Jr., and Peter Petre. *Father, Son & Co.: My Life at IBM and Beyond.* New York: Bantam, 1990.

Georges Doriot

Ante's biography is an engaging read.

Ante, Spencer E. *Creative Capital: Georges Doriot and the Birth of Venture Capital.* Cambridge, MA: Harvard Business, 2008.

Ken Olsen

Ken Olsen has been mostly forgotten, but he was pivotal in bringing entrepreneurship out from under the shadow of big professionally managed businesses.

Anderson, John J. "Dave Tells Ahl." *Creative Computing 10*, no. 11 (November 1984). Accessed at https://www.atarimagazines.com/creative/v10n11/66_Dave _tells_Ahl__the_hist.php.

Rifkin, Glenn, and George Harrar. *Ultimate Entrepreneur; The Story of Ken Olsen and Digital Equipment Corporation.* Rocklin, CA: Prima Communications, 1989.

This highly illustrated book is very informative and fun to read.

Evans, Harold, Gail Buckland, and David Lefer. *They Made America: From the Steam Engine to the Search Engine: Two Centuries of Innovators.* Boston: Little, Brown, 2004, particularly 376–77.

Silicon

The story of semiconductors is seminal to the story of our modern ideas about entrepreneurs and entrepreneurship. Here are four classic books that describe that story and many of the entrepreneurs involved.

Malone, Michael S. *The Intel Trinity: How Robert Noyce, Gordon Moore, and Andy Grove Built the World's Most Important Company.* New York: Harper Collins, 2014.

Lécuyer, Christophe. *Making Silicon Valley: Innovation and the Growth of High Tech, 1930–1970.* Cambridge, MA: MIT Press, 2006.

Reid, Thomas R. *The Chip: How Two Americans Invented the Microchip and Launched a Revolution.* New York: Random House, 2001.

Seitz, Frederick, Norman G. Einspruch, and Norman G. Einspruch. *Electronic Genie: The Tangled History of Silicon.* Urbana: University of Illinois Press, 1998.

Dan Bricklin

Bricklin's own sincere reflections and recollections are a great source for understanding the birth of the spreadsheet.

Livingston, Jessica. *Founders at Work: Stories of Startups' Early Days.* Berkeley, CA: Apress, 2008, 73–88.

Chapter 9

The following pieces on ancient slavery are good overviews.

Mesopotamian Slaves

Michel, Cécile. "Economy, Society, and Daily Life in the Old Assyrian Period." In *A Companion to Assyria*, ed. Eckart Frahm, chap. 4. Hoboken, NJ: Wiley, 2017, particularly 80.

Greek Slavery

Bresson, Alain. *The Making of the Ancient Greek Economy: Institutions, Markets, and Growth in the City-States*. Princeton, NJ: Princeton University Press, 2015.

Roman Slavery

Temin, Peter. *The Roman Market Economy*. Princeton University Press, 2017.

This chapter in Tchernia's book explains how slaves were captured and used by Gauls to pay for their Roman wine.

Tchernia, André. "Wine Exporting and the Exception of Gaul." In *The Romans and Trade*. Oxford: Oxford University Press, 2016.

Isaac Franklin and John Armfield

Franklin and Armfield have unfortunately slipped under the radar as examples of horrific entrepreneurial slave owners.

Gudmestad, Robert H. "The Troubled Legacy of Isaac Franklin: The Enterprise of Slave Trading." *Tennessee Historical Quarterly* 62, no. 3 (2003): 193.
Howell, Isabel. "John Armfield, Slave-Trader." *Tennessee Historical Quarterly* 2, no. 1 (1943): 3–29.

Mesopotamian Loans and Ammisaduqa

Michael Hudson is the scholar to read regarding loans in the ancient Mideast.

Finkelstein, Jacob J. "The Edict of Ammiṣaduqa: A New Text." *Revue d'Assyriologie et d'archéologie orientale* 63, no. 1 (1969): 45–64.

Hudson, Michael. "How Interest Rates Were Set, 2500 BC–1000 AD: Máš, Tokos and Fœnus as Metaphors for Interest Accruals." *Journal of the Economic and Social History of the Orient* 43, no. 2 (2000): 132–61.

Hudson, Michael. *The Lost Tradition of Biblical Debt Cancellations.* New York: Henry George School of Social Science, 1993.

Deforestation

These are two good articles with different perspectives on ancient entrepreneurially induced deforestation.

Harris, William V. "Plato and the Deforestation of Attica." *Athenaeum* 99 (2011): 479–82.

Harris, William Vernon. "Defining and Detecting Mediterranean Deforestation, 800 BCE to 700 CE." In *The Ancient Mediterranean Environment Between Science and History*, 173–194. Leiden: Brill, 2013.

Air Pollution

These three articles will get you up to speed on the sources of ancient air pollution.

Hong, Sungmin, et al. "History of Ancient Copper Smelting Pollution During Roman and Medieval Times Recorded in Greenland Ice." *Science* 272, no. 5259 (1996): 246–49.

Makra, László. "Anthropogenic Air Pollution in Ancient Times." In *Toxicology in Antiquity*, 2nd ed., ed. Peter Wexler, 267–87. Cambridge, MA: Academic, 2018.

Nriagu, Jerome O. "A History of Global Metal Pollution." *Science* 272, no. 5259 (1996): 223.

This book is clunky, but it contains many interesting facts about London's air quality.

Brimblecombe, Peter. *The Big Smoke: A History of Air Pollution in London Since Medieval Times.* London: Routledge, 2011.

Accum

Accum is a very interesting entrepreneur who deserves much more attention. His book really opens your eyes to how far entrepreneurs go when unconstrained in exploiting their customers.

Accum, Friedrich Christian. *A Treatise on Adulterations of Food and Culinary Poisons: Exhibiting the Fraudulent Sophistications of Bread, Beer, Wine, Spirituous Liquors, Tea, Coffee, Cream, Confectionery, Vinegar, Mustard, Pepper, Cheese, Olive Oil, Pickles and Other Articles Employed in Domestic Economy; and Methods of Detecting Them.* London: Longman, 1820.

Browne, Charles Albert. "The Life and Chemical Services of Fredrick Accum." *Journal of Chemical Education* 2, no. 11 (1925): 1008.

Cole, R. J. "Friedrich Accum (1769–1838). A Biographical Study." *Annals of Science* 7, no. 2 (1951): 128–43.

Adulterated Milk

If you want to study how and why entrepreneurs adulterated food, you'll also need to read Mullaly's book.

Mullaly, John. *The Milk Trade of New York and Vicinity: Giving an Account of the Sale of Pure and Adulterated Milk.* New York: Fowlers & Wells, 1853.

Johannes Gutenberg

These four references give a well-rounded perspective of the impact of Gutenberg's innovations.

Buringh, Eltjo, and Jan Luiten Van Zanden. "Charting the 'Rise of the West': Manuscripts and Printed Books in Europe, A Long-Term Perspective from the Sixth Through Eighteenth Centuries." *Journal of Economic History* 69, no. 2 (2009): 409–45.

Febvre, Lucien, and Henri-Jean Martin. *The Coming of the Book: The Impact of Printing 1450–1800*, trans. David Gerard. London: Verso, 1997.

Man, John. *The Gutenberg Revolution.* New York: Random House, 2010.

Pettegree, Andrew. *The Book in the Renaissance.* New Haven, CT: Yale University Press, 2010.

Louis Réard

Réard is a classic example of the success that entrepreneurs can find by offering salacious products.

Alac, Patrik. *Bikini Story*. New York: Parkstone, 2012.

Chapter 10

Debate on Iron and Salt

Loewe's narration of the debate on salt and iron is the most readable and complete, other than reading a translation of the original.

Gale, Esson M. *Discourses of Salt and Iron: A Debate on State Control of Commerce and Industry in Ancient China: Chapters I-XIX Translated from the Huan K'uan, with Introduction and Notes*. Leiden: Brill, 1931.
Loewe, Michael. "The Grand Inquest—81 BC." In *Crisis and Conflict in Han China: 104 BC to AD 9*. London: Routledge, 2013.

Hammurabi's Code

Fordham University, *Ancient History Sourcebook: Code of Hammurabi, ca. 1780 BCE*. https://sourcebooks.fordham.edu/ancient/hamcode.asp.

Standards and Weights and Market Supervision

This is a fascinating study of early weights and measures, indicating what lengths and levels of technology were invested in keeping entrepreneurs in check.

Petruso, Karl M. "Early Weights and Weighing in Egypt and the Indus Valley." *M Bulletin* (Museum of Fine Arts, Boston) 79 (1981): 44–51.

Caveat Emptor

Reitz's account of the emergence of consumer law is complete and clear.

Reitz, John C. "A History of Cutoff Rules as a Form of Caveat Emptor: Part II—From Roman Law to the Modern Civil and Common Law." *American Journal of Comparative Law* 37, no. 2 (1989): 247–99.

Evelyn Welch's book is interesting to read, and its fantastic illustrations make it fun to browse.

Welch, Evelyn S. *Shopping in the Renaissance: Consumer Cultures in Italy 1400–1600*. New Haven, CT: Yale University Press, 2005.

Bubble Act

These two articles do a good job of describing the South Sea bubble and the impact of government intervention and legislation.

Harris, Ron. "The Bubble Act: Its Passage and Its Effects on Business Organization." *Journal of Economic History* 54, no. 3 (1994): 610–27.
Temin, Peter, and Hans-Joachim Voth. "Riding the South Sea Bubble." *American Economic Review* 94, no. 5 (2004): 1654–68.

Blue Sky Laws

The quote in this section comes from the following.

Hall v. Geiger-Jones Co., 242 U.S. 539 (1917).

Religion

My section on religion focuses on the constraints imposed on entrepreneurs by religions. Because I found no clear linkages between the emergence, structure, and impact of entrepreneurship with religion, I have not featured such a discussion. There have been some famous books linking religion to entrepreneurial success, most notably Max Weber's *The Protestant Ethic and the Spirit of Capitalism*, but more recent and thoughtful research has shown that the data he presented were more strongly correlated with literacy and levels of education than with specific religious teachings. We can see strong differences in entrepreneurial outcomes between communities. Those outcomes can arise due to differences in the value of education and in values that welcome or constrain change.

Dana's article is an excellent survey of research into the impact of religion on entrepreneurship. Seabright tackles the linkage from an evolutionary perspective; he wonders if the linkage could be fundamental to the way that human brains evolved a sense of trust that drives both religious thought and entrepreneurship.

Dana, Léo-Paul, ed. "Introduction: Religion as an Explanatory Variable for Entrepreneurship." In *Entrepreneurship and Religion*, 1–26. Cheltenham, UK: Edward Elgar, 2010.
Seabright, Paul. "Religion and Entrepreneurship: A Match Made in Heaven?" *Archives de sciences sociales des religions* 175 (2016): 201–19.

Widgery creates a great overview of Hindu ethics, in which entrepreneurship plays a distinct role.

Widgery, Alban G. "The Principles of Hindu Ethics." *International Journal of Ethics* 40, no. 2 (1930): 232–45.

Kuran explains how Islam favors traders but is suspicious of innovators.

Kuran, Timur. "The Scale of Entrepreneurship in Middle Eastern History: Inhibitive Roles of Islamic Institutions." In *The Invention of Enterprise: Entrepreneurship from Ancient Mesopotamia to Modern Times*, ed. David S. Landes, Joel Mokyr, and William J. Baumol, 62–87. Princeton, NJ: Princeton University Press, 2010.

Karl Marx

I found Wheen's biography on Marx most useful. Pipes's history of communism is terse and succinct.

Pipes, Richard. *Communism: A History*. New York: Modern Library, 2003.
Wheen, Francis. *Karl Marx: A Life*. New York: Norton, 1999.

Nepmen

This is a great article on why and how Lenin turned to entrepreneurs to help revive the Soviet economy.

Ball, Alan. "Lenin and the Question of Private Trade in Soviet Russia." *Slavic Review* 43, no. 3 (1984): 399–412.

Chapter 11

Pythagoras

Riedweg's chapter on Pythagoras's educational and spiritual enterprise is a good place to start in understanding what the great philosopher-mathematician was trying to accomplish.

Riedweg, Christoph. *Pythagoras: His Life, Teaching, and Influence.* Ithaca, NY: Cornell University Press, 2008, particularly 98–113.

Greek Liturgies

Bitros and Karayiannis have written extensively about classical Greek and Athenian entrepreneurship.

Bitros, George C., and Anastassios D. Karayiannis. "Values and Institutions as Determinants of Entrepreneurship in Ancient Athens." *Journal of Institutional Economics* 4, no. 2 (2008): 205.
Demosthenes, *Against Aphonus II*, 22.
Demosthenes, *Against Stephanus I*, 66.

Garland gives an excellent overview of life in ancient Greece and touches on liturgies.

Garland, Robert. *Daily Life of the Ancient Greeks.* Indianapolis, IN: Hackett, 2008.

Thomas Coram

The Foundling Hospital still exists. The institution maintains a site with plenty of Thomas Coram material.

Coram Story, https://coramstory.org.uk/thomas-coram/.

The Wagner biography is dense but a good place to learn more.

Hill, Hamilton Andrews. *Thomas Coram in Boston and Taunton.* Worcester, MA: American Antiquarian Society, 1893.
Wagner, Gillian. *Thomas Coram, Gent., 1668–1751.* Woodbridge, UK: Boydell, 2004.

Dr. V

It is surprising that nobody has yet written a biography of this inspiring individual.

Aravind Eye Care Center, https://aravind.org/our-story/.
Miller, Stephen. "McSurgery: A Man Who Saved 2.4 Million Eyes." *Wall Street Journal*, August 5, 2006. https://www.wsj.com/articles/SB115474199023727728.

Muhammad Yunus

There is plenty of online material about Muhammad Yunus. Start with what the Nobel Prize Committee said.

The Nobel Prize, https://www.nobelprize.org/prizes/peace/2006/yunus/biographical/.

Andrew Carnegie

You can find this version of Carnegie's famous article many places online. This is the original.

Carnegie, Andrew. "The Gospel of Wealth." *North American Review* 183, no. 599 (1906): 526–37.

Chapter 12

iPhone Consequences

It is hard to find analyses of the unintended consequences of our most popular products and services.

Merchant, Brian. *The One Device: The Secret History of the iPhone*. London: Bantam, 2017.

Acknowledgments

A veritable army of people have helped me with this project. First and foremost, I must acknowledge my wife, Diana, as my partner and muse in all I do and accomplish. Her inputs, suggestions, and patient readings of countless drafts have made this a vastly better book. Nobody could have a better muse and partner.

As I wrote in the introduction, many academics helped introduce me to the literature and data sets of their fields. The Princeton Department of Classics has been particularly supportive. I would like to specifically thank Andrew Feldherr, Caroline Cheung, and Dan-el Padilla Peralta for sharing insights on the daily life and mindsets of Roman and Greek consumers and entrepreneurs, as well as patiently answering questions. Anna Shields and Xin Wen in East Asian Studies pointed me to a treasure trove of literature and sources. My colleague David Miller has been an essential resource and mentor in understanding how religions think about entrepreneurs. I am very fortunate that archeologist Peter Bogucki's office is down the hall from mine, as he pointed me to many great references. I particularly appreciate Professor Fikri Kulakoglu for traveling from Ankara to spend two days briefing me and showing me the archeological sites at Kültepe and Kanesh, and Rob Pyatt's tour of and briefing on Grimes Graves. I am also grateful to Mogens Trolle Larsen for providing some additional insights beyond his book and articles. Marcos Hunt Ortiz's insights on Cabezo Juré were also very helpful. Valerie Hansen at Yale helped me unravel critical sources depicting the Qingming scroll. I also received critical help finding material from Andrew Garrard and Anthony Barbieri-Low. It took a small squadron of experts to help me track down the origin of the Chinese word for profit; I could not have done it without Joshua Seufert, head of collections at Princeton's East Asian Library, and Charles Aylmer, the head of Chinese Collections at Cambridge University, aided by Yuzhou Bai's expert translations. My colleague Sheila Pontis's mastery of the design of information was essential for creating the graphics that describe entrepreneurial swarming behavior and the EIC.

I am very grateful for the undying support I receive from Princeton's Keller Center's executive director, Cornelia Huellstrunk, and faculty directors Margaret Martonosi and Naveen Verma. My summer research interns, Nathan Bolanos and Nirakar Sapkota, helped me dig deep into relevant data sets.

Myles Thompson's enthusiasm for this project helped propel it to its conclusion; he provided very important advice and suggestions along the way. The encouragement and frank recommendations I received from Peter Dougherty on the first draft of the first chapter changed my approach but gave me the courage to carry on. His comments on my next-to-last draft and the title helped me further sharpen their impact. I am very thankful that Brian Smith has stayed close at hand to navigate Columbia's editing and publishing processes. Lisa Hamm was brilliant with her designs for the book. Getting permissions for the dozens of illustrations throughout the book was a major challenge that could not have been accomplished without the leadership of Sheri Gilbert. I am grateful to my editor, David Moldawer, at Bookitech, for challenging me to keep my prose terse and succinct. I have received many valuable and insightful suggestions from friends and colleagues who generously agreed to read drafts of the book as it took shape, including Larry Gilson, Anita Sands, Howard Aldrich, Don Bernstein, Rebecca De La Espriella, Ed Zschau, Alex Stewart, Cornelia Huellstrunk, Bill Gartner, Noam Wasserman, and Arel Lidow. The comments from three anonymous reviewers were particularly insightful and helped make this a better book.

I thank Barbara Hendricks and Megan Wilson for helping with the marketing efforts. Last but not least, my agent, Jud Laghi, is ever patient and always a delight to work with.

Index

Page numbers in *italics* indicate figures or tables.